English Grammar

for
dummies®
A Wiley Brand

English Grammar

3rd Edition

by Geraldine Woods

for
dummies®
A Wiley Brand

English Grammar For Dummies®, 3rd Edition

Published by: **John Wiley & Sons, Inc.**, 111 River Street, Hoboken, NJ 07030-5774, www.wiley.com

Copyright © 2017 by John Wiley & Sons, Inc., Hoboken, New Jersey

Published simultaneously in Canada

For general information on our other products and services, please contact our Customer Care Department within the U.S. at 877-762-2974, outside the U.S. at 317-572-3993, or fax 317-572-4002. For technical support, please visit https://hub.wiley.com/community/support/dummies.

Wiley publishes in a variety of print and electronic formats and by print-on-demand. Some material included with standard print versions of this book may not be included in e-books or in print-on-demand. If this book refers to media such as a CD or DVD that is not included in the version you purchased, you may download this material at http://booksupport.wiley.com. For more information about Wiley products, visit www.wiley.com.

Library of Congress Control Number: 2017935002

ISBN 978-1-119-37659-0 (pbk); ISBN 978-1-119-37661-3 (ebk); ISBN 978-1-119-37660-6 (ebk)

Manufactured in the United States of America

10 9 8 7 6 5 4 3 2 1

Contents at a Glance

Table of Contents

PART 3: CONVENTIONAL WISDOM: PUNCTUATION AND CAPITALIZATION

Introduction

Emoticons. Gifs. Instagram photos. Selfies. Snapchat. With these and so many other visual ways to communicate, you might think that grammar is as extinct as a dodo bird. You'd be wrong. In fact, texts, tweets, social media posts, and online comments have actually increased the amount of writing people do each day. Plus, pen-and-paper writing is still around. When writing is involved, grammar is involved, too.

In *English Grammar For Dummies,* 3rd Edition, I address all your grammar questions about written and spoken language, including a few you didn't know you had. I do so without loading you up with obscure terminology, defining terms only when you need them to understand *what* you're supposed to do as well as *why* you're supposed to do it. In this book, I also explain which rules of formal English you can ignore — sometimes or even all the time. The goal of *English Grammar For Dummies,* 3rd Edition, is to ensure that the language you use conveys your ideas accurately and makes a good impression on your reader or listener.

This book also has another, very practical purpose. Those who express themselves in proper English have a better shot at getting a job, keeping it, and moving into high-salary positions. If you're at a desk and *not* getting paid (in other words, you're in school), you also need good grammar. No matter what subject you're studying, teachers favor proper English. So do the designers of standardized tests. The SAT — that loveable exam facing college applicants — contains a substantial writing section, as does the ACT (another fun hurdle of the college-admissions process). Whether you're aiming for a great job or a good grade, *English Grammar For Dummies,* 3rd Edition, will help you reach your goal.

Foolish Assumptions

I wrote the third edition of *English Grammar For Dummies* with a specific person in mind. I assume that you, the reader, already speak English to some extent and that you want to speak it better. I also assume that you're a busy person with better things to do than worry about the pronouns in your profile for a dating app. (Though perhaps you should. One survey revealed that men who use the word *whom* in their profiles attract more "clicks" than those who don't.)

This book is for you if you want

>> Better grades

>> Skill in communicating exactly what you mean

>> A higher-paying or higher-status job

>> Speech and writing that presents you as an educated, intelligent person

>> A good score on the SAT, the ACT, and other standardized exams

>> The ability to create polished reports and presentations at work or at school

>> Texts, tweets, and posts that get the job done within tight word-limits

>> Stronger skills in English as a second language

Icons Used in This Book

TIP

Wherever you see this icon, you'll find helpful strategies for understanding the structure of the sentence or for choosing the correct word form.

WARNING

Not every grammar point has a built-in trap, but some do. This icon tells you how to avoid common mistakes as you construct a sentence.

POP QUIZ

Think you know how to find the subject in a sentence or choose the correct verb tense? Take the pop quizzes located throughout this book to find out what you know and what you may want to learn.

TEST ALERT

Are you hoping to spend some time behind ivy-covered walls? To put it another way: Are you aiming for college? Then you should pay special attention to the information next to this icon because college-admissions testers *love* this material.

REMEMBER

This icon identifies key grammar points to deposit in your memory bank.

Beyond the Book

Need crucial information, fast? Check out the *English Grammar For Dummies* Cheat Sheet. Simply go to `www.dummies.com` and type "English Grammar For Dummies Cheat Sheet" in the Search box.

Where to Go from Here

Every reader is different, and you don't want to waste time in a chapter that explains something you already know or will never use. Of course, you're welcome to read every single word I've written. If you do, you'll be my favorite person. But realistically, I know that you want to dip into *English Grammar For Dummies*, 3rd Edition, as efficiently as possible. Try these strategies:

» Look through the Contents at a Glance at the beginning of the book so you have an idea what's where. If you see something that has often puzzled you — commas or verb tense or something else — put that section on your "to read" list.

» Now get more specific. Zero in on the sections you may need in the detailed Table of Contents, which follows the Contents at a Glance. Again, choose whatever you like.

» Check out the last section of Chapter 1, where I present some grammar questions and the chapters that answer them. Read the chapters that correspond to the questions that stump you.

» Also keep an eye out for pop quizzes. Try the questions, and if you know the answers, skip that section. If you make a mistake, spend some quality time in that chapter.

» You can also ignore everything in the preceding bullets and simply flip through the book. If something catches your eye, stop. Read, learn, and have fun!

1

Building a Firm Foundation: The Parts of the Sentence

IN THIS PART . . .

Become familiar with the conventions of formal and informal language when speaking, texting, and writing.

Figure out how sentences are constructed, starting with verbs.

Identify the subjects in sentences.

Learn how to build complete and coherent sentences.

Explore an important building block of sentences: the complement.

Chapter **1**

Using the Right Words at the Right Time

In the Middle Ages, *grammar* meant the study of Latin, the language of choice for educated people. In fact, grammar was so closely associated with Latin that the word referred to any kind of learning. This meaning of *grammar* shows up when people of grandparent-age and older talk about their *grammar school,* not their elementary school. The term *grammar school* is a leftover from the old days. The very old days.

These days the word *grammar* refers to the nuts and bolts of language, specifically, how words are put together to create meaning. Most people also apply the term to a set of rules you have to follow in order to speak and write better. However, the definition of *better* changes according to situation, purpose, and audience.

In this chapter, I show you the difference between formal and informal English and explain when each is called for. I also tell you what apps, speech-to-text, and word-processing programs can and can't do to help you write proper English. I also give you some pointers about generally accepted grammar for texting, tweeting, emailing, and other forms of electronic communication.

What This Year's Sentence Is Wearing: Understanding Grammar and Style

Fresh from the shower, you're standing in front of your closet. What should you select? Some options aren't open to you. You can't show up at work wearing nothing — not if you want to keep your job and, in addition, stay out of jail. That's a law (in the real world) and a rule (in the world of grammar). You *can* choose a bright purple jacket and a fluorescent green scarf. The fashion police may object, but real cops will leave you alone. In both the real world and Grammar Land, this sort of decision is a matter of *style*. A style point is more flexible than a grammar rule. Take that jacket-scarf selection. Your friends may stare and suggest a subtler color combination, or they may praise you for team loyalty if your school colors are purple and green and you're cheering at a pep rally.

The grammar rules of proper English can and do change, but not often — maybe a few times every 500 years. (Sometimes people break grammar rules on purpose. See the next section, "Distinguishing Between the Three Englishes," for more information.) Style, on the other hand, shifts much more frequently. A sentence from the early 20th century may look odd to 21st century readers, and a sentence from the 19th century will seem even stranger. Style also changes with context. Science publications and literary journals, for example, capitalize titles differently. Geography matters, too. In the United States, a comma often appears before *and* in a list of three or more items. British writers generally omit that comma.

TIP

In *English Grammar For Dummies,* 3rd Edition, I discuss the most common style points. If I tackled every situation, though, you'd be reading a thousand-page book. For your most important writing projects, you may want to consult a manual of style. Many institutions publish this sort of book, listing their preferences for punctuation, capitalization, and a whole bunch of other *-ations* you've never heard of. A few popular style manuals are the *Modern Language Association Handbook* (for academic writing in the humanities), *The Chicago Manual of Style* (for general writing), the *Publication Manual of the American Psychological Association,* and the *MIT Guide to Science and Engineering Communication* (for science writing).

These examples illustrate the difference between grammar and style:

SENTENCE: Am going basketball game I to the.

WHAT'S WRONG: The word order is scrambled.

GRAMMAR OR STYLE? Grammar.

CORRECTED SENTENCE: I am going to the basketball game.

SENTENCE: She was born on March 18 2009.

WHAT'S WRONG: Most writers would insert a comma after *18.*

GRAMMAR OR STYLE? Style. Some writers prefer a completely different format for the date.

CORRECTED SENTENCE: She was born on March 18, 2009. Or, She was born on 18 March 2009.

SENTENCE: Them enjoy playing baseball.

WHAT'S WRONG: The word *them* isn't appropriate for that spot in the sentence. (Why? Check Chapter 8.)

GRAMMAR OR STYLE: Grammar.

CORRECTED SENTENCE: They enjoy playing baseball.

SENTENCE: Ann spends too much time surfing the Internet.

WHAT'S WRONG: When it was first invented, "Internet" was generally capitalized. These days, many publications prefer lowercase *(internet).*

GRAMMAR OR STYLE: Style.

CORRECTED SENTENCE: Ann spends too much time surfing the internet.

REMEMBER

When you're speaking or writing, you should take care not to break any grammar rules. You should also follow the style guidelines of the authority figure who's judging your work. However (there's always a *however* in life, isn't there?), your surroundings, audience, and purpose affect the grammar and style choices you make. For more information, read the next section, "Distinguishing Between the Three Englishes."

Distinguishing Between the Three Englishes

Good grammar sounds like a great idea, but *good* is tough to pin down. Why? Because you know several "Englishes," and the language that works in one situation is not suitable in another. Here's what I mean. Imagine that you're hungry. What do you say or write?

Wanna get something to eat? or c u in caf?

Do you feel like getting a sandwich?

Will you accompany me to the dining room?

These statements illustrate the three Englishes of everyday life. I call them friend-speak, conversational English, and formal English.

Before you choose, you need to know where you are and what's going on. Most important, you need to know your audience.

Wanna get something to eat? Friendspeak

Friendspeak is informal and filled with slang. Its sentence structure breaks all the rules that English teachers love. It's the language of *I know you and you know me and we can relax together.* In friendspeak, the speakers are on the same level. They have nothing to prove to each other, and they're comfortable with each other's mistakes. In fact, they make some mistakes on purpose, just to distinguish their personal conversation from what they say on other occasions. Here's a conversation in friendspeak:

Me and him are going to the gym. Wanna come?

He's like, I did 60 push-ups, and I'm like, no way.

I doubt that the preceding conversation makes sense to many people, but the participants understand it quite well. Because they both know the whole situation (the guy they're talking about gets muscle cramps after 4 seconds of exercise), they can talk in shorthand. They can write in shorthand, too, in texts such as *c u in caf* (which means "see you in the cafeteria"), tweets, instant messages, and similar communications between close friends.

For the most part, I don't deal with friendspeak in this book. You already know it. In fact, you've probably created a version of it with anyone who's your *bff* (best friend forever). In Chapter 16, I do explain some factors you should consider when you're writing online — to your friends or to anyone else.

FLEEK GRAMMAR

Want to be in the in-crowd? Easy. Just create an out-crowd and you're all set. How do you create an out-crowd? Manufacture a special language (slang) with your friends that no one else understands, at least until the media picks it up or someone *earjacks* you. (*Earjack* is slang for "secretly listen to.") Slang is the ultimate friendspeak. You and your pals are on the inside, talking about a *sketchy neighborhood* (*sketchy* means "dangerous"). Everyone else is on the outside, wondering what *fleek* (awesome, exactly right) means. Should you use slang in your writing? Probably not, unless you're dealing with a good friend. The goal of writing and speaking is communication, and slang may be a mystery to your intended audience. Also, because slang changes quickly, even a short time after you've written something, the meaning may be obscure. Instead of cutting-edge, you sound dated.

When you talk or write in slang, you also risk sounding uneducated. In fact, sometimes breaking the usual rules is the point of slang. In general, you should make sure that your readers know that you understand the rules before you start breaking them (the rules, not the readers) safely.

Do you feel like getting a sandwich? Conversational English

A step up from friendspeak is *conversational English*. Although not quite friend-speak, conversational English includes some warmth and informality. Conversational English doesn't stray too far from English class rules, but it does break some. You can relax, but not completely. It's the tone of most everyday speech, especially between equals. Conversational English is — no shock here — usually for conversations. Specifically, conversational English is appropriate in these situations:

>> Chats with family members, neighbors, and acquaintances

>> Informal conversations with teachers and co-workers

>> Friendly conversations (if there are any) with supervisors

Conversational English also shows up in writing, where it creates a "just us friends" or "no big deal" tone. I'm using conversational English in this book because I'm pretending that I'm chatting with you, the reader, not teaching grammar in a classroom situation. Look for conversational English in these communications:

>> Notes, emails, instant messages, tweets, and texts to acquaintances and friends

>> Posts or comments on social media, blogs, and so on

>> Friendly letters to relatives

>> Letters to acquaintances who enjoy a warm, friendly tone

Conversational English has a breezy sound. Letters are dropped in contractions (*don't, I'll, would've,* and so forth). In written form, conversational English breaks punctuation rules, too. Sentences run together, and commas connect all sorts of things. Multiple punctuation marks (two or three exclamation points, for example) show strong emotion, especially in social media posts and texts.

Will you accompany me to the dining room? Formal English

You're now at the pickiest end of the language spectrum: formal, grammatically correct speech and writing. Formal English displays the fact that you have an advanced vocabulary, a knowledge of etiquette, and command of standard rules of English usage. You may use formal English when you have less power, importance, and/or status than the other people in the conversation to demonstrate that you respect them. You may also speak or write in formal English when you have *more* power, importance, and/or status than the audience to create a tone of dignity or to provide a suitable role model for someone who is still learning. Situations that call for formal English include:

>> Business letters or emails (from or between businesses as well as from individuals to businesses)

>> Letters or emails to government officials

>> Online comments posted to publications or government websites

>> Office memos or emails

>> Reports

>> Homework

>> Communications to teachers

>> Speeches, presentations, oral reports

>> Important conversations (for example, job interviews, college interviews, parole hearings, congressional inquiries, inquisitions, sessions with the principal in which you explain that unfortunate incident with the stapler, and so on)

Think of formal English as business clothing. If you're in a situation where you want to look your best, you're also in a situation where your words matter. In business, homework, or any situation in which you're being judged, use formal English.

POP QUIZ

Can you adapt your writing to suit the situation and audience? Try this quiz. Which note is correct?

A. no hw — ttyl

B. Hi, Ms. Smith. Just a note to let you know I didn't do the homework. I'll explain later! Ralph

C. Dear Ms. Smith,

I was not able to do my homework last night. I will speak with you about this matter later.

Sincerely,

Ralph

Answer: The correct answer depends upon a few factors. How willing are you to be stuck in the corner of the classroom for the rest of the year? If your answer is "very willing," send A, a text written in friendspeak. (By the way, *hw* is short for "homework" and *ttyl* means "talk to you later.") Does your teacher come to school in jeans and sneakers? If so, note B is probably acceptable. Note B is written in conversational English. Is Ms. Smith prim and proper, expecting you to follow every rule ever created, including a few she made up? If so, note C, which is written in formal English, is your best bet.

Thumbing Your Way to Better Grammar

I live in New York City, and I seldom see thumbs that aren't tapping on very small screens — texting (sending written notes over the phone), IMing (instant messaging), tweeting (sending 140-character notes), posting comments on social media, or simply jotting down ideas and reminders. I can't help wondering what sort of grammar will evolve from these forms of communication. Perhaps the 19th edition of *English Grammar For Dummies* will be only ten pages long, with "sentences" like *u ok? lmk — bbl.* (Translation for the techno-challenged: "Are you okay? Let me know. I'll be back later.")

At present, however, match the level of formality in electronic communication to your situation, message, and audience. If you're dealing with a friend, feel free to abbreviate and shorten anything you like. If you're communicating with a co-worker or an acquaintance or a general audience on social media, conversational English is probably fine, and it may even be the best choice. Formal English, on some websites, comes across as stiff and artificial. In general, the more power the recipient has, the more careful you should be. When you're unsure of your audience or writing to someone you want to impress with your level of knowledge, play it safe and opt for formal English.

written. Chances are you'll iden- to fit in, match that style. Or be a ee more guidelines for electronic

Prob… …nar-Checking Softw…

…elevant because grammar-checking …sing programs make human knowl-

…can arrange those words trillions of ways. No app or device can catch all … mistakes, and many programs identify errors that aren't actually wrong. Worse, some apps automatically guess what you mean and make changes automatically. A friend of mine tried to sign up for an online *writing course,* which her phone changed to a *worrying vise.* (On second thought, writing does sometimes cause so much worry that you feel you're trapped in a vise! Maybe the phone was accurate after all.) Other programs show you a few choices in a tiny space, where it's all too easy to hit the wrong word. Imagine what happens when you type or tap "garage" and it shows up as "grave" in answer to the question "Where's Pam?" (Speech-to-text programs that try to capture your words on a screen frequently make mistakes like this one.)

True, *some* apps find *some* problems and *sometimes* suggest good alternatives. But *some* is not the same as *all.* Often, computers can't tell the difference between *homonyms* — words that sound alike but have different meanings and spelling. For example, if I type

> Eye through the bawl at hymn, but it went threw the window pain instead.

my word-processing program is perfectly satisfied. However, I was actually trying to say

> I threw the ball at him, but it went through the window pane instead.

REMEMBER

Machines aren't as smart as people (especially people who've already shown their intelligence by reading *English Grammar For Dummies*). Take a look at the words your device inserts, changes, or identifies as wrong. Then use your knowledge of spelling and grammar to say exactly what you mean, correctly.

What's Your Problem? Solutions to Your Grammar Gremlins

I love to stroll around my neighborhood pondering the meaning of life, my grocery list, and other important topics. With my head in the clouds, I sometimes stub my toe. Once I know where the sidewalk cracks are, though, I can avoid them. If you can figure out where the cracks are in your *grammatical neighborhood* — the gremlins likely to trip you up — your sentences will roll along without risk of falling flat. Table 1-1 shows common usage problems and the location of their solutions. Skim the first column until you recognize something that stumps you. Then turn to the chapter listed in the second column.

TABLE 1-1 **Problems and Solutions**

Problem	Solution Chapter
The winner is he? Is he the winner?	2
We may? might? be right.	2
Here is? are? five pencils.	3
Three deers? deer? Two dogcatchers-in-chief? dogcatcher-in-chiefs?	3
You used too much chocolate sauce, nevertheless, you can have a cherry. Correct? Incorrect?	4
The superhero is. Complete sentence? Incomplete?	4

(continued)

TABLE 1-1 *(continued)*

Problem	Solution Chapter
The IRS apologized? had apologized? in your dreams apologizes?	6
You was? were? my first choice.	6
Mary, in addition to Sam, has? have? a little lamb?	7
Everyone needs their? his? your? this? grammar book.	7
She told he? him? an incredibly ridiculous story.	8
Keep this secret between you and I? me? me and the tabloids?	8
Getting on? in? over? the plane.	9
Jack feels bad? badly? about climbing.	10
More clear? Clearer?	10
The mayor was better than any public official. Correct? Incorrect?	10
Bagels' ? Bagels are on sale.	11
Bo declared that he was "tired." Correct? Incorrect?	12
Say it isn't so Joe. Comma needed?	13
Grammatically correct sentence? Grammatically-correct sentence?	14
The pigeon flew East? east?	15
Are you and the boss bff? or best friends forever?	16
The window was broken by me. Correct? Incorrect?	17
While combing my hair, the world ended. Correct? Incorrect?	18
Down the hill tumbled Jill. Correct? Incorrect?	19
I like grammar, ice cream, and to be on vacation? vacations?	20
Being fifteen, the video game is great fun. Correct? Incorrect?	21
The way life is suppose? supposed? to be.	22
A good part of speech to end a sentence with?	22

Chapter **2**

Verbs: The[...] of the Sen[...]

> linking and action verbs
> helping verbs and main verbs
> verbs express action or state of being
> The subject is usually a noun.
> The "someone" or "something" being talked about or doing the action is the subject.

Think about a se[...] all your ideas on the tr[...]ce (your reader or your l[...]hout the verb, you may get your point across, but you're going to have a bumpy ride.

Every sentence needs a verb, so you start with the verb when you want to do anything to your sentence — including correct it. Verbs come in all shapes and sizes, and grammarians have come up with a few dozen names for every single one. In school, you may have learned about *predicates, modals, transitive, intransitive,* and other sorts of verbs. Don't worry about terminology. It's not as important as understanding what verbs add to your sentence.

In this chapter, I explain how to distinguish between linking and action verbs and how to sort helping verbs from main verbs. Then I show you how to choose the correct verb for all your sentences, including questions and negative statements.

Expressing Meaning with Verbs

What time is it? You can find out by checking a clock, your watch, your phone, or a verb. Surprised by that last one? Verbs express states of being (what is, was, or will be) and action (what someone or something does, did, or will do). In other words, a verb is a part of speech that expresses time, which grammarians call *tense*. Check out the italicized verbs in these example sentences. Notice what the verb tells the reader or listener about time:

Mark *spilled* ink on the quilt. (*spilled* — past)

Mark's mom *is* upset. (*is* — present)

Mark *will wash* the quilt, or his mom *will murder* him. (*will wash* and *will murder* — future)

These are just three simple examples, but you get the point. The verb puts the action or state of being on a time line. (Don't tense up about tense. You can find everything you need to know about this topic in Chapter 6.)

One more important thing you should know about verbs: In a sentence, the verb must match the subject, the person or thing performing the action or existing in the state of being. (See Chapter 3 for the lowdown on subjects.) If the subject is singular (just one), the verb is singular. If the subject is plural (more than one), the verb is plural. In these example sentences, the subject is in bold type and the verb is italicized:

The **poster** *is* on the wall of Sam's bedroom. (*poster* and *is* — singular)

Sam's **pets** *hate* the poster. (*pets* and *hate* — plural)

Sam's **cat** *has chewed* one corner of the poster. (*cat* and *has chewed* — singular)

My well-behaved **dogs** *do* not *chew* posters. (*dogs* and *do chew* — plural)

TIP

In the last example sentence, did you notice that the word *not* isn't italicized? *Not* changes the meaning of the verb from positive to negative, but it isn't an official part of the verb. It's an adverb, if you really want to know. (Turn to Chapter 10 for more about adverbs.)

For help with matching singular subjects to singular verbs and plural subjects to plural verbs, read Chapter 7.

Meeting the Families: Linking and Action Verbs

As everyone in a romantic relationship knows, when things turn serious, it's time to meet the family — the cousins, grandparents, and other relatives you'll be eating Thanksgiving dinner with for the rest of your life. Your relationship with verbs may not be romantic, but it *is* serious, because you can't make a sentence without a verb. In this section, you meet the two verb "families" — linking and action. You don't have to share holidays, but you do have to recognize and deal with them.

Linking verbs: The Giant Equal Sign

Linking verbs are also called *being verbs* because they express states of being — what is, will be, or was. Here's where math intersects with English. Linking verbs are like giant equal signs plopped into the middle of your sentence. For example, you can think of the sentence

Ralph's uncle *is* a cannibal with a taste for finger food.

as

Ralph's uncle = a cannibal with a taste for finger food.

Or, in shortened form,

Ralph's uncle = a cannibal

Just as in an algebra equation, the word *is* links two ideas and says that they are the same. Thus, *is* is a linking verb. Read on to find out about all sorts of linking verbs.

Forms of "to be"

Most linking verbs are forms of the verb *to be*, an essential but annoying verb that changes form frequently, depending on the subject of the sentence. Have a look at these example sentences:

Lulu *will be* angry when she hears about the missing sculpture.

Lulu = angry (*will be* is a linking verb)

I *am* unhappy about the theft also!

I = unhappy (*am* is the linking verb)

Stan *was* the last surfer to leave the water when the tidal wave approached.

Stan = last surfer (*was* is a linking verb)

Edgar *has been* depressed ever since the fall of the House of Usher.

Edgar = depressed (*has been* is a linking verb)

TIP

Unlike Hamlet, the Shakespearean character who worries whether "to be or not to be," you have no choice. You need a form of "to be" almost every time you speak or write. Try writing a paragraph or so without this verb. Tough, right? The most common forms of *to be* are the following: *am, are, is, was, were, will be, shall be, has been, have been, had been, could be, should be, would be, might have been, could have been, should have been, shall have been, will have been, must have been, must be.* (In Chapter 6, you can find all the forms of this irregular but essential verb.)

Synonyms of "to be"

"To be" is not the only linking verb — just the most popular. In fact, some people call linking verbs "being verbs." I prefer the term *linking* because some equal-sign verbs are not forms of the verb *to be*. Check out these examples:

With his sharp toenails and sneaky smile, Big Foot *seemed* threatening.

Big Foot = threatening (*seemed* is a linking verb)

A jail sentence for a misplaced comma *appears* harsh.

jail sentence = harsh (*appears* is a linking verb in this sentence)

The penalty for making a grammar error *remains* severe.

penalty = severe (*remains* is a linking verb in this sentence)

Loch Ness *stays* silent whenever monsters are mentioned.

Loch Ness = silent (*stays* is a linking verb in this sentence)

Seemed, appears, remains, and *stays* are similar to forms of the verb *to be* in that they express states of being. They also add shades of meaning to the basic concept. You may, for example, say that

With his sharp toenails and sneaky smile, Big Foot *was* threatening.

but now the statement is more definite. *Seemed* leaves room for doubt. Similarly, *remains* (in the third example sentence) adds a time dimension to the basic expression of being. The sentence implies that the penalty was and still is severe.

TIP

The most common words that express shades of meaning in reference to a state of being are *appear, seem, grow, remain,* and *stay*.

Savoring sensory verbs

Sensory verbs — verbs that express information you receive through the senses of sight, hearing, smell, taste, and so forth — may also be linking verbs:

> Two minutes after shaving, Ralph's chin *feels* scratchy.
>
> Ralph's chin = scratchy (*feels* is a linking verb)

> The ten-year-old lasagna in your refrigerator *smells* disgusting.
>
> lasagna = disgusting (*smells* is a linking verb)

> The ten-year-old lasagna in your refrigerator also *looks* disgusting.
>
> lasagna = disgusting (*looks* is a linking verb)

> Needless to say, the ten-year-old lasagna in your refrigerator *tastes* great!
>
> lasagna = great (*tastes* is a linking verb)

WARNING

Verbs that refer to the five senses are linking verbs only if they act as an equal sign in the sentence. If they aren't equating two ideas, they aren't linking verbs. In the preceding example sentence about Ralph's chin, *feels* is a linking verb. Here's a different sentence with the same verb:

> With their delicate fingers, Lulu and Stan *feel* Ralph's chin.

In this sentence, *feel* is not a linking verb because you're not saying that

> Lulu and Stan = chin.

Instead, you're saying that Lulu and Stan don't believe that Ralph shaved, so they checked by placing their fingers on his chin.

TIP

Some sensory verbs that function as linking verbs are *look*, *sound*, *taste*, *smell*, and *feel*.

Which sentence has a linking verb?

POP QUIZ

A. That annoying new clock sounds the hour with a loud heavy metal song.

B. That annoying new clock sounds extremely loud at four o'clock in the morning.

Answer: Sentence B has the linking verb. In sentence B, clock = extremely loud. In sentence A, the clock is doing something — sounding the hour — not being. (It's also waking up the whole neighborhood, but that idea isn't in the sentence.)

Try another. In which sentence is "stay" a linking verb?

A. Larry stays single only for very short periods of time.

B. Stay in the yard, Rover, or I cut your dog-biscuit ration in half!

Answer: Sentence A has the linking verb. In sentence A, Larry = single (at least for the moment). In sentence B, Rover is being told to do something — to stay in the backyard — clearly an action.

If you're dying to learn more grammar terminology, read on. Linking verbs connect the subject and the *subject complement*, also known as the *predicate nominative* and *predicate adjective*. For more on complements, read Chapter 5.

Completing linking-verb sentences correctly

A linking verb begins a thought, but it needs another word to complete the thought. Unless your listener is a mind reader, you can't walk around saying things like "the president is" or "the best day for the party will be" and expect people to know what you mean.

You have three possible completions for a linking verb: a descriptive word, a noun, or a pronoun (a word that substitutes for a noun). Take a look at some descriptions that complete the linking–verb equation:

> After running 15 miles in high heels, Renee's thigh muscles are *tired.*
>
> thigh muscles = *tired* (tired is a description, an adjective in grammatical terms)
>
> Renee's high heels are *stunning,* especially when they land on your foot.
>
> high heels = *stunning* (*stunning* is a description, also called an adjective)
>
> Oscar's foot, wounded by Renee's heels, seems particularly *painful.*
>
> foot = *painful* (*painful* is a description, an adjective)
>
> Lola's solution, to staple Oscar's toes together, is not very *helpful.*
>
> solution = *helpful* (*helpful* is a description, an adjective. The other descriptive words, *not* and *very,* describe *helpful,* not *solution.*)

You may also complete a linking verb equation with a person, place, or thing — a noun, in grammatical terms. Here are some examples:

The most important part of Lulu's diet is *popcorn*.

part of Lulu's diet = *popcorn* (*popcorn* is a thing, and therefore a noun)

Lulu's nutritional consultant has always been a complete *fraud*.

Lulu's nutritional consultant = *fraud* (*fraud* is a noun)

Sometimes you complete a linking verb sentence with a *pronoun*, a word that substitutes for the name of a person, place, or thing. For example:

The winner of the all-state spitball contest is *you!*

winner = *you* (*you* is a substitute for the name of the winner, and therefore a pronoun)

The murderer is *someone* in this room.

The murderer = *someone* (*someone* is a substitute for the name of the unknown killer and therefore a pronoun)

You can't do much wrong when you complete linking verb sentences with descriptions or with nouns. However, when you're writing, you can do a lot wrong when the completion of a linking verb sentence is a pronoun. (In speaking, most people don't worry about this rule.)

Think of a linking-verb sentence as reversible. That is, the pronoun you put after a linking verb should be the same kind of pronoun that you put before a linking verb. Here's what I mean. Read these sentence pairs:

The winner of the election is *him!*

Him is the winner of the election!

Uh oh. Something's wrong. You don't say *him is*. You say *he is*. Because you have a linking verb (*is*), you must put the same word after the linking verb that you would put before the linking verb. Try again:

The winner of the election is *he!*

He is the winner of the election!

Now you've got the correct ending for your sentence.

TIP

Subject pronouns, which complete linking-verb sentences correctly, are *I, you, he, she, it, we, they, who,* and *whoever*. Pronouns that are not allowed to be subjects include *me, him, her, us, them, whom,* and *whomever*. (In case you're curious, these pronouns act as objects. More on objects in Chapter 7.)

WARNING

In the previous examples, I discuss formal English, not conversational English. In conversational English, the following exchange is okay:

> Who's there?
>
> It is me. OR It's me.

In formal English, the exchange goes like this:

> Who is there?
>
> It is I.

Because of the linking verb *is*, you want the same kind of pronoun before and after the linking verb. You can't start a sentence with *me*, but you can start a sentence with *I*.

Now you've probably, with your sharp eyes, found a flaw here. You can't reverse the last reply and say

> I is it.

I takes a different verb — *am*. Both *is* and *am* are forms of the verb *to be* — one of the most peculiar creations in the entire language. So yes, you sometimes have to adjust the verb when you reverse a sentence with a form of *to be* in it. But the idea is the same: *I* can be a subject; *me* can't.

Lights! Camera! Action verb!

Linking verbs are important, but unless you've won the lottery, you just can't sit around being all the time. You have to do something. (And even if you did win the lottery, you'd be bored without something to do.) Here's where action verbs come into the picture. Everything that is not *being* is *action*, at least in the verb world. Unlike the giant equal sign associated with linking verbs (see "Linking Verbs: The Giant Equal Sign," earlier in the chapter), something *happens* with an action verb:

> Drew *slapped* the thief who *stole* the briefcase. (*Slapped* and *stole* are action verbs.)
>
> Fred *will run* to third base as soon as his sneezing fit *ends*. (*Will run* and *ends* are action verbs.)
>
> According to the teacher, Roger *has shot* at least 16 spitballs in the last ten minutes. (*Has shot* is an action verb.)

WARNING

Don't let the name *action* fool you. Some action verbs aren't particularly energetic: *think, sit, stay, have, sleep, dream,* and so forth. Besides describing my ideal vacation, these words are also action verbs! Think of the definition this way: If the verb is *not* a giant equal sign (a linking verb), it's an action verb.

Calling the Help Line for Verbs

You've probably noticed that some of the verbs I've identified throughout this chapter are single words and others are made up of several words. The extra words are called *helping verbs.* They don't carry out the trash or dust the living room, but they do help the main verb express meaning, usually changing the time, or *tense,* of the action. (For more on tense, see Chapter 6.)

Timing is everything: Creating a time frame with helping verbs

Helping verbs often signal when the action or state of being is occurring. Here are some sentences with helping verbs that create a time line:

> Alice *will sing* five arias from that opera tomorrow evening.
>
> (*Sing* is the main verb, and *will* is a helping verb. *Will* places the action at some point in the future.)
>
> Gwen *had moved* the vase, but the baseball *hit* it anyway.
>
> (*Moved* is the main verb, and *had* is a helping verb. *Hit* is a main verb without any helping verbs. *Had* places the action of moving sometime in the past.)
>
> Bob and Ellen *are admiring* Lola's new tattoo.
>
> (*Admiring* is the main verb, and *are* is a helping verb. *Are* places the action in the present.)

Don't ask! Questions and negative statements

To make your life more complicated, English often throws in a helping verb or two in order to form questions and negative statements. Usually the helping verb and the main verb are separated in this sort of sentence. In questions, the subject (the person or thing performing the action) comes between the helper and the main verb. *Not,* by the way, is NOT part of the verb. It's an adverb. (Check Chapter 10 for more about adverbs.) In negative statements, *not* shows up between the helper and the main verb. In Chapter 6, I explain more about forming questions and negative statements in various verb tenses. For now, check out these examples of questions and negative statements with helping verbs:

Does the ring in Lulu's bellybutton *rust* when she showers?

(*Does* is a helping verb, and *rust* is the main verb.)

Do Larry and Ella *need* a good divorce lawyer?

(*Do* is the helping verb, and *need* is the main verb.)

Did Zoe *play* the same song for eight hours?

(*Did* is the helping verb, and *play* is the main verb.)

Did the grammarians *complain* about that question?

(*Did* is the helping verb, and *complain* is the main verb.)

Will George remember all the old familiar places?

(*Will* is the helping verb, and *remember* is the main verb.)

Larry does not *drive* a sports car because he wants to project a wholesome image.

(*Does* is the helping verb, and *drive* is the main verb.)

The killer *bees do* not *chase* Roger because they are afraid of him.

(*Do* is the helping verb, and *chase* is the main verb.)

I will not *learn* anything else about verbs ever again.

(*Will* is the helping verb, and *learn* is the main verb.)

You've probably figured out that the main verbs in these example questions and negative statements are action verbs, with the helpers *do, does, did,* or *will.* You can't go wrong with *did* and *will,* because those helpers are the same for singular and plural subjects. *Does* and *do,* unfortunately, change according to the subject of the sentence. *Does* matches all singular subjects (when only one person is performing the action) and *do* works best in plural sentences, when more than one person is performing the action. *Do* is also the helper you want when the subject is *I* or *you.* (For more on matching singular and plural subjects and verbs, turn to Chapter 7.)

Questions or negative statements formed with the verb *to be* don't need *do* or *does*. In these examples, the verb is italicized:

> *Is* grammar a popular subject?
>
> *Am* I a good grammarian?
>
> *Were* the grammarians *analyzing* that sentence?

Change this statement into a question:

> Ella meets Larry's parents today.

Answer: *Does* Ella *meet* Larry's parents today? To form the question, add the helping verb *does*.

Now change this statement into a negative (opposite).

> George gave me help during the grammar test.

Answer: George *did* not *give* me help during the grammar test. You form the negative with the helping verb *did*.

Adding shades of meaning with helping verbs

Helping verbs also change the meaning of a sentence by adding a sense of duty, probability, willingness, and so forth. Concentrate on the italicized verbs in these examples. All are add-ons, or *helping verbs*. The main verbs appear in bold type. Notice how the meaning changes:

> Rita *may* **attend** the party. Her boss *might* **be** there.
>
> (The helping verbs *may* and *might* expresses possibility: Rita will go if she's in a good mood and stay home if she isn't. Same thing for the boss. *May* takes on another meaning, too. The same helping verb can express permission: Rita's father checked out the party and okayed it.)
>
> Rita *should* **attend** every official event. She *must* **go**.
>
> (The helping verbs *should* and *must* mean that attending is a duty or obligation. Even if Rita wants to sit on her sofa and knit socks, she has to attend.)

Rita *would* **stay** home if she *could* **do** so. She *can* **sleep** during the show, though.

(Two helpers appear in the first sentence. The helping verb *would* shows willingness or preference. The helping verb *could* makes a statement about ability. In the second sentence, *can* also refers to ability.)

Find the helping verbs in this sentence. Decide how the helping verb affects the meaning.

Would you consider a campaign for president if Lamar must step down?

Answer: *Would* is a helping verb that adds a sense of possibility to the main verb, *consider*. *Must* is a helping verb the implies an obligation. It is attached to the main verb *step*.

Some grammarians are very strict about the difference between some pairs of helpers — *can/may, can/could* and *may/might.* They see *can* as ability only, and *may* as permission. Similarly, a number of grammarians allow *can* and *may* for present actions only, with *might* and *could* reserved for past tense. These days, most people interchange all these helpers and end up with fine sentences. Don't worry too much about these pairs.

Distinguishing between helping verbs and main verbs isn't particularly important, as long as you get the whole thing when you're identifying the verb in a sentence. If you find only part of the verb, you may confuse action verbs with linking verbs. You want to keep these two types of verbs straight when you choose an ending for your sentence, as I explain in "Completing linking-verb sentences correctly" in the previous section.

To decide whether you have an action verb or a linking verb, look at the main verb, not at the helping verbs. If the main verb expresses action, the whole verb is action, even if one of the helpers is a form of *to be.* For example:

is going

has been painted

should be strangled

are all action verbs, not linking verbs, because *going, painted,* and *strangled* express action.

SHE DONE HIM WRONG

The word *done* is never a verb all by itself. A true party animal, this verb form insists on being accompanied by helping verbs. In grammarspeak, which you do NOT have to learn, *done* is a past participle of the verb *to do*. Naked, shivering, totally alone participles, such as *done*, never function as verbs. Here are some examples:

WRONG: He done all he could, but the sky fell anyway.

RIGHT: He had done all he could, but the sky fell anyway.

ALSO RIGHT: He did all he could, but the sky fell anyway.

WRONG: She done him wrong.

RIGHT, BUT A BAD SENTENCE: She has done him wrong.

ALSO RIGHT, ALSO A BAD SENTENCE: She did him wrong.

BETTER SENTENCE: What she has done to him is wrong.

ANOTHER OKAY: What she did to him is wrong.

You may blame the fact that so many people create sentences like the first example *(He done all he could)* on one of the many joys of English grammar. Some verb forms can stand alone or pair with a helping verb. Consider the verb *to walk*:

I *walked* twenty miles.

I *have walked* twenty miles.

These sentences both contain the word *walked*. It's a verb in the first example and part of a verb in the second example. Bottom line: Don't use *done* by itself as a verb. It's a combination form only!

Pop the Question: Locating the Verb

A scientific study by a blue-ribbon panel of experts found that 90 percent of all the errors in a sentence occurred because the verb was misidentified. Okay, there was no study. I made it up! But it is true that when you try to crack a sentence, you should always start by identifying the verb. To find the verb, read the sentence and ask two questions:

» What's happening?

» What is? (or, What word is a "giant equal sign"?)

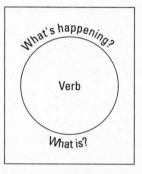

© John Wiley & Sons, Inc.

If you get an answer to the first question, you have an action verb. If you get an answer to the second question, you have a linking verb.

For example, in the sentence

Archie flew around the room and then swooped into his cage for a birdseed snack.

you ask "What's happening?" and your answer is *flew* and *swooped. Flew* and *swooped* are action verbs.

If you ask, "What is?" you get no answer, because there's no linking verb in the sentence.

Try another:

Lola's new tattoo will be larger than her previous fifteen tattoos.

What's happening? Nothing. You have no action verb. What is? *Will be. Will be* is a linking verb.

Pop the question and find the verbs in the following sentences. For extra credit, identify the verbs as action or linking.

A. Michelle scratched the cat almost as hard as the cat had scratched her.

B. After months of up-and-down motion, Lester is taking the elevator sideways, just for a change of pace.

C. The twisted frown on Larry's face seems strange because of the joyful background music.

Answers: A. *scratched* is an action verb, *had scratched* is an action verb. B. *is taking* is an action verb. C. *seems* is a linking verb.

You may hear English teachers say, "the verb *to sweep*" or some such expression. In fact, in this chapter I refer to "all forms of the verb *to be*." But *to be* is not actually a verb. It's an infinitive. An *infinitive* is *to + a verb*. (Some grammarians see the *to* as an add-on and count only the verb as an infinitive.) Don't worry about the terminology. The most important thing to know about infinitives is this: When you pop the question to find the verb, don't choose an infinitive as your answer. If you do, you'll miss the real verb or verbs in the sentence. Other than that, forget about infinitives!

Chapter **3**

Who's Doing What? How to Find the Subject

n Chapter 2, I describe the sentence as a flatbed truck carrying your meaning to the reader or listener. Verbs are the wheels of the truck, and subjects are the drivers. Why do you need a subject? Can you imagine a truck speeding down the road without a driver? Yes, I know that some tech companies are working to develop "self-driving cars." But even those vehicles, if they ever come on the market, will have a driver — the computer! The point is, someone or something has to be in charge. In a sentence, it's the subject.

Who's Driving the Truck? Why the Subject Is Important

All sentences contain verbs — words that express action or state of being. (For more information on verbs, see Chapter 2.) But you can't have an action in a vacuum. You can't have a naked, solitary state of being either. Someone or something must also be present in the sentence — the *who* or *what* you're talking about in relation to the action or state of being expressed by the verb. The "someone" or "something" doing the action or being talked about is the subject.

TIP

A "someone" must be a person and a "something" must be a thing, place, or idea. So guess what? The subject is usually a noun because a noun is a person, place, thing, or idea. I say *usually* because sometimes the subject is a pronoun — a word that substitutes for a noun or another pronoun — *he, they, it,* and so forth. (For more on pronouns, see Chapter 8.)

Teaming up: Subject and verb pairs

Another way to think about the subject is to say that the subject is the "who" or "what" part of the subject–verb pair. The subject–verb pair is the main idea of the sentence, stripped to essentials. A few sentences:

Jasper gasped at the mummy's sudden movement.

In this sentence, *Jasper gasped* is the main idea; it's also the subject–verb pair.

Justin will judge the beauty contest only if *his girlfriend competes.*

You should spot two subject–verb pairs in this sentence: *Justin will judge* and *girlfriend competes.*

Now try a sentence without action. This one describes a state of being, so it uses a linking verb:

Jill has always *been* an extremely efficient worker.

The subject–verb pair is *Jill has been.* Did you notice that *Jill has been* sounds incomplete? *Has been* is a linking verb, and linking verbs always need something after the verb to complete the idea. I give you more links in the verb chain in Chapter 2; now back to the *subject* at hand. (Sorry. I couldn't resist that pun.) The subject–verb pair in action-verb sentences may usually stand alone, but the subject–verb pair in linking verb sentences may not.

Compound subjects and verbs: Two for the price of one

Subjects and verbs pair off, but sometimes you get two (or more) for the price of one. You can have two subjects (or more) and one verb. The multiple subjects are called *compound subjects.* Here's an example:

Dorothy and *Justin* went home in defeat.

Here you notice one action (*went*) and two people (*Dorothy, Justin*) doing the action. So the verb *went* has two subjects.

Now take a look at some additional examples:

> *Lola* and *Lulu* prepared breakfast for George yesterday. (*Lola, Lulu* = subjects)
>
> The *omelet* and *fries* were very salty. (*omelet, fries* = subjects)
>
> *Snort* and *Squirm* were not allowed to join Snow White's band. (*Snort, Squirm* = subjects)

Another variation is one subject paired with two (or more) verbs. For example:

> Alex *screamed* and *cried* after the contest.

You've got two actions (*screamed, cried*) and one person doing both (*Alex*). *Alex* is the subject of both *screamed* and *cried*.

Some additional samples of double verbs, which in grammatical terms are called *compound verbs:*

> George *snatched* the flash drive and quickly *stashed* it in his pocket. (*snatched, stashed* = verbs)
>
> Larry *complained* for hours about Ella's insult and then *crept* home. (*complained, crept* = verbs)
>
> Luke *came* to school last week but *didn't stay* there. (*came, did stay* = verbs)

Pop the Question: Locating the Subject–Verb Pairs

Allow me to let you in on a little trick for pinpointing the subject–verb pair of a sentence: Pop the question! (No, I'm not asking you to propose.) Pop the question tells you what to ask in order to find out what you want to know. The correct question is all important in the search for information, as all parents realize.

> WRONG QUESTION FROM PARENT: What did you do last night?
>
> TEENAGER'S ANSWER: Nothing.

RIGHT QUESTION FROM PARENT: When you came in at 2 a.m., were you hoping that I'd ignore the fact that you went to the Carleton Club?

TEENAGER'S ANSWER: I didn't go to the Carleton Club! I went to the mall.

PARENT: Aha! You went out on a school night. You're grounded.

In Chapter 2, I explain that the first question to ask is not "Is this going to be on the test?" but "What's the verb?" (To find the verb, ask *what's happening?* or *what is?*) After you uncover the verb, put "who" or "what" in front of it to form a question. The answer is the subject.

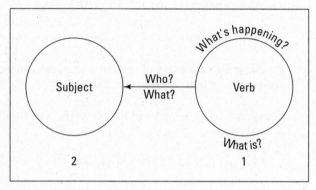

© John Wiley & Sons, Inc.

Check out this example: Jack polishes his dives during hours of practice.

1. Pop the question: What's happening? Answer: *polishes. Polishes* is the verb.

2. Pop the question: Who or what *polishes?* Answer: *Jack polishes. Jack* is the subject.

Ready for another?

The pool has been closed by the Health Department.

1. Pop the question: What's happening? Answer: *has been closed. Has been closed* is the verb.

2. Pop the question: Who or what *has been closed?* Answer: *pool. Pool* is the subject.

TIP

Did you notice anything different about the last example sentence? The verb, *has been closed*, asks about something that happened to the pool, not about something the pool did. *Has been closed* is a passive verb (the action happens to the subject), not an active one (the subject does the action). I explain more about active and passive verbs in Chapter 17. Fortunately, "pop the question" works the same way for sentences with either active or passive verbs.

POP QUIZ

A pop quiz on popping the question. What are the subject and verb in the following sentence?

Roger will soon be smiling because of all the treasure in his ship.

Answer: The verb is *will be smiling* and the subject is *Roger.* Try one more. Identify the subject and verb.

No matter what the weather, Roger never even considers wearing a hat.

Answer: The verb is *considers* and the subject is *Roger.*

What's a Nice Subject Like You Doing in a Place Like This? Unusual Word Order

Most of the sentences you encounter are in the normal subject–verb order, which is (surprise!) subject–verb. In other words, the subject usually comes before the verb. Not every sentence follows that order, though most do. Sometimes a subject hides out at the end of the sentence or in some other weird place. (Hey, even a subject needs a change of scenery sometime.)

If you pop the question and answer it according to the meaning of the sentence — not according to the word order — you'll be fine. The key is to put the subject questions (who? what?) in front of the verb. Then think about what the sentence is actually saying and answer the questions. Like magic, your subject will then appear.

Try this one:

Up the avenue and around the park trudged Godzilla.

1. Pop the question: What's happening? What is? Answer: *trudged. Trudged* is the verb.

2. Pop the question: Who *trudged?* What *trudged?* Answer: *Godzilla. Godzilla* is the subject. (I'll let you decide whether Godzilla is a who or a what.)

If you were answering by word order, you'd say *park.* But the *park* did not *trudge; Godzilla trudged.* Pay attention to meaning, not to placement in the sentence, and you can't go wrong.

What are the subjects and verbs in the following sentences?

A. Alas, what a sadly inadequate grammarian am I.

B. Across the river and through the woods to the grammarian's house go Ella and Larry.

Answers: In sentence A, *am* is the verb and *I* is the subject. In sentence B, the verb is *go* and the subjects are *Ella* and *Larry.*

Always find the verb first. Then look for the subject.

ME, MYSELF, AND I

In formal speech and writing, you can use *I* as a subject, but not *me* or *myself.*

> Wrong: Bill and me are going to rob that bank. Bill and myself will soon be in jail.

> Right: Bill and I are going to rob that bank. Bill and I will soon be in jail.

Me doesn't perform actions; it receives actions. To put this rule another way: *Me* is an object of some action or form of attention. He gave the stolen money to *me.* (Check Chapter 8 for more on the difference between *I* and *me.*)

Myself is appropriate only for actions that double back on the person performing the action: I told *myself* not to be such a nerd! *Myself* may also be used for emphasis (though some grammarians object to the repetition), along with the word *I: I myself* will disclose the story to the tabloid offering the most bucks.

In informal conversation, you can get away with pairing *myself* or *me* with another subject. Between friends, you may hear "Me and Bob have a getaway plan" or "Bob and myself won't get caught." No problem there, at least no problem with language. Just don't rob the bank!

Find That Subject! Detecting You-Understood

"Sit still."

"Eat your vegetables."

"Clean your room."

What do these sentences have in common? Yes, they're all nagging comments you've heard all your life. More importantly, they're all commands. The verbs give orders: *sit, eat, clean.* So where's the subject in these sentences?

If you pop the question, here's what happens:

1. Pop the question: What's happening? What is? Answer: *sit, eat, clean.*

2. Pop the question: Who *sit, eat, clean?* Answer: Uh . . .

The second question appears to have no answer, but appearances can be deceiving. The answer is *you. You* sit still. *You* eat your vegetables. *You* clean your room. What's that you say? *You* is not in the sentence? True. *You* is not written, but it's implied. And when your mom says, "Eat your vegetables," you understand that she means *you.* So grammarians say that the subject is *you-understood.* The subject is *you,* even though *you* isn't in the sentence and even though *you* don't intend to eat any of those lima beans your mom overcooked.

POP QUIZ

Pop the questions and find the subject–verb pairs in these three sentences.

A. Ella, dancing the cha-cha, forgot to watch her feet.

B. Stop, Ella!

C. Over the bandleader and across five violin stands fell Ella.

Answers: In sentence A, *forgot* is the verb and *Ella* is the subject. *Dancing* is a fake verb. (I discuss fake verbs and subjects later in this chapter.) In sentence B, *stop* is the verb and *you-understood* is the subject. The remark is addressed to *Ella,* but *you-understood* is still the subject. In sentence C, *fell* is the verb and *Ella* is the subject.

Searching for the Subject in Questions

Does everyone love grammar? Don't answer that! I started this section with that sentence not to check attitudes toward grammar (I'd rather not know) but to illustrate the subject's favorite location in a question. Most questions in English are formed by adding a helping verb — *do, does, will, can, should,* and so forth — to a main verb. (For everything you need to know about helping verbs, turn to Chapter 2.) The subject is generally tucked between the helping verb and the main verb, but you don't have to bother remembering that fascinating bit of trivia. To locate the subject in a question, simply "pop the question" the same way you do for any other sentence. Here's how to attack the first sentence of this paragraph:

1. Pop the question: What's happening? What is? Answer: *does love.*

2. Pop the question: Who *does love?* Answer: *everyone.*

TIP

When you're "popping the subject question" for a subject, the "popped question" may sound a little odd. Why? Because in a question, the subject usually isn't located in front of the verb. But if you ignore the awkwardness of the phrasing and concentrate on meaning, you can easily — and correctly — identify the subject of a question.

POP QUIZ

Pop the questions and find the subject–verb pairs in these three questions.

A. Has George ever been elected president?

B. Could I possibly care less about George's cherry tree?

C. Won't George's ax-sharpener charge extra?

Answers: In sentence A, *has been elected* is the verb and *George* is the subject. In sentence B, *could care* is the verb and the subject is *I.* Sentence C is a bit tricky. The word "won't" is short for "will not." So the verb in C is *will charge,* and the subject is *George's ax-sharpener.* You may be wondering what happened to the *not. Not* is an adverb, not that you need to know that fact. It changes the meaning of the verb from positive to negative. (For more on adverbs, turn to Chapter 10.)

Don't Get Faked Out: Avoiding Fake Verbs and Subjects

As I walk through New York City, I often see "genuine" Rolex watches (retail $10,000 or so) for sale from street peddlers for "$15 — special today only!" You need to guard against fakes when you're on the city streets (no surprise there).

Also (and this may be a surprise), you need to guard against fakes when you're finding subject–verb pairs.

Finding fake verbs

Verbs in English grammar can be a little sneaky sometimes. You may ask *who?* or *what?* in front of a verb and get no answer or at least no answer that makes sense. When this happens, you may gather that you haven't really found a verb. You've probably stumbled upon a lookalike, or, as I call it, a "fake verb." Here's an example:

> Wiping his tears dramatically, Alex pleaded with the teacher to forgive his lack of homework.

Suppose you pop the verb question *(What's happening? What is?)* and get *wiping* for an answer. A reasonable guess. But now pop the subject question: *Who wiping? What wiping?* The questions don't sound right, and that's your first hint that you haven't found a real verb. But the question is not important. The answer, however, is! And there is no real answer in the sentence. You may try *Alex*, but when you put him with the "verb," it doesn't match: *Alex wiping.* (*Alex is wiping* would be okay, but that's not what the sentence says.) So now you know for sure that your first "verb" isn't really a verb. Put it aside and keep looking. What's the real verb? *Pleaded.*

To sum up: Lots of words in the sentence express action or being, but only some of these words are verbs. (Most are what grammarians call verbals; check out Chapter 19 for more on verbals.) At any rate, if you get no answer to your pop-the-subject question, just ignore the "verb" you think you found and look for the real verb.

Watching out for "here" and "there" and other fake subjects

Someone comes up to you and says, "Here is ten million dollars." What's the first question that comes into your mind? I know, good grammarian that you are, that your question isn't *Where can I buy a good yacht?* but rather *What's the subject of that sentence?* Well, try to answer your question in the usual way, by popping the question.

> Here is ten million dollars.

1. Pop the question: What's happening? What is? Answer: *is.*
2. Pop the question: Who *is?* What *is?* Answer: ?

What did you say? *Here is?* Wrong. *Here* can't be a subject. Neither can *there*. Both of these words are fake subjects. What's the real answer to the question *What is?* *Ten million dollars. Here* and *there* are fill-ins, place markers; they aren't what you're talking about. *Ten million dollars* — that's what you're talking about!

Choosing the correct verb for "here" and "there" sentences

If you write *here* and *there* sentences, be sure to choose the correct verb. Because *here* and *there* are never subjects, you must always look *after* the verb for the real subject. When you match a subject to a verb (something I discuss in detail in Chapter 7), be sure to use the real subject, not *here* or *there*. Example:

> Here are ten anteaters. NOT Here is ten anteaters. (anteaters = subject)

TIP

If you want to check your choice of verb, try reversing the sentence. In the sample sentence above, say *ten anteaters is/are*. Chances are your "ear" will tell you that you want *ten anteaters are*, not *ten anteaters is*.

TEST ALERT

Standardized tests often check whether you can detect the right verb for a "here" or "there" sentence. Test-taker beware!

POP QUIZ

Which sentence is correct?

A. There are 50 reasons for my complete lack of homework.

B. There's 50 reasons for my complete lack of homework.

Answer: Sentence A is correct. In sentence B, *there's* is short for *there is*, but *reasons*, the plural subject, takes a plural verb.

Subjects Aren't Just a Singular Sensation: Forming the Plural of Nouns

Distinguishing between singular and plural subjects is a really big deal, and I go into it in detail in Chapter 7. But before I go any further, I want to explain how to form the plural of nouns (words that name persons, places, or things) because most subjects are nouns. If you learn how to form plurals, you'll also be able to recognize them.

Regular plurals

Plain old garden-variety nouns form plurals by adding the letter *s*. Check out Table 3-1 for some examples.

TABLE 3-1

Examples of regular plurals

Singular	Plural
zebra	zebras
stripe	stripes
cat	cats
nerd	nerds
lollipop	lollipops
eyebrow	eyebrows

Singular nouns that end in *s* already, as well as singular nouns ending in *sh, ch,* and *x* form plurals by adding *es*. Some examples are shown in Table 3-2.

TABLE 3-2

Examples of regular plurals ending in -s, -sh, -ch, and -x

Singular	Plural
splash	splashes
box	boxes
kiss	kisses
watch	watches
mess	messes
catch	catches

The -IES and -YS have it

If a noun ends in the letter *y*, and the letter before the *y* is a vowel (a, e, i, o, u), just add *s*. For examples, see Table 3-3.

TABLE 3-3

Examples of regular plurals ending in a vowel plus y

Singular	Plural
monkey	monkeys
turkey	turkeys
day	days
boy	boys
honey	honeys
bay	bays

If the noun ends in *y* but the letter before the –*y* is not a vowel, form the plural by changing the *y* to *i* and adding *es*. For examples, see Table 3-4.

TABLE 3-4

Examples of regular plurals ending in a consonant plus -y

Singular	Plural
sob story	sob stories
unsolvable mystery	unsolvable mysteries
a cute little belly	cute little bellies
pinky	pinkies
activity	activities
penny	pennies

WARNING

Never change the spelling of a name when you make it plural. The plural of *Sammy* is *Sammys*, not *Sammies*.

No knifes here: Irregular plurals

This topic wouldn't be any fun without irregulars, now would it? Okay, you're right. Irregulars are always a pain. However, they're also always around. Table 3-5 gives you examples of irregular plurals.

TABLE 3-5

Examples of irregular plurals

Singular	Plural
knife	knives
sheep	sheep
man	men
woman	women
child	children
deer	deer

TIP

Listing all the irregular plurals is an impossible task. Check the dictionary for any noun plural that puzzles you.

The brother-in-law rule: Hyphenated plurals

If you intend to insult your relatives, you may as well do so with the correct plural form. Remember: Form the plural of hyphenated nouns by adding *s* or *es* to the important word, not to the add–ons. These words are all plurals:

» mothers-in-law

» brothers-in-law

» vice-presidents

» secretaries-general

» dogcatchers-in-chief

TIP

You may hear references to "attorney generals." If you do, call the grammar police. An "attorney general" is a lawyer, not a military officer. Therefore, *attorney* is the important part of this title, and it's a noun. The *general* is a description — a reference to the rank of the *attorney*. To form a plural, you deal with the noun, not with the descriptive word. Therefore, you have one *attorney general* and two or more *attorneys general* — and probably a large number of lawsuits.

Chapter **4**

When All Is Said and Done: Complete Sentences

Everyone knows this important rule of English grammar: All sentences must be complete. But everyone breaks the rule. I just did! *But everyone breaks the rule* is not a complete sentence; it's a sentence *fragment*. At times, fragments are perfectly acceptable, and in this chapter I show you when you can get away with writing one. (Hint: Hardly anyone texts and tweets in complete sentences.) The other extreme — more than one complete sentence improperly glued together — is a *run-on sentence*. A run-on sentence — and its variation, a *comma splice* — are grammatical felonies. Never fear: In this chapter, I explain how to join ideas without risking a visit from the Grammar Police. I also provide everything you need to know about *endmarks*, the punctuation separating one sentence from another. I even explain when you can omit an endmark entirely or double — even triple — it to emphasize your point.

Completing Sentences: The Essential Subjects and Verbs

A complete sentence has at least one subject–verb pair. They're a pair because they match. They both enjoy taking long walks on the beach, playing video games, and making fun of reality-show contestants. Just kidding. They match because, well, they work smoothly as a team. One half of the pair (the verb) expresses action or being, and the other half (the subject) is whatever or whoever does the action or exists in the state of being. (For more information on verbs, see Chapter 2; for more information on subjects, see Chapter 3.) A few subject–verb pairs that match are

> Egbert scrambled
>
> Ms. McAnnick has repaired
>
> Eva will be

Just for comparison, here's one mismatch:

> Egbert scrambling

TIP

When you're texting, tweeting, or IMing (instant messaging), space is tight. Every character counts, including spaces. Therefore, many people opt for "sentences" that contain only verbs, so long as the meaning is clear. Check out this sample text:

> Went home. Fed cow. Cleaned barn.

The missing subject, *I*, is obvious. If you're talking about someone else, however, you need to supply a subject:

> Abner went home. Fed cow. Cleaned barn.

Now the person receiving the message understands that Abner did all the work, not the texter — who, of course, was too busy texting to tackle chores. By the way, I used capital letters in the preceding examples. Lots of people opt for lowercase in messages like these, and many also drop the periods. Check Chapter 16 for a guide to capitalization and punctuation in electronic media.

You may find some mismatches in your sentences when you go subject–verb hunting. Mismatches are not necessarily wrong; they're simply not subject–verb pairs. Take a look at the preceding mismatch, this time inside its sentence:

> Egbert, scrambling for a seat at the counter, knocked over an omelet plate.

TIP

When you're checking a sentence for completeness, ignore the mismatches. Keep looking until you find a subject–verb pair that belongs together. If you can't find one, you don't have a complete sentence.

Complete sentences may also include more than one subject–verb pair:

Dorothy fiddled while the orchestra pit burned. (*Dorothy* = subject of the verb *fiddled, orchestra pit* = subject of the verb *burned*)

Because Lester jumped on the trampoline, the earth shook. (*Lester* = subject of the verb *jumped, earth* = subject of the verb *shook*)

Not only did George swim, but he also sipped the pool water. (*George* = subject of the verb *did swim, he* = subject of the verb *sipped*)

Complete sentences may also match one subject with more than one verb, and vice versa:

The cute green lizard appeared in three commercials but sang in only two. (*lizard* = subject of verbs *appeared, sang*)

Alice and Archie tweet at least once an hour, all day and all night. (*Alice, Archie* = subjects of the verb *tweet*)

Roger and I have put your crayons on the radiator. (*Roger, I* = subjects of the verb *have put*)

Complete sentences that give commands may match an understood subject (you) with the verb:

Give me a coupon. (*you-understood* = subject of the verb *give*)

Visit Grandma, you little brat! (*you-understood* = subject of the verb *visit*)

TIP

To find the subject–verb pair, start with the verb. Pop the verb question: *What's happening?* or *What is?* The answer is the verb. Then pop the subject question: Ask *who?* or *what?* in front of the verb. The answer is the subject. (For a more complete explanation, see Chapter 3.)

POP QUIZ

The sentence below contains one true subject–verb pair and one mismatch. Can you find the subject–verb pair?

The angry ant caught in a blob of glue vowed never to walk near a model airplane again.

Answer: The subject–verb pair is *ant vowed.* The mismatch is *ant caught.* The sentence isn't saying that the *ant caught* something, so *ant caught* is not a match.

TIP

In the preceding pop quiz, *to walk* is not the verb. *To walk* is an infinitive, the basic form from which verbs are made. Infinitives never function as verbs in a sentence.

Complete Thoughts, Complete Sentences

What's an incomplete sentence? It's the moment in the television show just before the last commercial. You know what I mean. *The hero slowly edges the door open a few inches, peeks in, gasps, and . . . FADE TO DANCING CEREAL BOX.* You were planning to switch to a different show, but instead you wait to see if the villain stabs the hero. You haven't gotten to the end, and you don't know what's happening. A complete sentence is the opposite of that moment in a television show. You have gotten to the end, and you do know what's happening. In other words, a complete sentence must express a complete thought. (You've probably noticed that grammar terminology is not terribly original; in fact, it's terribly obvious.)

Check out these complete sentences. Notice how they express complete thoughts:

> Despite Egbert's fragile appearance, he proved to be a tough opponent.
>
> Ms. McAnnick will repair your car while you wait.
>
> I can't imagine why anyone would want to ride on top of a bus.
>
> Did Lola apply for a job as a tattoo artist?

For comparison, here are a few incomplete thoughts:

> The reason I wanted a divorce was.
>
> Because I said so.

I can guess what you're thinking. Both of those incomplete thoughts may be part of a longer conversation. Yes, in context those incomplete thoughts may indeed express a complete thought:

> Sydney: So the topic of conversation was the team's chances for a trophy?
>
> Alice: No! The reason I wanted a divorce was!

and

Nick: Why do I have to do this dumb homework?

Alice: Because I said so.

Fair enough. You can pull a complete thought out of the examples. However, the context of a conversation is not enough to satisfy the complete thought/complete sentence rule. To be "legal," your sentence must express a complete thought.

Check out these examples:

The reason I wanted a divorce was the topic of our conversation, even though his real interest was the team's chances for a trophy.

You have to do this dumb homework because I said so.

Final answer: Every complete sentence has at least one subject–verb pair and must express a complete thought.

TEST ALERT

Standardized tests frequently require you to recognize and sometimes correct incomplete sentences. Test writers like to include a long, but incomplete sentence fragment — or an extremely short complete sentence — in the answer choices. If the thought is complete, the sentence is fine, even if it's as short as two words. If the thought isn't complete, despite rambling on for ten lines, you've got a fragment, not a sentence. Bottom line: Don't worry about length. Use logic instead.

WARNING

In deciding whether you have a complete sentence or not, you may be led astray by words that resemble questions. Consider these three words: *who knits well.* A complete thought? Maybe yes, maybe no. Suppose those three words form a question:

Who knits well?

This question is understandable and its thought is complete. Verdict: legal. Suppose these three words form a statement:

Who knits well.

Now they don't make sense. This incomplete sentence needs more words to make a complete thought:

The honor of making Elizabeth's sweater will go to the person who knits well.

The moral of the story? Don't change the meaning of what you're saying when deciding whether a thought is complete. If you're *questioning*, consider your sentence as a *question*. If you're *stating*, consider your sentence as a *statement*.

Occasionally a complete sentence ends with an ellipsis — three spaced dots. Such sentences show up in dramatic works, to add suspense or to indicate hesitation or confusion. These sentences appear incomplete, but because they fulfill the author's purpose, they *are* complete. For more information on ellipses, see "Reaching the End of the Line: Endmarks" later in this chapter.

Which sentence is complete?

A. Martin sings.

B. Martin, who hopes to sing professionally some day but can't get beyond the do-re-mi level despite fifteen years with an excellent teacher and many hours of practice.

Answer: Even though it is short, sentence A is complete. *Martin sings* is a complete idea and includes the necessary subject–verb pair. In sentence B, one subject is paired with two verbs (*who + hopes, can get*), but no complete thought is stated.

WHY CLARITY IS IMPORTANT

One of my favorite moments in teaching came on a snowy January day. A student named Danny ran into the lunchroom, clearly bursting with news. "Guess what?" he shouted triumphantly to his friends. "A kid on my bus's mother had a baby last night!"

This situation wasn't critical. After all, the baby had already been born. But imagine if Danny had been greeting an ambulance with "Quick! Over here! A kid on my bus's mother is having a baby!" I think everyone agrees that the best reaction from an emergency medical technician isn't "Your bus has a mother?"

Being clear is the most important rule of English grammar. Faced with a choice between confusion and incomplete sentences, for example, incomplete sentences win. Here's the news Danny should have spread that cold January day:

This kid on my bus? His mother had a baby last night.

Of course, he could also have told his story correctly by saying:

The mother of a kid on my bus had a baby last night.

Either way, everyone would've yawned, finished lunch, and filed out to math class. Hearing either of these statements, the students would've understood what Danny was trying to say.

So remember: First comes meaning. Second comes everything else.

Joining Forces: Combining Sentences Correctly

Listen to a toddler and you may hear something like "I played with the clay and I went to the zoo and Mommy said I had to take a nap and I fell asleep and then I woke up." Monotonous, yes. But — surprise, surprise — grammatically correct. Take a look at how the information would sound if that one sentence turned into five: *I played with the clay. I went to the zoo. Mommy said I had to take a nap. I fell asleep. Then I woke up.* The information sounds choppy. When the sentences are combined, the information flows more smoothly. Granted, joining everything with *and* is not a great idea. Read on for better ways of attaching one sentence to another.

TEST ALERT

Standardized test-makers enjoy plopping run-on sentences and comma splices into paragraphs and checking whether you can identify the run-ons as grammatically incorrect. (A *run-on sentence* is two or more complete thoughts joined improperly. A *comma splice* is a run-on in which a comma attempts to unite two complete thoughts.) Teachers who score the essay section of the SAT also frown on run-ons and comma splices. The best way to avoid this type of grammar error is to figure out how to connect sentences legally, as explained in this section.

Connecting with coordinate conjunctions

The words used to join elements in a sentence are *conjunctions.* You're surely familiar with these common words: *for, but, yet, so, nor, and,* and *or.* (*And* is the most popular, for those of you keeping track.) These little powerhouses, which are called *coordinate conjunctions,* eat kale and work out every day. Their healthful habits make them strong enough to join complete sentences. (They may also unite other types of grammatical elements, including individual words.) Check out these coordinate conjunctions in action, joining complete sentences:

The rain pelted Abner's hair, *and* his suede shoes were completely ruined.

The CEO told Tanya to text the address of the restaurant to everyone, *but* Tanya had no idea where the restaurant was.

You can take a hike, *or* you can jump off a cliff.

Ben did not know how to shoe a horse, *nor* did he understand how hard a horse can kick.

Thousands of people filled the square, *for* they had received a tweet about a flash mob.

Coordinate conjunctions give equal emphasis to the elements they join. In the preceding sentences, the ideas on one side of the conjunction have no more or less importance than the ideas on the other side of the conjunction.

TIP

When the conjunctions *and, but, or, nor,* and *for* unite two complete sentences, a comma precedes the conjunction. For the lowdown on commas, turn to Chapter 13.

REMEMBER

Some words appear to be strong enough to join sentences, but in reality they're just a bunch of couch potatoes who've never seen the inside of a gym. They may look good, but the minute you need them to pick up a truck or something, they're history. False joiners include *however, consequently, therefore, moreover, also,* and *furthermore.* Use these words to add meaning to your sentences but not to glue the sentences together. When you see these words on a standardized exam, be careful! A favorite test-maker trick is to plop these words into a run-on. Take a look at these examples:

RUN-ON: Lennie gobbled the steak, consequently, Robbie had nothing to eat.

CORRECTED VERSION #1: Lennie gobbled the steak; consequently, Robbie had nothing to eat.

CORRECTED VERSION #2: Lennie gobbled the steak. Consequently, Robbie had nothing to eat.

Notice the semicolon in the first corrected sentence? Semicolons are equivalent to coordinate conjunctions. According to the Governing Council on Grammar (which doesn't exist), semicolons can join two complete sentences under certain conditions. See the next section for more details.

TIP

With your sharp eyes, you probably spotted a comma after *consequently* in each of the preceding examples. Grammarians argue about whether you must place a comma after a false joiner. (For the record, false joiners are *conjunctive adverbs.* No one in the entire universe needs to know that term.) Some grammarians say that the comma is necessary. Others (I'm one) see the comma as optional — a question of personal style. If you're writing for authority figures, ask what they prefer. If you have no one to please but yourself, insert or omit a comma whenever you want.

Attaching thoughts: Semicolons

The semicolon is a funny little punctuation mark; it functions as a pit stop between one idea and another. It's not as strong as a period, which in Britain is called a "full stop" because, well, that's what a period does. It stops the reader. A semicolon lets the reader take a rest, but just for a moment. This punctuation mark is strong enough to attach one complete sentence to another.

I've seen writing manuals that proclaim, "Never use semicolons!" with the same intensity of feeling as, say, "Don't blow up the world with that nuclear missile." I've also read articles proclaiming (with no proof whatsoever) that only people old enough to collect a pension use this punctuation mark and that no sane person ever places one in a text. My advice is to use semicolons if you like them. Avoid them if you don't.

If you do put a semicolon in your sentence, be sure to attach related ideas. Here's an example:

> RIGHT: Grover was born in Delaware; he moved to Virginia when he was 4.

> WRONG: I put nonfat yogurt into that soup; I like Bob Dylan's songs.

In the first example, both parts of the sentence are about Grover's living arrangements. In the second, those two ideas are, to put it mildly, not in the same universe. (At least not until Bob Dylan writes a song about a container of yogurt. Hey, it could happen.)

POP QUIZ

Punctuate the following, adding or subtracting words as needed:

> Abner will clip the thorns from that rose stem he is afraid of scratching himself.

Answer: Many combinations are possible, including these two:

> Abner will clip the thorns from that rose stem. He is afraid of scratching himself.

> Abner will clip the thorns from that rose stem; he is afraid of scratching himself.

Boss and Employee: Joining Ideas of Unequal Ranks

In the average company, the boss runs the show. The boss has subordinates who play two important roles. They must do at least some work, and they must make the boss feel like the center of the universe. Leave the boss alone in the office, and everything's fine. Leave the employees alone in the office, and pretty soon someone is riding on the ceiling fan.

Some sentences resemble companies. The "boss" part of a sentence is all right by itself; it expresses a complete thought. The "employee" can't stand alone; it's an incomplete thought. (In case you're into grammar lingo: The boss is an *independent clause*, and the employee is a *subordinate clause*. For more information on independent and subordinate clauses, see Chapter 18.) Together, the "boss" and the "employee" create a more powerful sentence. Check out some examples:

> BOSS: Jack ate the bagel.
>
> EMPLOYEE: After he had picked out all the raisins.
>
> JOINING 1: Jack ate the bagel after he had picked out all the raisins.
>
> JOINING 2: After he had picked out all the raisins, Jack ate the bagel.

> BOSS: George hacked the government's computer network.
>
> EMPLOYEE: Because he felt traitorous.
>
> JOINING 1: George hacked the government's computer network because he felt traitorous.
>
> JOINING 2: Because he felt traitorous, George hacked the government's computer network.

> BOSS: The book bag is in the garage.
>
> EMPLOYEE: That Larry lost.
>
> JOINING: The book bag that Larry lost is in the garage.

The joined example sentences are grammatically legal because they contain at least one complete thought, which can stand on its own as a complete sentence.

Choosing Subordinate Conjunctions

The conjunctions in the boss–employee type of sentence I describe in the preceding section do double duty. These conjunctions emphasize the importance of one idea (the "boss," an *independent clause,* the equivalent of a complete sentence). They also show that the other (the "employee" or *subordinate clause*) is less important. The conjunctions joining boss and employee give some information about the relationship between the two ideas. These conjunctions are called *subordinate conjunctions.* Some common subordinate conjunctions are *while, because, although,*

though, since, when, where, if, whether, before, until, than, as, as if, in order that, so that, whenever, and *wherever.*

Check out how conjunctions are used in these examples:

Sentence 1: Michael was shaving. (not a very important activity)

Sentence 2: The earthquake destroyed the city. (a rather important event)

If these two sentences are joined as equals with a coordinate conjunction, the writer emphasizes both events:

Michael was shaving, *and* the earthquake destroyed the city.

Grammatically, the sentence is legal. But do you really think that Michael's work with a razor is equal in importance to an earthquake that measures 7 on the Richter scale? Better to join these clauses as unequals with the help of a subordinate conjunction, making the main idea about the earthquake the boss:

While Michael was shaving, the earthquake destroyed the city.

or

The earthquake destroyed the city *while* Michael was shaving.

The *while* gives you *time* information, attaches the employee sentence to the boss sentence, and shows the greater importance of the earthquake. Not bad for five letters.

Here's another:

Sentence 1: Esther must do her homework now.

Sentence 2: Mom is on the warpath.

In combining these two ideas, you have a few decisions to make. Depending on how you join them, the reader will grasp a different meaning. First, check out these ideas with a coordinate conjunction — a word that unites equals:

Esther must do her homework now, and Mom is on the warpath.

The combined sentence leaves so much room for interpretation that readers may wonder why the two ideas appear in the same sentence. Try again:

Esther must do her homework now, *but* Mom is on the warpath.

This joining of equals is better because *but* adds meaning. Most likely, Mom is running around the house screaming at the top of her lungs. Esther has to concentrate on her history homework, but she finds that concentrating is impossible during her mom's tantrum.

Try another joining:

Esther must do her homework now *because* Mom is on the warpath.

This sentence is more definite: Esther's mother got one of those little pink notes from the teacher *(Number of missing homeworks: 323)*. Esther knows that if she wants to survive through high school graduation, she'd better get to work now. One more joining to check:

Mom is on the warpath *because* Esther must do her homework now.

In this version, Esther's mother has asked her daughter to clean the garage. She's been asking Esther every day for the last two years. Now the health inspector is due and Mom's really worried. But Esther told her that she couldn't clean up now because she had to do her homework. World War III erupted immediately.

Do you see the power of these joining words? These conjunctions strongly influence the meanings of the sentences.

REMEMBER

Choose a joining word that makes your meaning clear.

Using Pronouns to Combine Sentences

A useful trick for combining short sentences legally is "the pronoun connection." (A *pronoun* substitutes for a noun, which is a word for a person, place, thing, or idea. See Chapter 8 for more information.) Check out these combinations:

Sentence 1: Amy read the book.

Sentence 2: The book had a thousand pictures in it.

Joining: Amy read the book *that* had a thousand pictures in it.

Sentence 1: The paper map stuck to Will's shoe.

Sentence 2: We plan to use the map to take over the world.

Joining: The paper map, *which* we plan to use to take over the world, stuck to Will's shoe.

Sentence 1: Margaret wants to hire a carpenter.

Sentence 2: The carpenter will build a new ant farm for her pets.

Joining: Margaret wants to hire a carpenter *who* will build a new ant farm for her pets.

Sentence 1: The tax bill was passed yesterday.

Sentence 2: The tax bill will lower taxes for the top .00009% income bracket.

Joining: The tax bill *that* was passed yesterday will lower taxes for the top .00009% income bracket.

Alternate joining: The tax bill that was passed yesterday will lower taxes for Bill Gates and Mark Zuckerberg. (Okay, I interpreted a little.)

That, which, and *who* are pronouns. In the combined sentences, each takes the place of a noun. *(That* replaces *book, which* replaces *map, who* replaces *carpenter, that* replaces *tax bill.)* These pronouns serve as thumbtacks, attaching a subordinate or less important idea to the main body of the sentence. For grammar trivia contests: *that, which,* and *who* (as well as *whom* and *whose*) are pronouns that may relate one idea to another. When they do that job, they are called *relative pronouns.*

TEST ALERT

Relative pronouns — like real relatives, at least in some families! — can cause lots of problems. Therefore, the SAT, the ACT, and other standardized exams hit this topic hard. Chapter 18 tells you everything you need to know about relative pronouns.

POP QUIZ

Combine these sentences with a pronoun.

Sentence 1: Charlie slowly tiptoed toward the poisonous snakes.

Sentence 2: The snakes soon bit Charlie right on the tip of his nose.

Answer: Charlie slowly tiptoed toward the poisonous snakes, *which* soon bit Charlie right on the tip of his nose. The pronoun *which* replaces *snakes* in sentence 2.

Understanding Fragments

I use incomplete sentences, or *fragments,* here and there throughout this book, and (I hope) these incomplete sentences aren't confusing. Especially in electronic communication, quick cuts and short comments are the rule. Fragments, though, sometimes *aren't* the best choice. To decide when fragments are acceptable, read on.

Placing fragments in the right context

In conversational English (see Chapter 1), fragments are usually acceptable. The most common type of fragment begins with the words *and, or, but,* or *nor.* These words are *conjunctions.* As I explain in "Joining Forces: Combining Sentences Correctly" earlier in this chapter, these conjunctions may combine two complete sentences (with two complete thoughts) into one longer sentence:

> Egbert went to his doctor for a cholesterol check, *and* then he scrambled home.

For centuries, writers have begun sentences with *and, or, but,* and *nor,* especially in informal writing or for dramatic effect. For example, the previous sentence may be turned into

> Egbert went to his doctor for a cholesterol check. And then he scrambled home.

No one misunderstands the meaning. The fragment's separation creates a punch line and adds a bit of drama. Verdict: This fragment is fine.

So are fragments that make sense in the context of a larger conversation, especially in conversational English. Have a look at this example:

> MARIA: Is that toaster on sale now?

> JOE: No, next week.

Joe's comment is clear only because Maria led the way. If Joe suddenly declares, "No, next week" with no context, he's likely to be met with a puzzled look. (See "Complete Thoughts, Complete Sentences" earlier in this chapter for more examples and additional explanation.)

Fragments are especially useful in electronic media — in some situations. When you're texting, complete sentences may appear overly formal and even disrespectful of your reader's time. Why make your reader plow through a complete sentence on a tiny screen when a few words can make the same point? Take a look at these texts between two friends making plans for the evening. For the sake of comparison, the complete, grammatically correct version appears in parentheses after each text:

> LOLA: tonight? (What are the plans for tonight?)

> GEORGE: dinner at my house (We are eating at my house.)

> LOLA: bringing wine (I am bringing wine.)

> GEORGE: ordered food (I ordered the food.)

English teachers may groan, but George and Lola understand each other perfectly. Fragments are perfectly acceptable here.

Steering clear of inappropriate fragments

Don't write sentence fragments that a reader may misunderstand. This sort of fragment usually begins with a subordinate conjunction. (See "Choosing Subordinate Conjunctions" earlier in this chapter for a complete explanation.) Here are some examples of this type of sentence fragment, so you know what to avoid:

> When it rained
>
> As if he were king of the world
>
> After the ball was over but before it was time to begin the first day of the rest of your life and all those other clichés that you hear every day in the subway on your way to work
>
> Before Al left
>
> Because I want to
>
> Whether you like it or not, and despite the fact that you don't like it, although I am really sorry that you are upset
>
> If hell freezes over

and so on.

Avoid fragments when your most formal English is necessary. If your reader expects perfect grammar, place fragments on your avoid-at-all-costs list.

REMEMBER

When you're answering error-recognition or sentence-improvement questions on standardized tests, watch out for answer choices beginning with *and, but, or, nor,* or a similar word. In standardized tests, consider this usage incorrect. When you're writing an essay for school, you should also avoid fragments. English teachers grade these essays, and they tend to prefer complete sentences.

POP QUIZ

Which is a sentence fragment? Which is a complete sentence? Which is a comma splice (a run-on)?

A. Cedric sneezed.

B. Because Cedric sneezed in the middle of the opera, just when the main character removed that helmet with the little horns from on top of her head.

C. Cedric sneezed, I pulled out a handkerchief.

Answers: Sentence A is complete. Sentence B is not really a sentence; it's a fragment with no complete idea. Sentence C is a comma splice because it contains two complete thoughts joined only by a comma.

Reaching the End of the Line: Endmarks

When you speak, your body language, silences, and tone act as punctuation marks. You wriggle your eyebrows, stop at significant moments, and raise your voice when you ask a question.

When you write, you can't raise an eyebrow or stop for a dramatic moment. No one hears your tone of voice. That's why grammar uses endmarks. This punctuation takes the place of live communication and tells your reader how to "hear" the words correctly. Plus, you need endmarks to close sentences legally in formal, written English. The rules for texting and tweeting, as well as other forms of electronic communication, are different. In this section, I explain your choices.

Traditional, formal sentences end with a period (.), question mark (?), exclamation point (!), or ellipsis (. . .). The following examples show how to use endmarks correctly.

The period is for ordinary statements, declarations, and commands:

> I can't do my homework.
>
> I refuse to do my homework.
>
> Do not assign homework again.

The question mark is for questions:

> Why are you torturing me with this homework?
>
> Is there no justice in the world for students?
>
> Does no one know how much work in listed in my assignment pad?

The exclamation point adds a little drama to sentences that would otherwise end in periods:

> I can't do my homework!
>
> I absolutely positively refuse to do it!
>
> Oh, the agony of homework I've seen!

An ellipsis (three dots) signals that something has been left out of a sentence. When missing words occur at the end of a sentence, use four dots (three for the missing words and one for the end of the sentence):

> Michael choked, "No, not that . . ."

> Roger complained, "If you don't shut up, I. . . ."

TIP

In formal writing, don't put more than one endmark at the end of a sentence, unless you're trying to create a comic effect:

> He said my cooking tasted like what?!?!?!

Don't put any endmarks in the middle of a sentence. You may find a period inside a sentence as part of an abbreviation; in this case, the period is not considered an endmark. If the sentence ends with an abbreviation, let the period after the abbreviation do double duty. Don't add another period:

> WRONG: When Ella woke me, it was six a.m..

> RIGHT: When Ella woke me, it was six a.m.

Blog posts and comments on social media sites often follow the standard endmark rules. On some sites and in texts and tweets, writers insert or omit endmarks following different standards:

» In the midst of a text conversation, many people omit periods at the end of a sentence. Inserting a period appears angry or insincere, according to some studies.

» A period may signal the end of a texting exchange, the final message before the texters go on to some other activity or a different conversation.

» Periods within a sentence make the statement more emphatic (Best. Cat video. Ever.) This usage is informal but increasingly common.

» Texters often use double or triple (or even more) question marks and exclamation points to express strong emotion. "I'm here!" is less excited than "I'm here!!!" Some writers also combine question marks and exclamation points to show doubt or amazement: "You're there?!?!?"

WARNING

Be careful when you stray from formal English rules for punctuation (or for anything else). If you're writing to a boss, teacher, or anyone else who may expect traditional, proper English, creative use of endmarks may count against you.

POP QUIZ

Can you punctuate this example correctly?

> Who's there Archie I think there is someone at the door Archie it's a murderer Archie he's going to

Answer: Who's there? Archie, I think there is someone at the door. Archie, it's a murderer! (A period is acceptable here also.) Archie, he's going to. . . .

Chapter **5**

Handling Complements

Speeding down the grammar highway, the sentence is a flatbed truck carrying meaning to the reader. The verbs are the wheels, and the subject is the driver. Complements are the common, not-always-essential parts of the truck — perhaps the defroster or the speedometer. These words are a little more important than those fuzzy dice some people hang from their rearview mirrors or bumper stickers declaring *I stop at railroad tracks.* (What do they think the rest of us do? Leap over the train?) You can sometimes create a sentence without complements, but their presence is generally part of the driving — sorry, I mean *communicating* — experience.

Four kinds of complements show up in sentences: direct objects, indirect objects, objective complements, and subject complements This chapter explains all of them. The first three types of complements are related to the *object* of a sentence. (Notice that the word *object* is part of the name.) The fourth type of complement is related to the *subject* of a sentence. (Thus the word *subject* is part of its name.) Distinguishing between these two groups helps you choose the proper pronoun, when the sentence calls for that part of speech — a favorite question on standardized tests.

Before I continue, it's time to straighten out the compliment/complement divide. The one with an "i" is just a word meaning "praise." *Complement* with an "e" is a grammatical term. A complement adds meaning to the idea that the subject and verb express. That is, a complement completes the idea that the subject and verb begin.

Getting a Piece of the Action: Complements for Action Verbs

Action verbs express — surprise! — action. No action verb needs a complement to be grammatically legal. But an action-verb sentence without a complement may sound bare. The complements that follow action verbs — the direct object, indirect object, and objective complement — enhance the meaning of the subject-verb pair.

Receiving the action: Direct objects

Imagine that you're holding a baseball, ready to throw it to your friend. In your fantasy, you're facing a Hall-of-Fame hitter. You go into your windup and pitch. The ball arcs gracefully against the clear blue sky — and crashes right through the kitchen window.

> You broke the kitchen window!

Before you can retrieve your ball, your phone rings. It's your mom, who has radar for situations like this. *What's going on?* she asks. You mutter something containing the word *broke.* (There's the verb.) *Broke? Who broke something?* she demands. You admit that *you* did. (There's the subject.) *What did you break?* You hesitate. You consider a couple of possible answers: *a bad habit, the world's record for the hundred-meter dash.* Finally you confess: *the kitchen window.* (There's the complement.)

Here's another way to think about the situation (and the sentence). *Broke* is an action verb because it tells you what happened. The action came from the subject *(you)* and went to an object *(the window).* As some grammarians phrase it, *the window* receives the action expressed by the verb *broke.* Conclusion? *Window* is a *direct object* because it receives the action directly from the verb.

Try another.

> With the force of 1,000 hurricanes, you pitch the baseball.

Pitch is an action verb because it expresses what is happening in the sentence. The action goes from the subject (*you*, the pitcher) to the object *(the baseball)*. In other words, *baseball* receives the action of *pitching*. Thus, baseball is the *direct object* of the verb *pitch*.

Here are a few examples of sentences with action verbs. The direct objects are italicized.

> The defective X-ray machine took strange *pictures* of my toe. (*took* = verb, *X-ray machine* = subject)
>
> George hissed the secret *words* to a fellow spy. (*hissed* = verb, *George* = subject)
>
> My best crayons draw beautiful *lines*. (*draw* = verb, *crayons* = subject)
>
> Leroy's laser printer spurted *toner* all over his favorite shirt. (spurted = *verb*, printer = *subject*)

You may be able to recognize direct objects more easily if you think of them as part of a pattern in the sentence structure: subject (S) – action verb (AV) – direct object (DO). This S–AV–DO pattern is one of the most common in the English language; it may even be the most common. (I don't know if anyone has actually counted all the sentences and figured it out!) At any rate, think of the parts of the sentence in threes, in the S–AV–DO pattern:

> machine took pictures
>
> George hissed words
>
> crayons draw lines
>
> printer spurted toner

Of course, just to make your life a little bit harder, a sentence can have more than one DO. Check out these examples:

> Al autographed *posters* and *books* for his many admirers.
>
> Roger will eat a dozen *doughnuts* and a few *slabs* of cheesecake for breakfast.
>
> The new president of the Healthy Heart Society phoned *Egbert* and his *brother*.
>
> George threw stained *shirts* and smelly *socks* across his bedroom.
>
> Ella bought *orange juice, tuna, aspirin,* and a *coffee table.*

Some sentences have no direct object. Take a look at this example:

> Throughout the endless afternoon and into the lonely night, Al sighed sadly.

No one or nothing receives the sighs, so the sentence has no direct object. Perhaps that's why Al is lonely.

The grammar point: This sentence doesn't have a direct object, though it is powered by a verb and expresses a complete thought.

Rare, but sometimes there: Indirect objects

Another type of object is *indirect* because the action doesn't flow directly to it. The *indirect object*, affectionately known as the IO, is an intermediate stop along the way between the action verb and the direct object. Read this sentence, in which the indirect object is italicized:

> Knowing that I'm on a diet, Maggie sent *me* some nonfat snacks.

The action is *sent*. My friend *Maggie* performed the action, so *Maggie* is the subject. What received the action? *Snacks. Snacks* is the direct object. That's what was *sent*, what received the action of the verb directly. But *me* also received the action, indirectly. *Me* received the sending of the snacks. *Me* is the indirect object.

The sentence pattern for indirect objects is subject (S) – action verb (AV) – indirect object (IO) – direct object (DO). Notice that the indirect object always precedes the direct object: S–AV–IO–DO. Here are a few sentences with the indirect objects italicized:

> Gloria will tell *me* the whole story tomorrow. (*will tell* = verb, *Gloria* = subject, *story* = direct object)

> As a grammarian, I should have given *you* better example sentences. (*should have given* = verb, *I* = subject, *sentences* = direct object)

> Ella sent *Larry* a harsh text. (*sent* = verb, *Ella* = subject, *text* = direct object)

> The opponent's coach offered *Annie* a bribe for dropping out of the race. (*offered* = verb, *coach* = subject, *bribe* = direct object)

Indirect objects, like salesclerks in a discount store, don't appear very often. When indirect objects do show up, they're always in partnership with a direct object. Unless you're a fan of grammar terminology, you don't need to worry about distinguishing between direct and indirect objects. As long as you understand that these words are objects, completing the meaning of an action verb, you recognize the basic composition of a sentence.

No bias here: Objective complements

Finally, a grammar rule that's hard to bungle. Here's the deal: Sometimes a direct object doesn't get the whole job done. A little more information is needed or desired, and the writer doesn't want to bother adding a whole new subject–verb pair. The solution? An *objective complement* — an added fact about the direct object.

The *objective complement* (italicized in the following sentences) may be a person, place, or thing. In other words, the objective complement may be a noun:

> Egbert named Lester *editor* of the Healthy Heart Society Bulletin. (*named* = verb, *Egbert* = subject, *Lester* = direct object)
>
> Gloria and the other club members unanimously elected Roger *president*. (*elected* = verb, *Gloria and members* = subjects, *Roger* = direct object)
>
> Al called his dog *Al-Too*. (*called* = verb, *Al* = subject, *dog* = direct object)

The objective complement may also be a word that describes a noun. (A word that describes a noun is called an *adjective*; see Chapter 10 for more information.) Take a peek at these sample sentences:

> Nancy considered her *unqualified* for the job. (*considered* = verb, *Nancy* = subject, *her* = direct object)
>
> George dubbed Al-Too *ridiculous*. (*dubbed* = verb, *George* = subject, *Al-Too* = direct object)
>
> Roger called George *heartless*. (*called* = verb, *Roger* = subject, *George* = direct object)

As you see, the objective complements in each of the sample sentences give the sentence an extra jolt. You know more with it than you do without it, but the objective complement is not a major player in the sentence.

Completing the Equation: Subject Complements

Subject complements are major players in sentences. A *linking verb* begins a word equation; it expresses a state of being, linking two ideas. The complement completes the equation. Because a complement following a linking verb tells you something about the *subject* of the sentence, it is called a *subject complement*. In each of the following sentences, the first idea is the subject, and the second idea (italicized) is the complement:

Ms. McAnnick is *upset* by the bankruptcy of the auto-parts manufacturer. *(Ms. McAnnick = upset)*

Gloria was a *cheerleader* before the dog bite incident. *(Gloria = cheerleader)*

The little orange book will be *sufficient* for all your firework information needs. *(book = sufficient)*

It is *I,* the master of the universe. *(It = I)*

Subject complements can take several forms. Sometimes the subject complement is a descriptive word (an *adjective,* for those of you who like to know the correct terminology). Sometimes the subject complement is a *noun* (person, place, thing, or idea) or a *pronoun* (a word that substitutes for a noun). The first example sentence equates *Ms. McAnnick* with a description (the adjective *upset*). The second equates *Gloria* with a position (the noun *cheerleader*). In the third sample sentence, the subject *book* is described by the adjective *sufficient*. The last sentence equates the subject *it* with the pronoun *I*. Don't worry about these distinctions. They don't matter! As long as you can find the subject complement, you're grasping the sentence structure.

The linking verbs that I mentioned in the previous paragraph are forms of the verb "to be." Other verbs that give sensory information (*feel, sound, taste, smell,* and so on) may also be linking verbs. Likewise, *appear* and *seem* are linking verbs. (For more information on linking verbs, see Chapter 2.) Have a look at a couple of sentences with sensory linking verbs. The complements are italicized:

Larry sounds *grouchier* than usual today. *(Larry = grouchier)*

After solving an algebra problem, Anna feels *proud. (Anna = proud)*

You can't mix types of subject complements in the same sentence, completing the meaning of the same verb. (English teachers refer to this rule as "parallelism." For more about parallelism, check out Chapter 20.) Use all descriptions (adjectives) or all nouns and pronouns. Take a look at these examples:

WRONG: Gramps is grouchy but a good artist.

RIGHT: Gramps is a grouch but a good artist.

ALSO RIGHT: Gramps is grouchy and artistic.

WRONG: Lester's pet spider can be annoying and a real danger.

RIGHT: Lester's pet spider can be an annoyance and a real danger.

ALSO RIGHT: Lester's pet spider can be annoying and really dangerous.

Pop the Question: Locating the Complement

In Chapter 2, I explain how to locate the verb by asking the right questions. *(What's happening? What is?)* In Chapter 3, I show you how to pop the question for the subject. *(Who? What?* before the verb). Now it's time to pop the question to find the complements. You ask the same question to find the direct object, the objective complement, and the subject complement. Indirect objects are a bit different; I explain their "pop questions" in the next section.

Before you look for a complement, locate the subject and the verb first. Say the subject and verb and tack on these complement questions:

Who or whom?

What?

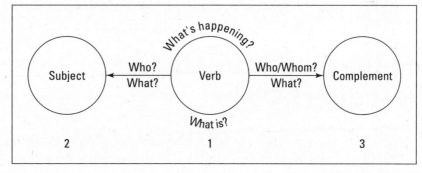

© John Wiley & Sons, Inc.

Watch these questions in action:

Flossie maintains the cleanest teeth in Texas.

1. Pop the verb question: What's happening? Answer: *maintains. Maintains* is the action verb.

2. Pop the subject question: Who or what *maintains?* Answer: *Flossie maintains. Flossie* is the subject.

3. Pop the complement question: *Flossie maintains* who/whom? No answer. *Flossie maintains* what? Answer: Flossie maintains *the cleanest teeth in Texas* (*teeth* for short). *Teeth* is the direct object.

Time for you to try another:

The actor recovering from the flu appeared tired and worn.

1. Pop the verb question: What's happening? No answer. What is? Answer: *Appeared. Appeared* is the linking verb.

2. Pop the subject question: Who or what *appeared?* Answer: *Actor appeared. Actor* is the subject.

3. Pop the complement question: *Actor appeared* who? No answer. *Actor appeared* what? Answer: *Tired* and *worn. Tired* and *worn* are the subject complements.

REMEMBER

Objects follow action verbs and subject complements follow linking verbs.

Pop the Question: Finding the Indirect Object

Though indirect objects seldom appear, you can check for them with another "pop the question." After you locate the action verb, the subject, and the direct object, ask

To whom? For whom?

To what? For what?

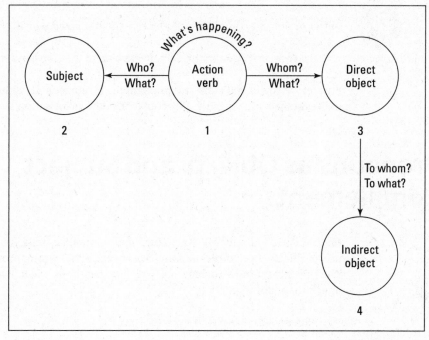

If you get an answer, it should reveal an indirect object. Here's an example:

Mildred will tell me the gossip.

1. Pop the verb question: What's happening? Answer: *will tell. Will tell* is an action verb.

2. Pop the subject question: Who will tell? Answer: *Mildred. Mildred* is the subject.

3. Pop the DO question: *Mildred will tell* whom? or what? Answer: *Mildred will tell the gossip. Gossip* is the direct object.

4. Pop the IO question: *Mildred will tell the gossip* to whom? Answer: to *me. Me* is the indirect object.

TIP

You may come up with a different answer when you pop the DO question in number 3 (*Mildred will tell* whom? or what?). You can answer *Mildred will tell me.* True. The only problem is that the sentence then has *gossip* flapping around with no label. Your attempt to determine the sentence structure has reached a dead end. Luckily for you, all you need to know is that both are objects. Only obsessive grammarians like me worry about which one is direct and which one is indirect.

Object or subject complement? Identify the italicized words.

Sal seemed *soggy* after his semi-final swim, so we gave *him* a *towel.*

Answer: *Soggy* is the subject complement. (*Seemed* is a linking verb.) *Him* is the indirect object. *Towel* is the direct object. (*Gave* is an action verb.)

Pronouns as Objects and Subject Complements

He told I? He told me? Me, of course. Your ear usually tells you which pronouns to use as objects (both direct and indirect) because the wrong pronouns sound funny. The object pronouns include *me, you, him, her, it, us, them, whom,* and *whomever.* Check them out in context:

Rickie splashed *her* with icy water.

The cobra hissed *them* a warning.

The talkative burglar told *her* everything.

REMEMBER

Your ear may not tell you the correct pronoun to use after a linking verb. That's where you want a *subject* pronoun, not an *object* pronoun. (Just for the record, the subject pronouns include *I, you, he, she, it, we, they, who,* and *whoever.*) Why do you need a subject pronoun after a linking verb? In conversational English (see Chapter 1), you don't. The rules relax when you're speaking with or writing to friends. In formal English, though, you should follow this rule: What's before the verb should be equal to what's after the verb (S = SC). You put subject pronouns before the verb as subjects, so you put subject pronouns after the verb, as subject complements. (For more information on linking verbs and the sentences they appear in, see Chapter 2. I discuss subject and object pronouns in Chapter 8.)

POP QUIZ

Which sentence is correct?

A. According to the witness, the burglar is her, the one with the bright orange eyes!

B. According to the witness, the burglar is she, the one with the bright orange eyes!

Answer: Sentence B is correct if you're writing formally. *Is* is a linking verb and must be followed by a subject pronoun, *she.* Sentence A is acceptable in conversation.

2

Clearing Up Confusing Grammar Points

Chapter **6**

Relax! Understanding Verb Tense

Are you obsessed with time: how to save it, race against it, borrow it, or watch it fly? Most people are. Perhaps that's one reason verbs are so important in the English language. They place the information in the sentence on a timeline stretching from the past through the present and into the future. This quality of verbs is known as *tense*.

Verbs take different forms in each tense, and to make life even harder for you, verbs also change, at times, according to the subject paired with them. (For more information on subjects, turn to Chapter 3.)

Never fear. In this chapter, I explain all six verb tenses — when to use them and how to form them properly. I also give you examples of regular verbs in every tense, as well as the most common irregular verbs.

Simplifying Matters: The Simple Tenses

Three of the six English tenses are called *simple.* (I discuss the other three, the *perfect* tenses, in the next section. Trust me, the perfect tenses are far from it.)

The three simple tenses are *present, past,* and *future.* Each of the simple tenses (just to make things even *more* fun) has two forms. One is the unadorned, no-frills, plain tense. This form doesn't have a special name; it is just called present, past, or future. It shows actions or states of being at a point in time, but it doesn't always pin down a specific moment. The other form is called *progressive.* It shows actions or a state of being *in progress.*

Present tense

Present tense tells you what is going on right now. The present form shows action or a state of being that is occurring now, that is generally true, or that is always happening. The present progressive form is similar, but it often implies a process. (The difference between the two is subtle. I go into more details about using these forms in the next section, "Using the Simple Tenses Correctly.") For now, take a look at a couple of sentences in the no-frills, plain present tense:

> Reggie often *rolls* his eyes in annoyance. (*rolls* is in present tense)

> George *plans* nothing for New Year's Eve because he never *has* a date. (*plans, has* are in present tense)

Now here are two sentences with present progressive verbs:

> Luciana *is axing* the proposal to cut down the national forest. (*is axing* is present progressive)

> Miguel and Lulu *are skiing* far too fast toward that cliff. (*are skiing* is present progressive)

The simple present tense for regular verbs changes at times, depending on who or what is doing the action or existing in the state of being expressed by the verb. In Table 6-1, you see the plain and progressive forms of the regular verb *walk,* paired with subjects. (Check out "The Rebels: Dealing with Irregular Verbs" later in this chapter for verbs that don't follow this pattern.) The pronouns *he, she, it,* or *they* represent every possible noun. In other words, use the *he/she/it* form for *Bob, lady, dog, box,* or any other singular noun. Use the verb form paired with *they* for *students, ladies, boys, books,* and any other plural noun.

TABLE 6-1   **Present Tense**

Singular Subject	Plain Present	Present Progressive	Plural Subject	Plain Present	Present Progressive
I	walk	am walking	we	walk	are walking
you	walk	are walking	you	walk	are walking
he, she, it	walks	is walking	they	walk	are walking

TIP

As you see, the pronoun *you* may be either singular or plural. I've placed the pronoun *they* in the plural column, its traditional spot. That tradition has been changing in recent years, as some people use *they* as a gender-neutral singular pronoun. In Chapter 7, I discuss this issue in detail.

Past tense

Past tense tells you what happened before the present time. This simple tense also has two forms — plain and chocolate-sprinkled. Sorry, I mean plain, which is called *past*, and *past progressive*. Consider these two past-tense sentences:

> When the elastic in Professor Belli's girdle *snapped,* the students *woke* up. (*snapped* and *woke* are in past tense)

> Despite the strong tape, the package *split* and *spilled* onto the conveyor belt. (*split* and *spilled* are in past tense)

Here are two more examples, this time in the past progressive form:

> While Buzz *was sleeping,* his cat, Nipper, *was destroying* the sofa. (*was sleeping* and *was destroying* are in the progressive form of the past tense)

> Lola's friends *were passing* tissues to Lulu at a rate of five per minute. (*were passing* is in the progressive form of the past tense)

The plain past tense is super-easy, and the past progressive is only a little bit harder. Have a glance at Table 6-2, which shows the past tense of the regular verb *walk.* The pronouns *he, she, it,* or *they* represent every possible noun. In other words, use the *he/she/it* form for *Luis, gentleman, cat, pencil,* or any other singular noun. Use the verb form paired with *they* for *robbers, cops, children, flowers,* and any other plural noun.

TABLE 6-2   **Past Tense**

Singular Subject	Plain Past	Past Progressive	Plural Subject	Plain Past	Past Progressive
I	walked	was walking	we	walked	were walking
you	walked	were walking	you	walked	were walking
he, she, it	walked	was walking	they	walked	were walking

WARNING

You can't go wrong with the past tense, except for the irregular verbs, which I address later in this chapter. But one very common mistake is to mix past and present tenses in the same story. Here's an example:

> So I go to the restaurant looking for Cindy because I want to tell her about Grady's date with Eleanor. I walk in and I see a film crew! So I went up to the director and said, "Do you need any extras?"

The speaker started in present tense — no problem. Even though an event is clearly over, present tense is okay if you want to make a story more dramatic. But the last sentence switches gears — suddenly we're in past tense. Problem! Don't change tenses in the middle of a story. And don't bother film directors either.

Future tense

Future tense talks about what has not happened yet. This simple tense is the only one that always needs helping verbs to express meaning, even for the plain version.

TIP

Helping verbs (see Chapter 2) such as *will, shall, have, has, should,* and so forth change the meaning of the main verb.

Future tenses — this may shock you — come in two forms. I'm not talking about alternate universes here; this book is about grammar, not sci-fi adventures! One form of the future tense is called *future,* and the other is *future progressive.* The unadorned form of the future tense goes like this:

> Nancy *will position* her campaign poster in the center of the bulletin board. (*will position* is in future tense)

> Lisa and I *will* never *part,* thanks to that bottle of glue. (*will part* is in future tense)

A couple of examples of the future progressive:

> During the post-election period, George *will be pondering* his options. (*will be pondering* is in the progressive form of the future tense)

> This summer, Lola *will be watering* her garden every day for two hours. (*will be watering* is in the progressive form of the future tense)

Table 6-3 shows the future and future progressive forms of the regular verb *walk*. The pronouns *he, she, it,* or *they* represent every possible noun. In other words, use the *he/she/it* form for *Peter, accountant, bird, show,* or any other singular noun. Use the verb form paired with *they* for *wrestlers, princesses, men, papers,* and any other plural noun.

TABLE 6-3 **Future Tense**

Singular Subject	Plain Future	Future Progressive	Plural Subject	Plain Future	Future Progressive
I	will walk	will be walking	we	will walk	will be walking
you	will walk	will be walking	you	will walk	will be walking
he, she, it	will walk	will be walking	they	will walk	will be walking

TIP

The helping verb *shall* also creates a future or future progressive verb. Traditionally, *shall* pairs with *I* and *we* and *will* pairs with other subjects. These days, most people prefer *will* for all subjects.

POP QUIZ

Find the verbs and sort them into present, past, and future tenses.

A. When a tornado whirls overhead, we snap selfies and post them online.

B. Will Mark inflate the balloons?

C. When you were 3, you blew out all the candles on your birthday cake.

Answers: In sentence A, the present tense verbs are *whirls, snap,* and *post.* In sentence B, the future tense verb is *will inflate.* In sentence C, the past tense verbs are *were* and *blew.*

POP QUIZ

Now find the verbs and sort them into present progressive, past progressive, and future progressive forms.

A. Exactly 5,000 years ago, a dinosaur was living in that mud puddle.

B. Zeus and Apollo are establishing a union of mythological characters.

C. The pilot will be joining us as soon as the aircraft clears the Alps.

Answers: In sentence A, the past progressive verb is *was living.* In sentence B, the present progressive verb is *are establishing.* In sentence C, the future progressive verb is *will be joining.*

Using the Simple Tenses Correctly

What's the difference between each pair of simple tense forms? Not a whole lot. People often interchange these forms without creating any problems. But shades of difference in meaning do exist.

Present and present progressive

The single-word form of the present tense may be used for things that are generally true at the present time but not necessarily happening right now. For example:

Ollie *attends* wrestling matches every Sunday.

If you try to reach Ollie on Sunday, you'll get an annoying voicemail message because he always turns off his phone when he's at the arena (*attends* is in present tense). Now read this sentence:

Ollie *is playing* hide-and-seek with his dog Spot.

This sentence means that right now (*is playing* is in the progressive form of the present tense), as you write or say this sentence, Ollie is running around the living room looking for Spot, who is easy to find ever since he ran through a tray of orange paint.

Past and past progressive

The difference between the plain past tense and the past progressive tense is pretty much the same as in the present tense. The single-word form often shows what happened in the past more generally. The progressive form may pinpoint action or a state of being at a specific time or occurring in the past on a regular basis.

Greg *went* to the store and *bought* clothes for all his friends.

This sentence means that at some point in the past Greg whipped out his charge card and finished off his Christmas list (*went* and *bought* are in past tense).

While Greg *was shopping,* his friends *were planning* their revenge.

This sentence means that Greg shouldn't have bothered because at the exact moment he was spending his allowance, his friends were deciding whether to pour ink into his lunchbox or to rip up Greg's homework (*was shopping* and *were planning* are in the progressive form of the past tense).

Greg *was shopping* until he *was drooping* with exhaustion, despite his mother's strict credit limit.

This sentence refers to one of Greg's bad habits, his tendency to go shopping every spare moment (*was shopping* and *was drooping* are in the progressive form of the past tense). The shopping was repeated on a daily basis, over and over again. (Hence, Greg's mom imposed the strict credit limit.)

Future and future progressive

You won't find much difference between these two. The progressive gives you slightly more of a sense of being in the middle of things. For example:

The actor *will be playing* Hamlet with a great deal of emotion.

The actor's actions in the sentence above may be a little more immediate than

The actor *will play* Hamlet with a great deal of emotion.

In the first example, *will be playing* is in the progressive form of the future tense. In the second example, *will play* is in future tense.

TIP

Understanding the difference between the two forms of the simple tenses entitles you to wear an Official Grammarian hat. But if you don't catch on to the distinction, don't lose sleep over the issue. If you can't discern the subtle differences in casual conversation, your listeners probably won't either. In choosing between the two forms, you're dealing with shades of meaning, not Grand Canyon-sized discrepancies.

TIP

When you're dealing with a pair (or more) of statements about the same time period, you probably need one of the simple tenses. Look at the italicized verbs in each of these example sentences:

> Maya *swiped* a handkerchief and daintily *blew* her noise. (*swiped* and *blew* = two events happening at almost the same moment; both verbs are in past tense)

> Maya *will be* in court tomorrow, and the judge *will rule* on her case. (*will be* and *will rule* = two events happening at the same time; both verbs are in future tense)

> Maya *is* extremely sad about the possibility of a criminal record, but she *remains* hopeful. (*is* and *remains* = states of being existing at the same time; both verbs are in present tense)

If two actions take place at the same time (or nearly the same time), use the same tense for each verb.

Not Picture Perfect: Understanding the Perfect Tenses

Now for the perfect tenses, which, I must tell you, are not always used perfectly. In fact, these three tenses — *present perfect, past perfect,* and *future perfect* — may give you gray hair, even if you are only 12 years old. And they have progressive forms too! As with the simple tenses, each tense has a no-frills version called by the name of the tense: *present perfect, past perfect,* and *future perfect.* The progressive form adds an "ing" to the mix. The progressive is a little more immediate than the other form, expressing an action or state of being in progress. In this section, I give you some examples of these tenses so you can identify each. In the next section, "Using the Perfect Tenses Correctly," I go into detail about when and how to use each tense.

Present perfect and present perfect progressive

The two present perfect forms show actions or states of being that began in the past but are still going on in the present. These forms are used whenever any action or state of being spans two time zones — past and present.

First, check out examples with plain present perfect tense:

> Roger and his friends *have spent* almost every penny of the inheritance. (The verb *have spent* is in present perfect tense.)

For years, Lulu's best friend, Roger, *has pleaded* with her to stop robbing banks. (The verb *has pleaded* is in present perfect tense.)

Now glance at these progressive examples:

Roger *has been studying* sculpture for 15 years without learning any worthwhile techniques. (The verb *has been studying* is in the progressive form of the present perfect tense.)

Lulu and Lola *have been counting* sheep all night. (The verb *have been counting* is in the progressive form of the present perfect tense.)

Table 6-4 shows the correct form of the regular verb *walk* in the present perfect and present perfect progressive. The pronouns *he, she, it,* or *they* represent every possible noun. In other words, use the *he/she/it* form for *Maria, dancer, lion, seat,* or any other singular noun. Use the verb form paired with *they* for *lawyers, kings, teenagers, hams,* and any other plural noun.

TABLE 6-4   **Present Perfect Tense**

Singular Subject	Plain Present Perfect	Present Perfect Progressive	Plural Subject	Plain Present Perfect	Present Perfect Progressive
I	have walked	have been walking	we	have walked	have been walking
you	have walked	have been walking	you	have walked	have been walking
he, she, it	has walked	has been walking	they	have walked	have been walking

As you see in the table, all present perfect verbs rely on the helping verb *have* — except for the one that pairs with *he, she,* and *it* (and the nouns those pronouns represent). For that pairing, you need *has.*

Past perfect and past perfect progressive

Each of these forms places an action in the past in relation to another action in the past. In other words, these tenses create a timeline that begins some time ago and ends at some point before NOW. At least two events are on the timeline. Here are some examples of the past perfect tense:

After she *had sewn* up the wound, the doctor realized that her watch was missing. (The verb *had sewn* is in past perfect tense.)

The watch *had ticked* for ten minutes before the nurse discovered its whereabouts. (The verb *had ticked* is in past perfect tense.)

Compare the preceding sentences with examples of the past perfect progressive:

> The patient *had been considering* a malpractice lawsuit but changed his mind. (The verb *had been considering* is in the progressive form of the past perfect tense.)

> The doctor *had been worrying* about legal penalties, but her patient dropped his case. (The verb *had been worrying* is in the progressive form of the past perfect tense.)

Check out Table 6-5 for the past perfect tense, both plain and progressive. The pronouns *he, she, it,* or *they* represent every possible noun. In other words, use the *he/she/it* form for *William, plumber, tiger, pillow,* or any other singular noun. Use the verb form paired with *they* for *politicians, teachers, babies, sketches,* and any other plural noun.

TABLE 6-5   **Past Perfect Tense**

Singular Subject	Plain Past Perfect	Past Perfect Progressive	Plural Subject	Plain Past Perfect	Past Perfect Progressive
I	had walked	had been walking	we	had walked	had been walking
you	had walked	had been walking	you	had walked	had been walking
he, she, it	had walked	had been walking	they	had walked	had been walking

Isn't this a lovely tense? Every subject pairs with the same plain or progressive verb. Little to learn and much to love — that's the past perfect tense when you're choosing a form. Lots to learn and much to hate — that's the past perfect tense when you're deciding when it's needed. I tackle that topic in the next section, "Using the Perfect Tenses Correctly."

Future perfect and future perfect progressive

These two forms talk about events or states of being that have not happened yet in relation to another event even further in the future. In other words, these forms create another timeline, with at least two events or states of being on it, all after the present moment.

First, take a look at the plain version of the future perfect:

> Appleby *will have eaten* the entire pie by the time recess ends. (The verb *will have eaten* is in future perfect tense.)

> When Appleby finally arrives at grammar class, the teacher *will have* already *outlined* at least 504 grammar rules. (The verb *will have outlined* is in future perfect tense.)

Now take a look at the progressive form of the future perfect tense:

> When the clock strikes four, Appleby *will have been chewing* for 29 straight minutes. (The verb *will have been chewing* is in the progressive form of the future perfect tense.)

> By the time he finishes dessert, Appleby's teacher *will have been explaining* the virtues of a healthy diet to her class for a very long time. (The verb *will have been explaining* is in the progressive form of the future perfect tense.)

Ready for a table? Table 6-6 presents the future and future progressive forms of the regular verb *walk.* The pronouns *he, she, it,* or *they* represent every possible noun. In other words, use the *he/she/it* form for *Olaf, artist, worm, bus,* or any other singular noun. Use the verb form paired with *they* for *mayors, heads, taxis, pickles,* and any other plural noun.

TABLE 6-6 **Future Perfect Tense**

Singular Subject	Plain Future Perfect	Future Perfect Progressive	Plural Subject	Plain Future Perfect	Future Perfect Progressive
I	will have walked	will have been walking	we	will have walked	will have been walking
you	will have walked	will have been walking	you	will have walked	will have been walking
he, she, it	will have walked	will have been walking	they	will have walked	will have been walking

As you probably noticed, all the plain future perfect forms are the same, and so are all the future progressive forms. You can relax when you're selecting the proper form to match a subject. Sadly, you can't relax when you're deciding when to use the future perfect. I tackle that issue in the next section, "Using the Perfect Tenses Correctly."

Using the Perfect Tenses Correctly

As anyone who watches crime dramas knows, figuring out when events happened is not always an easy task. The perfect tenses are (sorry, I can't resist) a *perfect* example of this fact. But investigators do know how to put events in order. Read on, and you'll know too.

TIP

To clarify what's happening when, timelines accompany some of the examples in this section. Match the events on the timeline to the verbs in the sentence to see where in time each tense places an action.

TEST ALERT

Standardized tests, such as the SAT and the ACT, obsess about verb tense. Expect to see at least a few questions containing the verb-tense issues described in this section.

Case 1: Beginning in the past and continuing in the present

You started something, and you haven't stopped. What do you need for this situation? Present perfect tense. This tense mixes two words. One appears to be present (the helping verbs *has* and *have*) and the other past (*walked, told, been, smashed,* and so on). Take a look at these examples:

> I *have gone* to the school cafeteria every day for six years, and I *have* not yet *found* one tasty item.

This sentence means that at present I am still in school, still trying to find something to eat, and for the past six years I was in school also, trudging to the cafeteria each day, searching for a sandwich that doesn't taste like wallpaper paste.

> Bertha *has* frequently *texted* Charles, but Charles *has* not *texted* Bertha back.

This sentence means that in the present Bertha hasn't given up yet; she's still trying to reach Charles. In the past, Bertha also texted Charles. In the present and in the past, Charles hasn't bothered to check his phone, which now contains 604 messages from Bertha. Check out Bertha's activity on this timeline:

```
                    Bertha keeps texting         NOW
              |――――――――――――――――――――――――――――――――――――|

          Bertha                               Bertha
          begins            PAST                 is
          texting                               still
                                               texting
```

© *John Wiley & Sons, Inc.*

As with the simple present tense, the present perfect tense takes two forms. One is called *present perfect*, and the other *present perfect progressive*. Shades of difference in meaning exist between the two — the progressive is a little more immediate — but nothing you need to worry about.

Which one is correct?

A. Isabel moved into that building in 2010 and lived there ever since.

B. Isabel has moved into that building in 2010 and lived there ever since.

C. Isabel moved into that building in 2010 and has lived there ever since.

Answer: Sentence C is correct. You cannot use the simple past, as in sentence A, because a connection to the present exists (the fact that Isabel still lives in that building). Sentence B is wrong because the moving isn't connected to the present. Because it's over and done with, you can't use present perfect for the move. Sentence C has the right combination — the move, now over, should be expressed in simple past. The event that began in the past and is still going on (Isabel's living in the building) needs present perfect tense.

Case 2: Events at two different times in the past

Everything in the past happened at exactly the same moment, right? Oh, if only this statement were true. History tests would be much easier, and so would grammar. To describe events in the past randomly, without worrying about when one occurred in relation to another, simple past tense is fine. To put more than one past event in order, you need past perfect tense. Check out the italicized verbs in this sentence:

> Maya *had* already *swiped* the handkerchief when she *discovered* the joys of honesty.

There are two events to think about, one taking place before the other. (Unfortunately for Maya, the joy of honesty came after the theft, for which she's doing two years in the penitentiary.) Note the timeline:

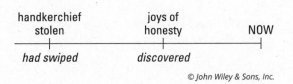

© *John Wiley & Sons, Inc.*

For two events in the past, write the earlier event with *had* and the more recent event in simple past tense (without *had*). Scan these examples:

> Because of Lulu's skill with a needle, where a hole in the sock *had gaped,* a perfect heel now *enclosed* her tender foot. (Event 1: the hole in the sock gapes; event 2: the mended sock covers the foot.)

> After Roger *had inserted* the microfilm, he *sewed* the hole in the now illegal teddy bear. (Event 1: Roger inserts the microfilm; event 2: Roger sews the bear.)

> After the song *had* been *played* at least 12 times, Michael *shouted,* "Enough!" (Event 1: The song is played 12 times; event 2: Michael loses it.)

WARNING

A common error is using *had* for everything. Wrong! Don't use *had* unless you're consciously putting two events in order:

> WRONG: Maya had dried her eyes and then she had gone to see the judge.

> RIGHT: After Maya had dried her eyes, she went to see the judge.

Note: You may encounter one other use of *had,* the subjunctive. See Chapter 17 if you have to know absolutely everything about *had* — and believe me, you don't.

POP QUIZ

Which sentence tells you about events that happened at different times?

A. When Maya slipped the judge a $50 bill, she hoped for mercy.

B. Because Maya had slipped the judge a $50 bill, she hoped for mercy.

Answer: Sentence B reports events at different times. Maya tried the bribe at 10 a.m. and spent the rest of the day planning a trip to Rio (cancelled when her jail term was announced). In sentence A, Maya bribes and hopes at the same time.

Case 3: More than two past events, all at different times

This rule, which also relies on past perfect tense, is similar to the one described in Case 2. Apply this rule when you talk about more than two events in the past if — and only if — the order matters:

> Maya *had baked* a cake and *had inserted* a sharp file under the icing before she *began* her stay in jail.

Now the timeline is as follows:

baking	file	jail	NOW
had baked	had inserted	began	

© John Wiley & Sons, Inc.

What do you notice? The most recent event *(began her stay in jail)* is written without *had.* In other words, the most recent event is in simple past tense. Everything that happened earlier is written with *had* — that is, in past perfect tense.

Here are some examples:

> Michael *had planned* the shower, and Lola *had* even *planned* the wedding by the time Ella *agreed* to marry Larry. (Events 1 and 2: Michael and Lola visit the wedding coordinator. Event 3: Ella makes the biggest mistake of her life.)

> Elizabeth *had composed* a sonata, *played* it for royalty, and *signed* a recording contract before she *reached* her tenth birthday. (Events 1, 2, and 3: Elizabeth writes the music, performs it, and makes big bucks. Event 4: Elizabeth's mom puts ten candles on the cake.)

In the last example three verbs — *composed, played,* and *signed* — form a list of the actions that Elizabeth performed before her tenth birthday. They all have the same subject *(Elizabeth)*. With your sharp eyes, you probably noticed that the word *had* precedes only *composed,* the first verb of the three. You may omit the word *had* in front of *played* and *signed* because they are part of the same list and they all have the same subject. The reader knows that the word *had* applies to all three of the verbs. In other words, the reader understands that *Elizabeth had composed, had played,* and *had signed.*

TIP

Whenever you may want to talk about events in the past without worrying about specific times, go for simple past tense. You *went* on vacation, *had* a great time, *sent* some postcards, *ate* a lot of junk food, and *came* home. No need for *had* in this description because the order isn't the point. You're just making a general list. Use *had* when the timing matters. Don't overuse it.

POP QUIZ

Identify the events in this sentence and put them in order.

> Where patriots had fought and wise founders had written a constitution, a fast-food restaurant stood.

Answer: Events 1 and 2: People with a better idea fight the old government and write a plan for a new government. Event 3: In the free and successful society that results, someone builds a restaurant after suing the landmarks preservation commission for the right to tear down a historic building.

Case 4: Two events in the future

Leaving the past behind, it's time to turn to the future. Read this sentence:

Nicky *will have completed* all 433 college applications before they are due.

Nicky's applications will be error-filled — he spelled his name *Niky* on at least three — but they will be done before the deadline. *Deadline* is the important word here, at least regarding verb tense. The *will have* form of the future, also called *future perfect tense*, involves a deadline. You don't necessarily see two verbs in the sentence, but you do learn about two events:

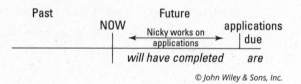

© *John Wiley & Sons, Inc.*

Use the future perfect tense to talk about the earlier of the two events.

Here are a few examples:

By nine tonight, Egbert *will have* successfully *scrambled* the secret message. (The deadline in the sentence is nine o'clock.)

Anna *will have left* for Mount Everest by the time the mountaineering supply company sends her gear. (The deadline in the sentence is the delivery of mountain-climbing supplies.)

POP QUIZ

Which sentence is correct?

A. Bernard will have tossed the salad tonight.

B. Bernard will have tossed the ball out the window before anyone has a chance to catch it.

Answer: Sentence B is correct. Future perfect tense involves a deadline, which in this sentence is *before anyone has a chance to catch it.*

Reporting Information: Verbs Tell the Story

Got a good story? Fine. Now all you need is the proper verb tense to tell it. In this section, I explain a few rules for reporting events, including some events that never happened.

Summarized speech

If you're like most people, you spread gossip. Not that you're a bad person. But if you hear a good tale, you pass it along. Check out this example:

> Flipping his hair over each of his three shoulders, the Martian *told* us about the explosion on his planet. The gas of three rocket tanks *caught* fire and *destroyed* the spaceport terminal, he *said.* He *went* on to explain that almost everyone on the planet *was affected,* including the volleyball team, which *sustained* significant losses. All their courts, he *said, were covered* with rubble, and they *forfeited* the intergalactic tournament.

The Martian's story is summarized speech. I'm not quoting him directly. If I were, I'd insert some of his exact words:

> "Oh, the humanity!" he cried.

In the previous summarized speech, the verbs are all in past tense. Although rare, it's possible to summarize speech in present tense also. Present tense adds an extra dose of drama:

> Flipping his hair over each of his three shoulders, the Martian *tells* us about the explosion on his planet. The gas of three rocket tanks *catches* fire and *destroys* the spaceport terminal, he *says.* He *goes* on to explain that almost everyone on the planet *is affected,* including the volleyball team, which *sustains* significant losses. All their courts, he *says, are covered* with rubble, and they *forfeit* the intergalactic tournament.

WARNING

When reporting information, either present or past tense is acceptable. However, mixing tenses is *not* acceptable. Don't move from one to the other, except for one special case, which I describe in the next section, "Eternal truths."

> WRONG: Bernard *said* that he *had tossed* the ball out the window. It *hits* a pedestrian, who *sues* for damages. (The first two verbs are in past tense, and the next two are in present tense.)

RIGHT: Bernard *said* that he *had tossed* the ball out the window. It *hit* a pedestrian, who *sued* for damages. (All verbs are in a form of the past tense.)

POP QUIZ

Correct the verb tense in this paragraph. The verbs are in italics.

Lola *testified* that she *excavated* at the town dump every Tuesday afternoon before she *attends* choir practice. She often *found* arrow heads, broken pottery, discarded automobile tires, and other items of interest. One day she *discovers* a metal coil about two feet long. On one end of the coil *was* a piece of gum. As she thoughtfully *removes* the gum and *starts* to chew, a whistle *blew*. Roger *sprinted* into the dump at top speed. "Get your hands off my gum," he *exclaims*. Roger *smiles*. His anti-gum-theft alarm *had worked* perfectly.

Answer: The story is in two different tenses, past and present. To correct it, choose one of the two. Here is the past tense version, with the changed verbs underlined:

Lola *testified* that she *excavated* at the town dump every Tuesday afternoon before she *attended* choir practice. She often *found* arrow heads, broken pottery, discarded automobile tires, and other items of interest. One day she *discovered* a metal coil about two feet long. On one end of the coil *was* a piece of gum. As she thoughtfully *removed* the gum and *started* to chew, a whistle *blew*. Roger *sprinted* into the dump at top speed. "Get your hands off my gum," he *exclaimed*. Roger *smiled*. His anti-gum-theft alarm *had worked* perfectly.

Here is the present tense version, with the changed verbs underlined:

Lola *testifies* that she *excavates* at the town dump every Tuesday afternoon before she *attends* choir practice. She often *finds* arrow heads, broken pottery, discarded automobile tires, and other items of interest. One day she *discovers* a metal coil about two feet long. On one end of the coil *is* a piece of gum. As she thoughtfully *removes* the gum and *starts* to chew, a whistle *blows*. Roger *sprints* into the dump at top speed. "Get your hands off my gum," he *exclaims*. Roger *smiles*. His anti-gum-theft alarm *has worked* perfectly.

TIP

One special note: When you're not reporting what someone says, you can make a general statement about something that always happens (someone's custom or habit) using present tense. You can easily combine such a statement with a story that focuses on one particular incident in the past tense. Therefore, the preceding story may begin in present tense and move to past tense in this way:

Lola *excavates* at the town dump every Tuesday afternoon before she *attends* choir practice. She often *finds* arrow heads, broken pottery, discarded automobile tires, and other items of interest.

Up to here in the story, all the verbs are in present tense because the story tells of Lola's habits. The story isn't reporting what someone said. In the next sentence, the story switches to past tense because it examines one particular day in the past.

> One day she *discovered* a metal coil about two feet long. On one end of the coil *was* a piece of gum. As she thoughtfully *removed* the gum and *started* to chew, a whistle *blew*. Roger *sprinted* into the dump at top speed. "Get your hands off my gum," he *exclaimed*. Roger *smiled*. His anti-gum-theft alarm *had worked* perfectly.

Eternal truths

Much changes in life, but not everything. Verbs reflect this fact. How? Take a look at these sentences. Can you figure out what's wrong with them?

> Anna explained that one plus one *equaled* two.
>
> Ms. Belli said that the earth *was* round.
>
> She added that diamonds *were made* of carbon.

Well, you may be thinking,

> *Equaled* two? What does it equal now? Three?
>
> *Was* round? And now it's a cube?
>
> *Were* made of carbon? Now they make diamonds from pastrami?

In others words, the verb tense is wrong. All of these statements represent eternal truths — statements that will never change. When you write or say such statements, you must always write in present tense, even if the statement was made in the past:

> Anna explained that one plus one *equals* two.
>
> Ms. Belli told us that the earth *is* round.
>
> She went on to say that diamonds *are made* of carbon.

The historical present

Not surprisingly, you use present tense for actions that are currently happening. But (surprise!) you may also use present tense for some actions that happened a long time ago and for some actions that never happened at all. The historical present is a way to write about history or literature:

> On December 7, 1941, President Franklin Delano Roosevelt *tells* the nation about the attack on Pearl Harbor. The nation immediately *declares* war.

> Harry Potter *faces* three tests when he *represents* Hogwarts in the tournament.

In the first sentence, *tells* and *declares* are in present tense, even though the sentence concerns events that occurred decades ago. Here the historical present makes the history more dramatic. (Non-historians often tell a story in present tense also, just to make the account more vivid.) In the second sentence, *faces* and *represents* are in present tense. The idea is that for each reader who opens the book, the story begins anew. With the logic that we have come to know and love in English grammar, the events are always happening, even though Harry Potter is a fictional character and the events never happened.

The Rebels: Dealing with Irregular Verbs

In earlier sections of this chapter, I provide charts showing you how regular verbs change in each tense. If only all verbs were regular! But in grammar, as in life, some rebels don't follow the rules. In this section, I show you some common irregular verbs, starting with three you need nearly every time you speak or write: *be, have,* and *do.* Then I show you some irregular *participles.*

To be, to have, to do

To be is possibly the weirdest verb in the English language. The verb *to be* changes more frequently than any other. Here it is, tense by tense. Note: In each table, the pronouns *he, she,* and *it* represent all the singular nouns in the language (*lamp, Charlie, Jean, cow,* and so on). The pronoun *they* represents all plural nouns (*trains, drivers, clouds,* and so forth).

Present

Singular	Plural
I am	we are
you are	you are
he, she, it is	they are

Present Progressive

Singular	Plural
I am being	we are being
you are being	you are being
he, she, it is being	they are being

TIP

Note that the singular forms are in the first column and plural forms are in the second column. Singulars are for one person or thing, and plurals for more than one. "You" is listed twice because it may refer to one person or to a group. (Just one more bit of illogic in the language.)

Past

Singular	Plural
I was	we were
you were	you were
he, she, it was	they were

Past Progressive

Singular	Plural
I was being	we were being
you were being	you were being
he, she, it was being	they were being

Note: I am not including a chart of the verb *be* in the future progressive or the perfect tenses because I can't think of any situation that would require you to say "I will be being" or "you had been being" or something similar. In theory, those verbs exist. In practice, you don't need them.

Future Tense

Singular	Plural
I will be	we will be
you will be	you will be
he, she, it will be	they will be

Present Perfect

Singular	Plural
I have been	we have been
you have been	you have been
he, she, it has been	they have been

Past Perfect

Singular	Plural
I had been	we had been
you had been	you had been
he, she, it had been	they had been

Future Perfect

Singular	Plural
I will have been	we will have been
you will have been	you will have been
he, she, it will have been	they will have been

Luckily for you, the verb *to have* is much simpler than *to be. To have* takes only three forms: *has, have,* and *had. Has* pairs for all singular subjects except for the pronouns *I* and *you. Have* pairs with all plural subjects, as well as the pronouns *I* and *you. Had* matches up with both singular and plural subjects. Isn't that nice?

To do is another easy irregular verb. It also has three forms: *does, do,* and *did.* Use *does* for all singular subjects except for *I* and *you.* Use *do* for all plural subjects, in addition to *I* and *you.* Select *did* for both singular and plural subjects.

For more information on pairing singular and plural subjects properly with verbs, turn to Chapter 7.

Irregular past forms and participles

Don't let the name scare you. Participles are not very mysterious; as you may guess from the spelling, a *participle* is simply a *part* of the verb. Each verb has two participles — a present participle and a past participle. The present participle is the *ing* form of the verb. Sometimes the spelling changes a bit (an *e* may disappear or a letter may double), but other than spelling, present participles won't give you any trouble. Table 6-7 shows a selection of regular present participles.

TABLE 6-7

Examples of Regular Present Participles

Verb	Present Participle
ask	asking
beg	begging
call	calling
dally	dallying
empty	emptying
fill	filling
grease	greasing

Are you having fun yet? Now the true joy begins. Dozens and dozens of English verbs have irregular past tense forms, as well as irregular past participles. I won't list all the irregular verbs here, just a few you may find useful in everyday writing. If you have questions about a particular verb, check your dictionary.

In Table 6-8, the first column is the infinitive form of the verb. (The infinitive is the "to + verb" form — *to laugh, to cry, to learn grammar*, and so on.) The second column is the simple past tense. The third column is the past participle, which is combined with *has* (singular) or *have* (plural) to form the present perfect tense. The past participle is also used with *had* to form the past perfect tense.

TABLE 6-8

Forms of Irregular Participles

Verb	Past	Past Participle
bear	bore	borne
become	became	become
begin	began	begun
bite	bit	bitten
break	broke	broken
bring	brought	brought
catch	caught	caught
choose	chose	chosen
come	came	come
do	did	done
drink	drank	drunk
drive	drove	driven
eat	ate	eaten
fall	fell	fallen
feel	felt	felt
fly	flew	flown
freeze	froze	frozen
get	got	got or gotten
go	went	gone
know	knew	known
lay	laid	laid
lead	led	led
lend	lent	lent
lie	lay	lain
lose	lost	lost
ride	rode	ridden
ring	rang	rung
rise	rose	risen

Verb	Past	Past Participle
run	ran	run
say	said	said
see	saw	seen
set	set	set
shake	shook	shaken
sing	sang	sung
sink	sank or sunk	sunk
sit	sat	sat
sleep	slept	slept
speak	spoke	spoken
steal	stole	stolen
swim	swam	swum
take	took	taken
throw	threw	thrown
wear	wore	worn
win	won	won
write	wrote	written

Chapter 7

Nodding Your Head: All About Agreement

ollywood filmmakers and about a million songwriters have tried to convince the public that opposites attract. Grammarians have clearly not gotten that message. Instead of opposites, the English language prefers matching pairs — singular with singular and plural with plural. Matching, in grammar terminology, is known as *agreement.*

In this chapter, I show you how to make subjects and verbs agree. I also deal with another part of speech — pronouns — and show you how to make sure they follow the rules of agreement.

Agreeing Not to Disagree

Agreement in the real world means that you share the same beliefs. In Grammar Land, the concept of *agreement* rests on these principles:

>> Verbs may be singular or plural. Sometimes the verb form is the same for both singular and plural expressions, and sometimes it's different.

>> Nouns (the part of speech that names people, places, things, and ideas) may also be singular or plural.

>> Pronouns (the part of speech that replaces or refers to nouns or other pronouns) may also be singular or plural. A few pronouns keep the same form for both singular and plural situations; most don't.

>> When you're writing a sentence, you need a subject — a noun or a pronoun. A singular subject pairs with a singular verb. A plural subject pairs with a plural verb. For more information on subjects and verbs, check out Chapter 2 (for verbs) and Chapter 3 (for subjects).

>> A pronoun must agree with its *antecedent*, the word the pronoun refers to or replaces. Singular pronouns match up with singular nouns or other singular pronouns. Plural pronouns pair with plural nouns or other plural pronouns.

>> Pronouns also must agree with their antecedents' *gender*. In general, masculine pronouns refer to males, and feminine pronouns refer to females. Neutral or *neuter* pronouns refer to either or both, or to objects that have no gender. (Pronoun gender is a complex topic, which I discuss in detail later in this chapter in "Dealing Sensitively with Pronoun Gender.")

These principles are simple. And in most situations, applying them is simple also. Once in a while, though, you face some complicated pairs. (Grammar resembles life in this regard, doesn't it?) In this chapter, you see how to deal with both the easy and the tough decisions about agreement.

Making Subjects and Verbs Agree

If you grew up speaking English, your "ear" usually helps you correctly match singular and plural subjects to their verbs. But even if English isn't your first language, you probably pair up lots of subjects and verbs correctly because most tenses use the same verb form for both singular and plural subjects. A few tenses use different forms, as do some irregular verbs. (Turn to Chapter 6 for a chart of every regular verb form, as well as charts of the most common irregular verbs.) Just as a reminder, in this section, I go over the basic principles.

The unchangeables

These regular verbs stay the same in both singular and plural situations. Because this topic is boring, I chose the regular verb *to snore* for the example sentences. Try to stay awake! Unchangeable verb forms occur in these tenses:

>> **Simple past tense:** Larry *snored* constantly, but his cousins *snored* only occasionally. (The simple past tense verb *snored* matches both the singular subject *Larry* and the plural subject *cousins*.)

>> **Simple future tense:** Ella *will snore* if she eats cheese before bedtime, but her bridesmaids *will snore* only after a meal containing sardines. (The simple future tense verb *will snore* matches both the singular subject *Ella* and the plural subject *bridesmaids*.)

>> **Future progressive tense:** I *will be snoring* the minute I hit the pillow. My roommates *will be snoring* soon too. (The future progressive verb *will be snoring* matches both the singular subject *I* and the plural subject *roommates*.)

>> **Past perfect tense:** Cedric *had snored* long before his tonsils were removed. His pet tigers *had snored* nightly before Cedric changed their diet. (The past perfect verb *had snored* matches both the singular subject *Cedric* and the plural subject *tigers*.)

>> **Future perfect tense:** By the time this chapter is over, Lola *will have snored* for at least an hour, and her friends *will have snored* for an even longer period. (The future perfect verb *will have snored* matches both the singular subject *Lola* and the plural subject *friends*.)

>> **Questions and negative statements in past tense:** *Did* Jane *snore* last night? No, she *did* not *snore*. *Did* her roommates *snore* instead? No, they *did* not *snore* either. (The past tense verb *did snore* matches the singular subjects *Jane* and *she*. The same verb matches the plural subjects *roommates* and *they*.)

Easy, right? You can't go wrong with an "unchangeable."

The changeables

Have you resolved to speak only in those unchanging tenses? Sorry! The other tenses are crucial to your communication skills. Fortunately, you need to know only a few principles to identify singular and plural verb forms that change:

>> **Simple present tense:** When the subject of the sentence names one person or one thing (the *he, she, it* form), the verb ends with an added letter *s*. Sentences with *I, we, you,* or any plural subject, all use the same verb, with no added *s*.

- Andy *snores* when he sleeps on a soft pillow. His friends *snore* when their pillows are too hard. (The singular present tense verb *snores* matches the singular subject *Andy*. The plural present tense verb matches the plural subject *friends*.)

- I *snore* when I'm overtired. (The simple present verb *snore* matches the subject *I*.)

- We *snore* if the bedroom is too hot, and the dogs *snore* if it is too cold. (The simple present verb *snore* matches the plural subjects *we* and *dogs*.)

- You *snore* too much! (The simple present verb *snore* works for the subject *you*, which may be either singular [talking to one person] or plural [talking to more than one person].)

» **Present and past progressive tenses:** Progressive tenses contain an *-ing* verb form and a form of the verb *to be*. The *-ing* portion of the verb stays the same, but *to be* changes drastically in the present and past tense, depending on its subject. Just be sure to match the subject to the correct form of the verb *to be*. (See Chapter 6 for all the forms of *to be*.) Check out these examples, based on the verb *to command:*

- I *am commanding*, you *are commanding*, Dan *is commanding*, and no one else *is commanding*. (The singular present progressive verbs are *am commanding, are commanding, is commanding,* and *is commanding*. These singular verbs pair with *I, you, Dan,* and *no one* — all singular subjects.)

- We *are commanding*, you *are commanding*, the tigers *are commanding*, and they *are commanding*. (The plural present progressive verb, *are commanding*, pairs with various plural subjects.)

- I *was commanding*, you *were commanding*, Dan *was commanding*, and no one else *was commanding*. (The singular past progressive verb is *was commanding*. This singular verb pairs with *I, you, Dan,* and *no one* — all singular subjects.)

- We *were commanding*, you *were commanding*, the tigers *were commanding*, and both *were commanding*. (The plural past progressive verb *were commanding* matches the plural subjects *we, you, tigers,* and *both*.)

» **Present perfect tense, both plain and progressive:** This tense uses *has* for singular subjects (except for the pronouns *I* and *you*) and *have* for plural subjects, as well as for *I* and *you*. The other portion of the verb, the participle, doesn't change. Some examples, all with the verb *to bite:*

- Sandra *has bitten* into my sandwich, Dracula *has been biting* a lot lately. (The singular present perfect verbs *has bitten* and *has been biting* match the singular subjects *Sandra* and *Dracula*.)

- We *have bitten* off more than we can chew. The tigers *have been biting* their cubs. You *have bitten* the dentist's finger. I *have been biting* my nails too much. (The present perfect verbs *have bitten* and *have been biting* match the subjects *we, tigers, you,* and *I.*)

» **Verbs in present-tense questions and negative statements:** Most present-tense questions and negative statements rely on the helping verb *to do.* Use *does* for singular subjects and *do* for plural subjects in a present tense question or negative statement. (For more information on questions and negative statements, turn to Chapter 2.)

  - *Does* your dog *bite?* (The singular verb *does bite* pairs with the singular subject *dog.*)

  - *Do* your cats *bite?* (The plural verb *do bite* pairs with the plural subject *cats.*)

  - My dog *does* not *bite.* (The singular verb *does bite* pairs with the singular subject *dog.*)

  - My cats *do* not *bite.* (The plural verb *do bite* pairs with the plural subject *cats.*)

TIP

Be extra careful when you're dealing with a verb that contains a form of *to be, to have,* or *to do.* Those verbs often change depending on whether they're paired with singular or plural subjects.

YOU GUYS UNDERSTAND, DON'T YOU?

You may have noticed that the word *you* is both singular and plural. I can say, "You are crazy" to Egbert when he claims that bacon is low in fat. I can also say, "You are crazy" to all those people who think Martians constructed the pyramids. In either case, I use the plural form of the verb *(are).* The fact that *you* is both singular and plural may be responsible for the popularity of such terms as *you all, y'all, youse* (very big in New York City), *you guys* (ditto), *and you people.* These terms are colorful but not correct in formal English. Use *you* for both singular and plural subjects, and if you care enough, make the meaning clear with context clues:

Today you must all wear clothes to the Introduction to Nudism class because the radiator is broken.

"I must have you and only you!" cried Larry to his soon-to-be sixth wife.

Matching Subjects and Verbs in Some Tricky Situations

Most of the time the subject–verb match is obvious. Occasionally, you have to put on your thinking cap and analyze the sentence to come up with the proper form. In this section, I show you how to deal with compound subjects and subjects that may be tough to locate.

Compound subjects

Sentences with two subjects joined by *and* take a plural verb, even if each of the two subjects is singular. (Think of math: one + one = two. One subject + one subject = plural subject.)

Here are some sample sentences with subjects joined by the word *and*:

> The sofa and the pillow are very comfortable. (*sofa + pillow* = plural subject, *are* = plural verb)

> The picture and its frame belong together. (*picture + frame* = plural subject, *belong* = plural verb)

> Romance and garlic do not mix. (*romance + garlic* = plural subject, *do mix* = plural verb)

When you join two subjects with *or*, however, you're not adding. You're offering two alternatives. Does that make your subject singular? Not necessarily. It depends on the two subjects.

» **If both subjects are singular, the verb is singular.** Polly or her parrot eats the leftover cracker. (*Polly, parrot* = singular subjects, *eats* = singular verb)

» **If both subjects are plural, the verb is plural.** The children or their parents prefer cookies. (*children, parents* = plural subjects, *prefer* = plural verb)

» **If one subject is singular and one is plural, match the verb to the closer subject.** Polly or the other children want extra snacks. (*Polly, children* = subjects, *children* is closer to the verb. Because *children* is plural, you need the plural verb *want*.)

POP QUIZ

Which sentence is correct?

A. The judge and the jury have shown no mercy in these cases.

B. The judge or her assistants has shown no mercy in these cases.

Answer: Sentence A is correct. The subject is plural (*judge and jury*) so a plural verb (*have shown*) is appropriate. In sentence B the verb (*has shown*) is singular, but the two subjects (*judge, assistants*) are joined by *or*, and the plural subject, *assistants*, is closer to the verb.

Locating subjects and ignoring distractions

Subjects and their verbs are like parents and babies on a stroll through the park; they always travel together. A passerby cooing at a baby may catch the kid's attention, but ultimately the passerby is a distraction — irrelevant to the essential parent–child bond. The sentence world has lots of passersby that show up, slip between a subject and its verb, and distract you. The best strategy is to identify distractions and then cross them out (at least mentally) to get to the bare bones of the sentence — the subject–verb pair.

TEST ALERT

Standardized exams often include sentences with camouflaged subject–verb pairs, to see whether you can make these elements of the sentence agree. Watch out for them!

The most common distractions, but not the only ones, are prepositional phrases. A *prepositional phrase* contains a preposition (*on, to, for, by,* and so on) and an object of the preposition (a noun or pronoun). These phrases may contain some descriptive words as well. Other distractions may be verbals or clauses. (For more information on prepositional phrases, see Chapter 9. I cover clauses in Chapter 18 and verbals in Chapter 19.)

In the following sentences, the distractions (not all prepositional phrases) are italicized.

> The accountant *with 10,000 clients and only two assistants* works way too hard.
> (accountant = subject, works = verb)

In this sentence, *accountant* is the singular subject. If you pay attention to the prepositional phrase, you may incorrectly focus on *clients* and *assistants* as the subject — both plural words.

> The IRS agent, *fascinated by my last three tax returns,* is ruining my vacation plans.
> (agent= subject, *is ruining* = verb)

By ignoring the distracting phrase about my tax returns in this sentence, you can easily pick out the singular subject–verb pair.

> The deductions, *not the tax rate,* are a problem. (*deductions* = subject, *are* = verb)

In this sentence, *deductions* is the plural subject. If you let yourself be distracted, you may incorrectly match your verb to *rate*, which is singular.

Final answer: Ignore all distracting phrases, and find the true subject–verb pair. Also, if any IRS employees are reading this book, please ignore my tax returns.

POP QUIZ

Which sentence is correct?

A. The boy in the first row, along with all the kids posting on Instagram, is ignoring the teacher.

B. The boy in the first row, along with all the kids posting on Instagram, are ignoring the teacher.

Answer: Sentence A is correct. The subject is *boy*. The boy *is ignoring. Along with all the kids posting on Instagram* is a distraction (in this case, a prepositional phrase).

Another: Which sentence is correct?

A. The girl in the last row, but not the football players in the hall, are taking selfies.

B. The girl in the last row, but not the football players in the hall, is taking selfies.

Answer: Sentence B is correct. The subject is *girl*. The verb must therefore be singular *(is taking)*. Ignore the words between the commas; they're distractions and don't affect the subject–verb match.

TIP

Sentences beginning with *here* or *there* can be tricky, too. *Here* and *there* look like subjects because they appear before the verb — the usual subject spot. But the true subject is *after* the verb in this sort of sentence. Take care to match the verb with the real subject:

Here is my favorite store. (*store* = singular subject, *is* = singular verb)

There are ten new messages on my phone. (*messages* = plural subject, *are* = plural verb)

For more information on *here/there* sentences, turn to Chapter 3. To find out more about some difficult subject–verb pairs, read "Agreeing in Tricky Situations" later in this chapter.

Reaching an Agreement with Pronouns

Think of pronouns as the ultimate substitute teachers. One day they're solving equations, and the next they're doing push-ups in the gym. Such versatility comes from the fact that pronouns don't have identities of their own; instead, they stand in for nouns or other pronouns. The word a pronoun refers to is its *antecedent*.

Although they're useful, pronouns can also be pesky because English has many different types of pronouns, each governed by its own set of rules. (See Chapter 8 for everything you need to know about subject, object, and possessive pronouns.) In this section, I first concentrate on making subject pronouns agree with the verbs they're paired with. Then I discuss agreement between pronouns and their antecedents.

Choosing subject pronouns

The basic rule for subject pronouns is simple: First find it! ("Pop the Question: Locating the Subject-Verb Pairs" in Chapter 3 tells you how.) If the subject pronoun is singular, pair it with a singular verb. If it's plural, use a plural verb. What's a singular subject pronoun? It's a word that replaces a singular subject noun, a word that names *one* person, place, thing, or idea. Plural subject pronouns replace plural subject nouns — those that name *more than one* person, place, thing, or idea. (Grammar terminology has flair, doesn't it?) Take a look at Table 7-1 for a list of some common singular and plural pronouns that may act as subjects.

TABLE 7-1   **Common Singular and Plural Pronouns**

Singular	Plural
I	we
you	you
he/she/it	they
who, whoever	who, whoever
what, whatever	what, whatever
which, whichever	which, whichever
that	that
either, neither	both
each, every	several
much	many
someone, something, somebody	few
anyone, anything, anybody	
no one, nothing, nobody	

TIP

Notice that some of the pronouns in Table 7-1 do double duty; they take the place of both singular and plural nouns or pronouns. Also, I should point out that the pronoun *they* is the subject (grammar pun intended) of much controversy these days. I discuss this issue in "Dealing Sensitively with Pronoun Gender" later in this chapter. For now, I've placed *they* in the plural column.

Most of the time choosing between singular and plural pronouns is easy. You're not likely to say

He are here.   or   They is gone.

because *he* (singular pronoun) and *are* (a plural verb) don't match. Nor do *they* (plural pronoun) and *is* (singular verb) pair up properly. Instead you say

He is here.   or   They are gone.

TIP

If you're learning English as a second language, your ear for the language is still in training. Put it on an exercise regimen of at least an hour a day of careful listening. A podcast or a television show in which reasonably educated people are speaking will help you to train your ear. You'll soon become comfortable hearing and choosing the proper subject–pronoun–verb pairs.

Matching pronouns to their antecedents

Pronouns aren't always subjects. They do many jobs in a sentence, acting as objects, showing possession, and so forth. In every situation, the pronouns must match their *antecedents* — the word or words they replace or refer to — in number and gender. *Number* is just a fancy grammar term for singular and plural. *Gender*, in the world of grammar, is masculine, feminine, or neuter (something that has no gender). Take a look at these examples, in which the pronoun is italicized and the antecedent is identified in parentheses:

Christine brought *her* new puppy home. (*her* refers to *Christine*)

Christine petted *him*. (*him* refers to *puppy*)

She often leaves the puppy in *her* yard. (*her* refers to Christine)

The neighbors aren't happy, and *they* have complained. The yard is too close to *their* windows and the puppy barks a lot. (neighbors)

She baked cookies for *them* and apologized. (Christine, neighbors)

Notice that sometimes the antecedent appears in the same sentence, and sometimes in a previous sentence. In the second example sentence, *him* replaces *puppy*, which appears in the first example sentence. No problem, so long as the reader or listener understands the meaning of the pronoun. (In Chapter 21, I talk more about making your pronouns crystal clear.)

TIP

When analyzing a sentence, you seldom find a noun that's been replaced by the pronouns *I* and *we*. The pronoun *I* always refers to the speaker and *we* refers to the speaker and someone else. Similarly, you won't often find a noun that's being replaced by *you*. That person refers to the person being spoken to, who may or may not be named in the sentence.

Similarly, the pronoun *it* sometimes has no antecedent:

> *It* is raining.

> *It* is obvious that Sylvia has not won the card-flipping contest.

In these sentences, *it* is just a place-filler, setting up the sentence for the true expression of meaning. (First example sentence: the rain. Second example sentence: Sylvia's loss in the contest.)

Back in Table 7-1, you saw singular and plural subject pronouns. Time to look at other sorts of pronouns. *Possessive pronouns* — those all-important words that indicate who owns something — also have singular and plural forms. You need to keep them straight. Table 7-2 helps you identify each type.

TABLE 7-2 ## Singular and Plural Possessive Pronouns

Singular	Plural
my	our
mine	ours
your	your
yours	yours
his	their/theirs
her	their
hers	theirs
its	their
whose	whose

Table 7-3 shows you pronouns that may serve as objects.

TABLE 7-3   **Some Common Singular and Plural Object Pronouns**

Singular	Plural
me, myself	us, ourselves
you, yourself	you, yourself
him, himself, her, herself, it, itself	them, themselves
whom, whomever	whom, whomever

Note: The way that people use the possessive pronouns *their* and *theirs* and the object pronouns *them* and *themselves* has been changing recently. Read "Dealing Sensitively with Pronoun Gender" later in this chapter for more information. For now, I've placed those pronouns in the plural column of Tables 7-2 and 7-3.

For more about subject, object, and possessive pronouns, turn to Chapter 8.

POP QUIZ

Identify the pronouns and their antecedents in this paragraph:

> Cedric arrived at his mother's charity ball, although it was snowing and no taxis had stopped to pick him up. When inside the ballroom, he glimpsed Lulu and her boyfriend dancing the tango. Their steps were strange indeed, for the orchestra was actually playing a waltz. As she sailed across the floor — her boyfriend had lost his grip — Lulu cried, "Help me!"

Answer: Cedric arrived at *his (Cedric's)* mother's charity ball, although *it* (no antecedent) was snowing and no taxis had stopped to pick *him (Cedric)* up. Once inside the ballroom, *he (Cedric)* glimpsed Lulu and *her (Lulu's)* boyfriend dancing the tango. *Their (Lulu and boyfriend's)* steps were strange indeed, for the orchestra was actually playing a waltz. As *she (Lulu)* sailed across the floor — *her (Lulu's)* boyfriend had lost *his (boyfriend's)* grip — Lulu cried, "Help *me!*" *(Lulu)*.

Agreeing in Tricky Situations

As anyone who's ever been in an argument knows, sometimes it's easy to come to an agreement, and sometimes it isn't. In this section, I show you some situations in which you have to pay extra attention to the subject–verb and the pronoun–antecedent pairs.

Five puzzling pronouns

Earlier in this chapter, I told you to ignore prepositional phrases when making subjects and verbs agree. Now I must confess that this rule has one small exception — well, five small exceptions. Five pronouns — five little words that just have to stir up trouble — change from singular to plural because of the prepositional phrases that follow them. The five troublemaking pronouns are

>> any

>> all

>> most

>> none

>> some

Here they are with some prepositional phrases and verbs. Notice how the prepositional phrase affects the verb number.

Singular	Plural
any of the information is	*any* of the magazines are
all of the pie is	*all* of the shoes are
most of the city is	*most* of the pencils are
none of the pollution is	*none* of the toenails are
some of the speech is	*some* of the politicians are

See the pattern? For these five words, the prepositional phrase is the determining factor. If the phrase refers to a plural idea, the verb is plural. If the phrase refers to a singular idea, the verb is singular.

That takes care of the verb issue. Now for pronouns. When you refer to one of these pronouns with another pronoun (in other words, if *any, all, most, none,* or *some* is an antecedent), follow the usual rule: Singular pairs with singular and plural pairs with plural. Take a look at these examples:

All of the pie is gone because I ate it. (*all* = singular, *it* = singular)

None of the birds are in their nest. (*none* = plural, *their* = plural)

Each and every

Each and *every* are very powerful words; they're strong enough to change any subject following them into a singular idea. Sneak a peek at these examples:

> *Each* shoe and sock *is* in need of mending, but Larry refuses to pick up a needle and thread.

> *Every* dress and skirt in that store *is* on sale, and Lulu's in a spending mood.

Do these sentences look wrong to you? Granted, they appear to have plural subjects: two things (*shoe and sock*) in sentence one, and another two things (*dress and skirt*) in sentence two. But when *each* or *every* is placed in front of a group, you take the items in the group one at a time. In the first example sentence, the subject consists of one *shoe*, one *sock*, another *shoe*, another *sock*, and so on. Therefore, the sentence needs a singular verb to match the singular subject. Ditto for the *dress and skirt* reference in the second example.

Keep these ideas in mind when you're matching other pronouns to *either* or *neither*. Traditionally, you choose a singular pronoun because the antecedents are singular:

> Each of my uncles will reveal *his* recipe for roast chicken. (*his* refers to one uncle)

> Every one of my aunts will tell you the recipe, if you ask *her* for it. (*her* refers to one aunt)

Recently, some grammarians have accepted the plural pronoun *their* or *they* in similar sentences. For more information on this trend, read "Dealing Sensitively with Pronoun Gender" later in this chapter.

Either and neither: Alone or with partners

Two more pain-in-the-pick-your-body-part pronouns are *either* and *neither*, when they're without their partners *or* and *nor*. When they're alone, *either* and *neither* are always singular, even if you insert a huge group (or just a group of two) between them and their verbs. Hence

> *Either* of the two armies *is* strong enough to take over the entire planet.

> *Neither* of the football captains *has shown* any willingness to accept Lola as quarterback.

Because the example sentences mention *armies* and *captains*, you may be tempted to choose plural verbs. Resist the temptation! No matter what the sentence says, if the subject is *either* or *neither,* singular is the correct way to go. That last statement applies to pronouns also:

> *Each* of the armies follows *its* own leader.

> *Neither* of the men will change *his* strategy.

Note: In the last example, I used the masculine words *men* and *his.* Pronoun–antecedent agreement is harder when you don't know the gender of the antecedent or when more than one gender is represented. See "Dealing Sensitively with Pronoun Gender" later in this chapter for guidance in these sorts of sentences.

When *either* and *neither* appear with their best buds, *or* and *nor,* two things happen. First, *either* and *neither* turn into conjunctions (joining words). Second, if they're joining two subjects, the subject that is closer to the verb determines whether the verb is singular or plural. Yes, that's right! This is a grammar problem you can solve with a ruler. Check out these examples:

> Either *Ella* or *her bridesmaids have eaten* the icing on the cake. (*bridesmaids* = closer subject, a plural; *have eaten* = plural verb)

> Neither *the waiters* nor *Larry is planning* to eat the leftovers. (*Larry* = closer subject, a singular; *is planning* = singular verb)

If the *either/or* and *neither/nor* sentence is a question, the subject closer to the part of the verb that changes governs the singular/plural decision. Take a look at these examples:

> *Does* either *Ella* or *her cousins want* antacids? (*Ella* = subject closer to the helping verb *does*; *Ella* = singular subject, *does want* = singular verb)

> *Do* neither *her cousins* nor *Ella know* how to cook? (*cousins* = subject closer to the helping verb *do*; *cousins* = plural subject, *do know* = plural verb)

Pairing a pronoun to an antecedent in an *either/or* and *neither/nor* sentence is simple. Just think about what you're trying to say and make the pronoun agree in number (singular or plural) and gender (masculine, feminine, neuter) with the word the pronoun represents:

> Do neither *Ella* nor her cousins know how to cook *her* favorite recipe? (The pronoun *her* pairs with the antecedent *Ella.*)

WARNING

In *either/or* and *neither/nor* sentences — in fact, in all sentences! — the meaning of the pronoun must be clear. If you write a sentence mentioning *Ella* and *Mary* and use the pronoun *her,* the reader won't know which woman *her* refers to. For help with this sort of sentence, turn to Chapter 21.

Politics and other irregular subjects

Besides dirty tricks and spin masters, the problem with politics is agreement. Specifically, *politics* looks plural because it ends in *s*. So do *mathematics, tactics, news, economics, civics, physics, athletics, measles, mumps,* and *analysis.* Surprise! All these words are singular and pair with singular verbs, and, if these words are antecedents, with singular pronouns:

> *Politics is* a dirty sport, and Bob devotes his life to *it.* (*politics, is, it* = singular)

> Roger thinks that *mathematics is* overrated, but he studies *it* anyway. (*mathematics, is, it* = singular)

> The *news* about the nutritional content of doughnuts *is* not encouraging. Did you read about *it?* (*news, is, it* = singular)

> "*Is measles is* a serious disease?" asked Egbert. "I think I have *it.* (*Is, measles, it* = singular)

Another word — *statistics* — may be either singular or plural. If you're talking about numbers, you're in plural territory:

> Check the *statistics. They show* that grammar knowledge is declining. (*statistics, they, show* = plural)

If you're talking about a course or a field of study, *statistics* is singular:

> *Statistics is* a difficult course. I took *it* last year. (*Statistics, is, it* = singular)

The English language also has words that are always *plural.* Here are a few of them: *eyeglasses, pants, trousers, jeans, shorts* and *scissors.* (Did you notice how many of those words refer to clothing? Strange.) Other common plural-only nouns are *credentials, acoustics, earnings, headquarters,* and *ceramics.* Plural verbs pair up with these words when they're subjects, and plural pronouns match them when they're antecedents:

> My *eyeglasses are broken.* I dropped *them* yesterday. (*eyeglasses, are broken, them* = plural)

TIP

When in doubt, check your dictionary and remember to match singular nouns with singular verbs and plural nouns with plural verbs.

The ones, the things, and the bodies

Three pronoun "families" — the *ones*, the *things*, and the *bodies* — create problems for anyone who wants to write proper English. Take a peek at the family tree:

The ones: *one, everyone, someone, anyone, no one*

The things: *everything, something, anything, nothing*

The bodies: *everybody, somebody, anybody, nobody*

These pronouns are always singular and match with singular verbs, even if they're surrounded by prepositional phrases that express plurals. Take a look at these examples:

So everybody *is* happy because *no one has caused* any trouble, and *anything goes.*

Anyone in the pool of candidates for mayor *speaks* better than Lulu.

One of the million reasons to hate you *is* your tendency to argue about grammar.

Not *one* out of a million spies *creates* as much distraction as George.

Matching these pronouns to other pronouns is a problem — and, increasingly, a sensitive issue. What was once considered correct became incorrect (in some grammarians' eyes) and then became correct again, sort of. I discuss this topic in more depth in "Dealing Sensitively with Pronoun Gender" later in this chapter. Here are some options for proper pronoun use now:

» In formal English, many grammarians call for a singular pronoun when you're referring to the "ones, the things, and the bodies." Because these pronouns don't reveal gender, you can include both, as in this sentence:

Everyone was asked to bring *his or her* gum to the bubble-popping contest.

» An older tradition calls for just the masculine pronoun, because a very long time ago, people assumed that masculine terms were universal and understood to include females. In this tradition, this sentence is correct, even if boys and girls participate in the contest:

Everyone was asked to bring *his* gum to the bubble-popping contest.

» More recently, grammarians have accepted *they, their,* and *theirs* when the antecedent is a member of the "ones, things, bodies" group. Using this guideline, here's a correct sentence:

Everyone was asked to bring *their* gum to the bubble-popping contest.

Which one should you use? Before you decide, consider your reader or listener. In conversational English, the third option *(they, their, theirs)* is commonly accepted. In formal written English, the first one may be a safer choice, though you should be careful not to create a clunky sentence. If your audience values inclusiveness more than grammatical consistency, you may wish to use the third option.

TIP

Sometimes an easy option is to avoid the pronoun entirely. In other words, try something like this sentence:

> Everyone was asked to bring gum to the bubble-popping contest.

See? No pronoun, no problem!

Who, which, and that

These pronouns can be either singular or plural, depending upon context. If they replace or refer to a singular noun or pronoun, they're singular. If they replace or refer to a plural pronoun, they magically turn into plural pronouns. When you match a verb or another pronoun to *who, which,* or *that,* think carefully about meaning. Then decide which verb or pronoun you need. Some examples:

> Elena, *who is* taking *her* first standardized test tomorrow, is very nervous. (*who = Elena* = singular, *is* and *her* = singular)

> The students *who are taking* the test next week have to devote *their* free time to studying. (*who = students* = plural, *are taking* and *their* = plural)

> The jug *that is falling* off the ledge is valuable, and I can't afford to replace *it.* (*that = jug* = singular, *is falling* and *it* = singular)

> The books *that interest* me are not in the library. I will have to buy *them.* (*that = books* = plural, *interest* and *them* = plural)

TIP

At times, locating the antecedent for *who, which,* or *that* can be very tough, unless you apply your best reading comprehension skills. Compare these sentences, which are similar but not at all the same:

> Lindy is one of the nurses who love to dance. (*who* refers to *nurses,* a plural, because more than one nurse loves to dance)

> Lindy is the only one of the nurses who wears dancing shoes to work. (*who* refers to *one,* a singular, because no one but Lindy wears dancing shoes to work)

REMEMBER

Find the antecedent — the word that *who, which,* or *that* refers to — and match the pronoun and verb to the antecedent.

Dealing Sensitively with Pronoun Gender

Historians write about war, and often, by disagreeing among themselves so forcefully, start their own wars over the correct version of historical events. Grammarians, too, have been known to fight. One long battle involves which pronoun suits a particular situation. The "problem areas," as they say in articles about dieting and exercise, generally focus on gender. In grammar, gender is masculine (for males), feminine (for females), or neuter (neither male nor female).

A brief outline of the pronoun wars: No one has trouble with neuter, genderless situations. The pronoun *it* refers to *cup* and *they* refers to *cups*. Everyone's happy. Nor do obviously plural pronouns cause problems. *They, them, their, theirs* match plural verbs and antecedents (the word the pronoun refers to). Finally, few people worry about an obvious masculine singular or feminine singular situation:

> William is a prince. He will inherit his grandmother's throne someday. (*William* is masculine, as are the pronouns *he* and *his*.)

> Elizabeth is the queen. She inherited her throne from her father. (*Elizabeth* is feminine, as are the pronouns *she* and *her*.)

But what happens when you're referring to a person whose gender is unknown, such as *person, officer, clerk,* or other singular noun? How should you refer to *someone, anybody,* and other singular pronouns? Remember, the general rule is that singular pairs with singular and plural with plural.

For many centuries, writers ignored the singular/plural issue and paired *person, everyone,* and any other word referring to someone of unknown gender with *they, them, their,* and *theirs.* Writers needed these non-gendered pronouns, and they used them in both singular and plural situations. Sometime in the 19th century, though, influential grammarians argued that *they, them, their,* and *theirs* should be used for plural situations only. These grammarians insisted that the singular masculine pronouns (*he, him, his*) were understood to include females.

You can easily see the problems with that solution to the pronoun wars. You can end up with sentences such as this one:

> Every new parent ignores his lack of sleep and his sore breasts because caring for a newborn baby is his top priority.

Many feminists have advocated *he or she, him or her,* and *his or her* when the gender of the antecedent is unclear. One problem is that a sentence with too many of these expressions is unbearably awkward:

> Call the clerk and tell him or her that his or her letter about the parking violation makes no sense at all and that I'm going to sue him or her for every penny he or she has.

WHEN IN ROME AND GREECE: CLASSICAL PLURALS

Granted, the Colosseum is a magnificent sight, and the Greek myths are pretty cool. But those languages! Thanks to the ancient Romans and Greeks, a number of English words form their plurals in an irregular way. Here are some singular/plural pairs:

- **Alumnus/alumni:** The singular, *alumnus,* is a masculine term. The plural, alumni, may refer to groups of males, or, if you accept the masculine term as universal, *alumni* may refer to both males and females. (See Chapter 8.)

- **Alumna/alumnae:** The singular, *alumna,* is a feminine term. The plural refers to groups of females.

- **Analysis/analyses:** *Analysis* is the singular, meaning "a course of psychological therapy" or, more generally, "a serious investigation or examination." The plural changes the *i* to *e.*

- **Parenthesis/parentheses:** (This sentence is in *parentheses,* but I try not to write with too many *parentheses* because readers find more than three *parentheses* confusing.)

- **Datum/data:** Technically, *data* is the plural of *datum* and takes a plural verb *(the data are clear).* However, more and more people are matching *data* with a singular verb *(the data is clear).* To impress all your grammarian friends, pair *data* with a plural verb.

- **Phenomenon/phenomena:** The singular term is *phenomenon,* a noun meaning "a marvel, a special occurrence or event." The plural term is *phenomena,* correct but so obscure nowadays that my computer thesaurus keeps trying to change it to *phenomenon.*

See what I mean? I bet you gave up halfway through the example. That's how bad it sounds! Another problem with *he or she* and similar expressions is their clearcut division of genders. In recent years, many people have come to see gender identity as complex — more multifaceted than *he or she* implies. These issues have led to a call for *they, them, their,* and *theirs* as the go-to pronouns for both singular and plural situations.

So what's a proper, grammatically correct sentence in the 21st century? My advice? Consider the arguments and then think about your reader or listener. Your personal beliefs are important, but you also have to take into account how your words will be received. If you like the *they-as-plural* rule, you may be misunderstood if you say *they have arrived* and only one person walks through the door. On the other hand, *everyone should cast their ballots* is easier to decode.

TIP

In writing for school or business, be careful. Whoever judges your work is likely to apply *his or her* or *their* standards, and beliefs about proper grammar, to your work. One way to avoid problems is to rewrite the sentence to make the antecedent plural:

> All the students must bring *their* gym shorts.

or to eliminate the problem pronoun:

> Bring *your* gym shorts, *you* little creeps!

Chapter **8**

Pronouns and Their Cases

or *me? Their* or *theirs? He* or *himself?* Or (gasp) *who* or *whom?* Millions of suffering grammar students have asked themselves these and similar questions, often gulping down an aspirin or two before they arrive at an answer. But there's actually a logic to pronoun choice, and a few tips go a long way toward making the proper form obvious. In this chapter, I explain the three major sets, or *cases*, of pronouns — *subject, object,* and *possessive.* Master the basic concepts, and you'll end up with the proper pronoun — and no headache — every time.

Me Like Tarzan: Choosing Subject Pronouns

The subject is the person or thing that is doing the action or being talked about in the sentence. (For more on locating the subject, see Chapter 3.) You can't do much wrong when you have the actual name of a person, place, or thing as the subject — in other words, a noun — but pronouns are another story.

Legal subject pronouns for formal English include *I, you, he, she, it, we, they, who,* and *whoever.* If you want to avoid a grammatical felony, stay away from *me, him, her, us, them, whom,* and *whomever* when you're selecting a subject. Also avoid the *−self* pronouns (*myself, himself, herself, ourselves,* and so forth) when you're scouting out a subject, unless you throw one next to another subject for emphasis, as in *I myself will select the proper pronoun.*

TIP

A bunch of lovely pronouns are suitable as subjects and as objects: *either, neither, each, every, some, any, most, none, all, many, everyone, someone, no one, everybody, somebody, nobody, everything, something, nothing, few, both,* and *several.*

Here are some examples of pronouns as the subject of a sentence:

I certainly did tell Lulu not to remove her nose ring in public! (*I* is the subject of the verb *did tell.*)

Nobody knows the answer to that question about pronouns. (*Nobody* is the subject of the verb *knows.*)

Al and *she* will bring their killer bees to the next meeting of the Unusual Pets Association. (*She* is one of the subjects of the verb *will bring.*)

Whoever marries Larry should negotiate a good prenuptial agreement. (*Whoever* is the subject of the verb *marries.*)

Compounding interest: Pairs of subjects

Most people do okay with one subject, but sentences with two subjects are a different story. For example, I often hear my otherwise grammatically correct students say such things as

Robert and *me* are going to the supermarket for some chips.

Although *her* and *I* have not met, Teresa sent me a friend request.

See the problem? In the first example sentence, the verb is *are going.* To find the subject, ask: *Who* or *what are going?* The answer right now is *Robert and me are going,* but *me* isn't a subject pronoun. Here's the correct version:

Robert and *I* are going to the supermarket for some carrots. (I couldn't resist correcting the nutritional content, too.)

In the second example sentence, the verb is *have met.* (*Not* isn't part of the verb.) *Who* or *what have met?* The answer, as it is now, is *her* and *I. I* is a legal subject pronoun, but *her* is not. The correct version is as follows:

Although *she* and *I* haven't met, Teresa sent me a friend request.

TIP

One good way to check pronouns is to look at each one separately. If you've developed a fairly good "ear" for proper English, isolating the pronoun helps you decide whether you've chosen correctly. You may have to adjust the verb a bit when you're speaking about one subject instead of two, but the principle is the same. If the pronoun doesn't sound right as a solo subject, it isn't right as part of a pair either. Here's an example:

ORIGINAL SENTENCE: *Ella* and *her* went to the grammar rodeo yesterday.

CHECK 1: *Ella* went to the grammar rodeo yesterday. Verdict: sounds okay.

CHECK 2: *Her* went to the grammar rodeo yesterday. Verdict: sounds terrible. Substitute *she.*

CHECK 3: *She* went to the grammar rodeo yesterday. Verdict: much better.

RECOMBINED, CORRECTED SENTENCE: *Ella* and *she* went to the grammar rodeo yesterday.

POP QUIZ

Which sentence is correct?

A. Bud, you, and me appointed the judges for the verb-tense event, so we have to live with their decisions, however wrong.

B. Bud, you, and I appointed the judges for the verb-tense event, so we have to live with their decisions, however wrong.

Answer: Sentence B is correct. *I* is a subject pronoun, and *me* is not. If you take the parts of the subject separately, you can usually hear the correct answer.

TIP

Subject pronouns may show up in another spot in the sentence — as a subject complement after a linking verb. Think of linking verbs as giant equal signs, equating two halves of the sentence. All forms of the verb *to be* are linking verbs, as well as verbs such as *seem, appear, smell, sound,* and *taste.* The type of pronoun that begins the equation (the subject) must, in formal speech and writing, also be the type of pronoun that finishes the equation. (For more information on finding linking verbs and the pronouns that go with them, see Chapter 5.)

Attracting appositives

Do you want to say the same thing twice? Use an appositive. An *appositive* is a noun or a pronoun that is exactly the same as the noun or pronoun that precedes it in the sentence. Check out these examples:

> Raven, the girl whose hair matches her name, is thinking of changing her name to Goldie.

> Tee Rex, holder of the coveted Dinosaur of the Year trophy, has signed an endorsement deal with a company that makes extra-large sneakers.

> Lola, a fan of motorcycles, acknowledges that life in the fast lane is sometimes hard on the complexion.

Do you see the pair of matching ideas in each sentence? In the first, *Raven* and *the girl whose hair matches her name* are the same. In the next sentence, *Tee Rex* and *holder of the coveted Dinosaur of the Year trophy* make a pair. In the third, *Lola* and *a fan of motorcycles* are the same. The second half of each pair (*the girl whose hair matches her name, holder of the coveted Dinosaur of the Year trophy*, and *a fan of motorcycles*) is an appositive.

Appositives fall naturally into most people's speech and writing, perhaps because human beings feel a great need to explain themselves. You probably won't make a mistake with an appositive unless a pronoun or a comma is involved. (See Chapter 13 for more information on appositives and commas.)

Pronouns can serve as appositives, and they show up mostly when you have two or more people or things to talk about. Here are some sentences with appositives and pronouns:

> The winners of the raffle — Ali and he — will appear on the *Tonight Show* tomorrow. (Appositive = *Ali* and *he*)

> The judges for the spitball contest, Sally and she, wear plastic raincoats. (Appositive — *Sally* and *she*)

> The dancers who broke their toenails, Lulu and I, will not appear in the closing number. (Appositive = *Lulu* and *I*)

Why are *he, she*, and *I* correct? In these sample sentences, the appositives are paired with the subjects of the sentence (*winners, judges, dancers*). In a sense, the appositives are potential substitutes for the subject. Therefore, you must use a subject pronoun.

TIP

The appositive pronoun must always match its partner; if you pair it with a subject, the appositive must be a subject pronoun. If you pair it with an object, it must be an object pronoun.

You can confirm pronoun choice with the same method that I describe in the previous section. Take each part of the pair (or group) separately. Adjust the verb if necessary, and then listen to the sentence. Here's the check for one of the sentences that I used earlier:

CHECK 1: The judges for the spitball contest wear plastic raincoats. Verdict: sounds okay.

CHECK 2: Sally wears plastic raincoats. (You have to adjust the verb because *Sally* is singular, not plural, but the pronoun sounds okay.)

CHECK 3: She wears plastic raincoats. (Again, you have to adjust the verb, but the pronoun sounds okay.)

Bottom line: Isolate the pronoun and say the sentence (either aloud or silently). If you have spent some time listening to educated speech or reading good books, your "ear" for good English should help you decide whether the pronoun is correct.

Picking pronouns for comparisons

Lazy people that we are, we all tend to take shortcuts, chopping words out of our sentences and racing to the finish. This practice is evident in comparisons. Read the following example sentences:

Lulu denies that she has as much facial hair as he.

That sentence really means

Lulu denies that she has as much facial hair as he has.

If you say the entire comparison, as in the preceding example, the pronoun choice is a cinch. However, when you drop the verb (*has*), you may be tempted to use the wrong pronoun, as in this sentence:

Lulu denies that she has as much facial hair as him.

Sounds right, doesn't it? But the sentence is wrong. The words you say must fit with the words you don't say. Obviously you aren't going to accept

Lulu denies that she has as much facial hair as him has.

Him has sounds improper, and it is. The technical reason? *Him* is an object pronoun, so you can't use it as the subject of *has.*

TIP

Whenever you have an implied comparison — a comparison that the sentence suggests but doesn't state completely — finish the sentence in your head. The correct pronoun becomes obvious.

Implied comparisons don't always require subject pronouns. With an object pronoun (see the next section for more information) the meaning of the sentence changes. Check out these examples:

IMPLIED: The dancers gave Michael more attention than she.

MEANING: The dancers gave Michael more attention than she gave Michael.

IMPLIED: The dancers gave Michael more attention than her.

MEANING: The dancers gave Michael more attention than the dancers gave to her.

As you see in these examples, three little letters can add quite a bit of meaning to your sentence. Choose your pronouns wisely.

POP QUIZ

Which sentence is correct?

A. Tee Rex broke more claws than I during the fight with Godzilla.

B. Tee Rex broke more claws than me during the fight with Godzilla.

Answer: Sentence A is correct. Read the sentence this way: Tee Rex broke more claws than *I did* during the fight with Godzilla. You can't say *me did.*

One more: Which is correct?

A. Roger told me more celebrity gossip than she.

B. Roger told me more celebrity gossip than her.

Answer: Both are correct, depending on the situation. Sentence A means that Roger told me more celebrity gossip than *she told me.* Sentence B means that Roger told me more celebrity gossip than *he told her.*

Using Pronouns as Direct and Indirect Objects

Up to this point in the chapter, I've concentrated on subject pronouns, but now it's time to turn to the receiver of the sentence's action — the object. Specifically, it's time to turn to *object pronouns.* (For more information on finding the object, see Chapter 5.) Pronouns that may legally function as objects include *me, you, him, her, it, us, them, whom,* and *whomever.* (A few pronouns work as both subject and object pronouns. Check "Me Like Tarzan: Choosing Subject Pronouns" in this chapter for a list of those worry-free words.)

Here are some examples of direct and indirect object pronouns, all in italics:

> Ticktock smashed *him* right on the nose for suggesting that "the mouse ran down the clock." (*smashed* is the verb; *Ticktock* is the subject; *him* is the object)

> Archie scolded *us* for ignoring his texts. (*scolded* is the verb; *Archie* is the subject; *us* is the object)

> Olivier, president of Grammarians 'R Us, sent *me* a horrifying *letter.* (*sent* is the verb; *Olivier* is the subject; *letter* and *me* are objects)

Here's some English teacher terminology for you, if you can stand it. (If not, don't worry. You don't need labels to use object pronouns correctly.) A *direct object* receives the action directly from the verb, answering the questions *whom?* or *what?* after the verb. An *indirect object* receives the action indirectly (clever, those grammar terms), answering the questions *to whom?* or *to what?* after the verb. In the previous example sentence, *letter* is the direct object and *me* is the indirect object. For more information on direct and indirect objects, see Chapter 5.

POP QUIZ

Which sentence is correct?

A. The principal punished we, the innocent, for the food fight in the cafeteria yesterday.

B. The principal punished us, the innocent, for the food fight in the cafeteria yesterday.

Answer: Sentence B is correct. *Us* is the object of the verb *punished.*

Are You Talking to I? Prepositions and Pronouns

Prepositions — words that express relationships such as *about, after, among, by, for, behind, since,* and others — may also have objects. (For a more complete list of prepositions, see Chapter 9.)

All object pronouns may act as objects of the preposition. The most common object pronouns are *me, you, him, her, it, us, them, whom,* and *whomever.* (Some pronouns do double-duty and are acceptable as both subjects and objects. Turn to "Me Like Tarzan: Choosing Subject Pronouns" earlier in this chapter for a list of those pronouns.)

Here are some examples of pronouns working as objects of prepositions, with both the preposition and the object pronoun italicized:

> Max, fearful for his pet tarantula, gave his dog *to us* yesterday.
>
> Michael's latest play received a critical review *from them.*
>
> Archie didn't like the window so he simply plastered *over it.*

TIP

The object of a preposition answers the usual object questions (*whom? what?*), as in these examples:

> Max, fearful for his pet tarantula, gave his dog to *whom*? Answer: to *us.*
>
> Michael's latest play received a critical review from *whom*? Answer: from *them.*
>
> Archie didn't like the window, so he simply plastered over *what*? Answer: over *it.*

Also notice that all the pronouns — *us, him, her, them, it* — come from the set of object pronouns.

POP QUIZ

Which sentence is correct?

A. According to Elton and she, the elephant's nose is simply too long.

B. According to Elton and her, the elephant's nose is simply too long.

Answer: Sentence B is correct. *According to* is the preposition. The object of the preposition is *Elton and her. Her* is an object pronoun. (*She* is a subject pronoun.)

WARNING

For some reason, the phrase *between you and I* has caught on. However, this usage is not yet considered correct in formal speech and writing. *Between* is a preposition, so object pronouns follow it. The pronoun *I* is for subjects, and *me* is for objects. So between you and me, *me* is the word you want.

Most of the tough pronoun choices come when the sentence has more than one object of the preposition (*Elton and her,* for example, in the pop quiz). In this situation, try this rule of thumb — and I really mean thumb, at least when you're writing or looking for errors in someone else's writing. Take your thumb and cover one of the objects. Say the sentence. Does it sound right?

> According to Elton

Okay so far. Now take your thumb and cover the other object. Say the sentence. Does it sound right?

>   According to she

Now do you hear the problem? Make the change:

>   According to her

Now put the two back together:

>   According to Elton and her

This method is not foolproof, but chances are good that you'll get a clue to the correct pronoun choices if you check the objects one by one.

Attaching Objects to Verbals

Isn't *verbal* a strange word? It sounds like something you keep in a little cage with an exercise wheel. But a *verbal* isn't a furry pet. It's a word derived from a verb (a word that expresses action or state of being) that functions as a noun or as a description (in other words, as an adjective or an adverb). I discuss verbals in detail in Chapter 19. In this section, I show you how to select a pronoun for that coveted role, object of a verbal. (Everyone in Hollywood is auditioning for the part.) Later in this chapter, in the section entitled "Dealing with Pronouns and '-Ing' Nouns," I address another way that pronouns interact with verbals.

Take a look at these verbals and their objects, both of which are italicized. Also notice the real verb in each sentence, which I've underlined:

>   Melanie <u>loves</u> *slapping him,* but Lulu favors nonviolence.
>
>   Lola briefly <u>left</u> the meeting *to call them.*
>
>   Oliver, *having watched us* at the party, <u>signed</u> up for singing lessons.

As you see, the verbals look like verbs. However, in the first sentence *slapping* isn't acting as a verb. *Slapping* is a thing that Melanie loves. In other words, it functions as a noun. In the second example, *to call* provides a reason why Lola left the meeting. Therefore *to call* describes the verb *left* (*left* why? *to call*). In the third example, *having watched us* gives you more information about *Oliver,* a noun. Anything that describes a noun is functioning as an adjective.

When your writing includes a verbal, ask the object questions: *whom? what?* after the verbal to locate its object. If the answer is a pronoun, be sure you've chosen an object pronoun.

Which sentence is correct?

A. Oliver loves to show I and Mel his new dance moves.

B. Oliver loves to show me and Mel his new dance moves.

Answer: Sentence B is correct. *To show* is a verbal. *To show whom? To show me and Mel. Me* is one of the objects of the verbal *to show. (Mel* is the other.)

Knowing the Difference Between Who and Whom

Many grammarians believe that no one cares these days about the difference between *who/whoever* and *whom/whomever*. In their view, *whom* and *whomever* are fading away. These grammarians may be right, but many people (including me) still see a role for these pronouns. If your listeners or readers are in that group, you should know when each is appropriate. First, the rule:

>> *Who* and *whoever* are for subjects.

  Who and *whoever* also follow and complete the meaning of linking verbs. (In grammarspeak, *who* and *whoever* serve as subject complements.)

>> *Whom* and *whomever* are for objects — all kinds of objects (direct, indirect, of prepositions, of infinitives, and so on).

For more information on subjects, see Chapter 3. For more information on objects and linking verb complements, see Chapter 5.

Before applying the rule concerning *who/whoever* and *whom/whomever*, check out these sample sentences:

  Whoever needs help from Roger is going to wait a long time. (*Whoever* is the subject of the verb *needs*.)

  Who is calling Lulu at this time of night? (*Who* is the subject of the verb *is calling*.)

  "Ask *whomever* you want to the prom," exclaimed Michael. (*Whomever* is the direct object of the verb *ask*.)

  To *whom* are you sending that email? (*Whom* is the object of the preposition *to*.)

Now that you know the rule and have seen the words in action, here's a trick for deciding between *who/whoever* and *whom/whomever*.

According to an old song, "love and marriage go together like a horse and carriage." Grammarians might sing that song with slightly different lyrics: "A subject and verb go together like a horse and carriage." (What do you think? Grammy material?) Follow these steps:

1. Find all the verbs in the sentence.

2. Don't separate the helping verbs from the main verb. Count the main verb and its helpers as a single verb.

3. Now pair each verb with a subject.

4. If you have a verb flapping around with no subject, chances are *who* or *whoever* is the subject you're missing.

5. If all the verbs have subjects, check them one more time. Do you have any linking verbs without complements? (For more information on complements, see Chapter 5.) If you have a lonely linking verb with no complement in sight, you need *who* or *whoever*.

6. If all subjects are accounted for and you don't need a linking verb complement, you've reached a final answer: *whom* or *whomever* is the only possibility.

Here are two example sentences, analyzed as described above:

SENTENCE ONE: *Who/Whom* shall I say is calling?

The verbs = *shall say, is calling.*

The subject of *shall say* = *I.*

The subject of *is calling* = Okay, here you go. You need a subject for *is calling* but you're out of words. You have only one choice: *who.*

CORRECT SENTENCE: *Who* shall I say is calling?

SENTENCE TWO: Jake is the ballplayer *who/whom* everyone thinks plays best.

The verbs = *is, thinks, plays.*

The subject of *is* = *Jake.*

The subject of *thinks* = *everyone*

The subject of *plays* = Um. . . m. Once again, a subject shortage occurs. Therefore, you need *who.*

CORRECT SENTENCE: Jake is the ballplayer *who* everyone thinks plays best.

Now you try. Which word is correct?

Agnes buys detergent in one-ton boxes for Roger, *who/whom* she adores in spite of his odor problem.

Answer: *Whom*, because it's the direct object of *adores*. *Agnes buys, she adores* = subject–verb pairs. Both are action verbs, so no subject complement is needed. Therefore, you need an object pronoun, *whom*.

People have led perfectly pleasant (though grammatically incorrect) lives without knowing the stuff in this section. However, the standardized test-makers consider these topics fair game — and big game, judging from the number of questions they ask about pronoun issues, especially *who* and *whom*.

Pronouns of Possession: No Exorcist Needed

Possessive pronouns show (pause for a drum roll) possession. Not the Hollywood evil demon kind of possession, but the kind where somebody owns something. Possessive pronouns include *my, your, his, her, its, our, their, mine, yours, hers, ours, theirs,* and *whose.* Check out the following sample sentences:

Michael took *his* apple out of the refrigerator marked "Open Only in Case of Emergency."

Sure that the computer had beeped *its* last beep, Lola shopped for a new model.

To *our* dismay, Roger and Lulu opened *their* birthday presents two days early.

Vengeance is *mine.*

Lester berated the dancer *whose* stiletto heels had wounded Lola's big toe.

The possessive pronouns in these examples show that the apple belongs to Michael, the beep belongs to the computer, the dismay belongs to us, and the presents belong to Roger and Lulu. Vengeance belongs to *me.* (*Mine* is the possessive pronoun that refers to something *I* own, something that belongs to *me.*) The last sentence is a little more complicated. The word *whose* refers to the *dancer.* The stiletto heels belong to the dancer. The big toe belongs to Lola, but possession is shown in this example with a possessive noun (*Lola's*) not a possessive pronoun (*her*).

Notice that none of the possessive pronouns have apostrophes. They never do! Ever! Never ever! Putting apostrophes into possessive pronouns is one of the most common errors. (*It's* doesn't mean *belongs to it. It's* means *it is.*)

Which sentence is correct?

A. Smashing the pumpkin on his mother's clean floor, Rocky commented, "I believe this gourd is yours."

B. Smashing the pumpkin on his mother's clean floor, Rocky commented, "I believe this gourd is your's."

Answer: Sentence A is correct. No possessive pronoun has an apostrophe, and *yours* is a possessive pronoun.

Dealing with Pronouns and "-Ing" Nouns

The rule concerning possessive pronouns and "–ing" nouns is easy, once you think about what you're trying to say — specifically, what you want to emphasize. Take a look at these two sentences:

Mom, look at us riding our bikes!

Mom objects to our riding our bikes in traffic.

In both sentences, the pronoun precedes *riding* — a noun that end in *-ing* and is created from a verb, *ride*. (In grammarspeak, *riding* is a *gerund*, a member of the verbal family I discuss in "Attaching Objects to Verbals" earlier in this chapter.) In the first example sentence, the speakers want their mother to look at them. Perhaps they've been struggling to learn how to ride, or perhaps they simply want attention. In either situation, the meaning is essentially complete after the pronoun:

Mom, look at us!

The phrase *riding our bikes* adds meaning, but it's not the point of the sentence. Now think about the second sentence. If you stop after the pronoun, the sentence is incomplete:

Mom objects to our.

Huh? *Our* what? You have to add the information about *riding our bikes in traffic* to end up with a statement that makes sense.

Consider for a moment what this sentence would mean:

Mom objects to us.

Now the sentence makes sense, but the meaning is different. The mother objects to the speakers. Perhaps she's always hated them — in which case grammar is the least of their problems. This is not the most likely meaning.

Bottom line: A possessive pronoun in front of an *-ing* noun formed from a verb (a gerund, in grammar terms) emphasizes the action, not the person the pronoun represents. If that's your intention, you must use a possessive pronoun.

TEST ALERT

Standardized test-makers love to check whether you know about possessives and gerunds. And now you do! Here are some examples:

> Lola knows that *their* creating a dress code has nothing to do with the fact that she recently pierced her toes. (not *them* creating)
>
> Egbert's wife likes *his* singing in the shower. (not *him* singing)
>
> The goldfish accept *our* placing food in the tank so long as we don't try to shake their fins. (not *us* placing)

TIP

Some *-ing* words weren't created from verbs, and some *-ing* words aren't nouns. Don't worry about distinguishing between one and the other. Just consider what you're trying to say, and choose a pronoun that helps you express your meaning.

POP QUIZ

Which sentence is correct?

A. The boss hates you answering the phone with "Whassup, dude?"

B. The boss hates your answering the phone with "Whassup, dude?"

Answer: Sentence B is correct. The boss doesn't know you enough to hate you (the meaning of Sentence A). Of course, if she got to know you better . . . but I won't go there. Sentence B places the emphasis on *answering.* The possessive *your* puts it there. The boss objects to "Whassup, dude?" as a client's introduction to the company. I can't imagine why.

Chapter **9**

Small Words, Big Trouble: Prepositions

How does the proverb go? Little things mean a lot? Whoever said that was probably talking about prepositions. Some of the shortest words in the language — at least most of them — these little guys pack a punch in your sentences. Unfortunately, prepositions attract mistakes as powerfully as catnip captures the attention of the meow-set. In this chapter, I explain everything you always wanted to know about prepositions and show you how to avoid the pitfalls associated with them.

Proposing Relationships: Prepositions

Imagine that you encounter two nouns: *elephant* and *book.* (A *noun* is a word for a person, place, thing, or idea.) How many ways can you connect the two nouns to express different ideas?

the book *about* the elephant

the book *by* the elephant

the book *behind* the elephant

the book *in front of* the elephant

the book *near* the elephant

the book *under* the elephant

The italicized words relate two nouns to each other. These relationship words are called prepositions. *Prepositions* may be defined as any word or group of words that relates a noun or a pronoun to another word in the sentence.

Sometime during the last millennium when I was in grammar school, I had to memorize a list of prepositions. (How quaint, right? We had inkwells, too.) I was so terrified of my seventh grade teacher that not only did I learn the list, I made it part of my being. In fact, I can still recite it. I don't think memorizing prepositions is worth the time, but a familiarity would be nice. In other words, don't marry the preposition list. Just date it a few times. Take a look at Table 9-1 for a list of some common prepositions:

TABLE 9-1 **Common Prepositions**

about	above	according to	across
after	against	along	amid
among	around	at	before
behind	below	beside	besides
between	beyond	by	concerning
down	during	except	for
from	in	into	like
of	off	on	over
past	since	through	toward
underneath	until	up	upon
with	within	without	

The Objects of My Affection: Prepositional Phrases and Their Objects

Prepositions never travel alone; they're always with an object. In the examples in the previous section, the object of each preposition is *elephant.* Just to get all the annoying terminology over with at once, a *prepositional phrase* consists of a preposition and an object. The object of a preposition is always a noun or a pronoun, or perhaps one or two of each. (A *pronoun* is a word that takes the place of a noun, such as *him* for *Raymond*, *it* for *hotel*, and so forth.)

Here's an example:

> In the afternoon the snow pelted Raymond on his little bald head.

This sentence has two prepositions: *in* and *on*. *Afternoon* is the object of the preposition *in*, and *head* is the object of the preposition *on*.

Why, you may ask, is the object *head* and not *little* or *bald*? Sigh. I was hoping you wouldn't notice. Okay, here's the explanation. You can throw a few other things inside a prepositional phrase — mainly descriptive words. Check out these variations on the plain phrase *of the elephant:*

> of the *apologetic* elephant
>
> of the *always annoying* elephant
>
> of the *antagonizingly argumentative* elephant

Despite the different descriptions, each phrase is still basically talking about an *elephant*. Also, *elephant* is a noun, and only nouns and pronouns are allowed to be objects of the preposition. So in the *Raymond* sentence, you need to choose the most important word as the object of the preposition. Also, you need to choose a noun, not an adjective. Examine *his little bald head* (the words, not Raymond's actual head, which is better seen from a distance). *Head* is clearly the important concept, and *head* is a noun. Thus *head* is the object of the preposition.

Sometimes a preposition may have more than one object, as in this sentence:

> Little Jane bounced the rubber ball in the hallway and bedroom.

In this sentence, *hallway* and *bedroom* are objects of the preposition *in*. You can think of this sentence as an abbreviated form of

> Little Jane bounced the rubber ball in the hallway and in the bedroom.

When you attach two or more objects to one preposition, you must be sure that both objects pair well with the preposition. Take a look at this sentence:

> Little Jane bounced the rubber ball in the street and the wall.

If you expand this sentence, you get

Little Jane bounced the rubber ball in the street and in the wall.

But how can you bounce a ball *in the wall?* Unless you're talking about a half-built house, you bounce a ball *on* or *against the wall*, not *in the wall*. The moral of the story is that a preposition with more than one object must make sense with each object separately. If it doesn't, write two separate prepositional phrases.

WARNING

Also be careful when you're choosing a pronoun as the object of a preposition. The pronouns cleared to act as objects of the preposition, are *me, you, him, her, it, us, them, whom,* and *whomever*. Stay away from *I, we, she, he, they, who,* and *whoever*. Those pronouns are for subjects and subject complements. (Turn to Chapter 5 for more information.)

Pop the question: Questions that identify the objects of the prepositions

All objects — of a verb or of a preposition — answer the questions *whom?* or *what?* To find the object of a preposition, ask *whom?* or *what?* after the preposition.

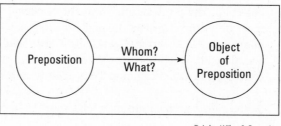

© John Wiley & Sons, Inc.

Marilyn thought that the selection of the elephant for the show was unfair.

In this sentence, you see two prepositional phrases. The first preposition is *of*. *Of* what? *Of the elephant. Elephant* is the object of the preposition *of*. The second preposition is *for*. *For* what? For the *show*. *Show* is the object of the preposition *to*.

POP QUIZ

What is the object of the preposition in this sentence?

The heroic teacher pounded the grammar rules into her students' tired brains.

Answer: *Brains* is the object of the preposition *into*. When you pop the question — *into* whom? or *into* what? — the answer is *her students' tired brains.* The most important word is *brains,* which is a noun.

Why pay attention to prepositions?

When you're checking subject–verb pairs, you need to identify and then ignore the prepositional phrases. The prepositional phrases are distractions. If you don't ignore them, you may end up matching the verb to the wrong word. (See Chapter 7 for more information on subject–verb agreement.) You may also find it helpful to recognize prepositional phrases because sometimes, when you "pop the question" to find an adjective or an adverb, the answer is a prepositional phrase. Don't panic. You haven't done anything wrong. Simply know that a prepositional phrase may do the same job as a single-word adjective or adverb. (See Chapter 10 for more on adjectives and adverbs.)

TIP

You should also pay attention to prepositions because choosing the wrong one may be embarrassing:

Person 1: May I sit *next* to you?

Person 2: (smiling) Certainly.

Person 1: May I sit *under* you?

Person 2: (sound of slap) Help! Police!

The task of selecting the proper preposition is often difficult because common expressions differ, depending upon the country or even area of a country in which the language is spoken. In New York City, for example, polite people wait *on line* (if they're impolite, they push through the crowd). In other parts of the United States, people wait *in line.* Also, sometimes more than one preposition is acceptable. You can *browse over* or *browse through* a magazine, reading bits here and there and deciding what you'd like to investigate thoroughly. Both prepositions, *over* and *through,* are correct.

Omitting a preposition can also change meaning. Can you see the difference between these two sentences?

Shirley swam the ocean.

Shirley swam in the ocean.

In the first example sentence, Shirley swam across the entire ocean — from, say, California to Japan or New York to Ireland. The second example sentence expresses a more likely meaning, that Shirley went to the beach and swam for a while in ocean water.

TEST ALERT

A few questions on standardized exams, including the SAT Writing and the ACT English tortures — sorry, I mean *test sections* — revolve around prepositions. You may encounter a misused preposition (*to* instead of *with*, for example) or a situation in which a preposition tries to do the job of another part of speech (*like* instead of *as*, for example). The best preparation for preposition questions is (a) a careful reading of this chapter and (b) general reading of good-quality writing. Why do I recommend *quality* writing? Language seeps into your brain when you read, and some of it stays there. If you're spending time with proper English, the correct use of prepositions simply sounds right. The reverse is also true. To dedicated readers, preposition errors stand out like ukuleles in an opera.

A Good Part of Speech to End a Sentence With?

As I write this paragraph, global warming is increasing, the stock market is tanking, and the Yankees' pitching staff is in deep trouble. In the midst of all these earth-shattering events, some people still walk around worrying about where to put a preposition. Specifically, they (okay, I must admit that sometimes I, too) worry about whether or not ending a sentence with a preposition is acceptable. Let me illustrate the problem:

> Tell me whom he spoke *about*.

> Tell me *about* whom he spoke.

Here's the verdict: Both sentences are correct, at least for most people and even for most grammarians. But not, I must warn you, for all. If you're writing for someone who loves to tsk-tsk about the decline and fall of proper English, avoid placing a preposition at the end of a sentence. Otherwise, put the preposition wherever you like, including at the end of a sentence.

INTERJECTIONS ARE EASY!

Grammarians usually give every part of speech a lot of attention — well, every part of speech except one. Interjections tend to fade into the background when you're analyzing a sentence grammatically. That's the opposite of what interjections do when you're listening to or reading a sentence that includes one. Why? *Interjections* are exclamations that often express intense emotion. These words or phrases aren't connected grammatically to the rest of the sentence, but they do add lots of meaning. Check out these examples, in which the interjections are italicized:

> *Ouch*. I caught my finger in the hatch of that submarine.

> *Curses,* foiled again.

> *Yes!* We've finally gotten to a topic that is foolproof.

Interjections may be followed by commas, but sometimes they're followed by exclamation points or periods. The separation by punctuation shows the reader that the interjection is a comment on the sentence, not a part of it. (Of course, in the case of the exclamation point or period, the punctuation mark also indicates that the interjection is not a part of the sentence at all.)

You can't do anything wrong with interjections, except perhaps overuse them. Interjections are like salt. A little salt sprinkled on dinner perks up the taste buds; too much sends you to the telephone to order take-out.

Chapter **10**

Two ~~Real~~ Really Good Parts of Speech: Adjectives and Adverbs

With the right nouns (names of persons, places, things, or ideas) and verbs (action or being words), you can build a pretty solid foundation in a sentence. The key to expressing your precise thoughts is to build on that foundation by adding descriptive words to your sentence. In this chapter, I explain the two basic types of descriptive words of the English language — the parts of speech known as *adjectives* and *adverbs*. I also show you how to use each properly, including when they're tucked into comparisons.

Clarifying Meaning with Descriptions

In case you doubt the significance of descriptive words, take a look at this sentence:

> Gloria sauntered past Lord & Taylor when the sight of a Ferragamo Paradiso Pump paralyzed her.

What must the reader know in order to understand this sentence fully? Here's a list:

>> The reader should know that Lord & Taylor is a department store.

>> The reader should be able to identify Ferragamo as an upscale shoe label.

>> The reader should be familiar with a Paradiso Pump (a shoe style I made up).

>> The reader should know that a pump is a type of shoe.

>> A good vocabulary — one that includes *saunter* and *paralyze* — is helpful.

If all of those pieces are in place, or if the reader has a good imagination and the ability to use context clues in reading comprehension, your message will get through. But sometimes you can't trust the reader to understand the specifics of what you're trying to say. In that case, descriptions are quite useful. Here's Gloria, version 2:

> Gloria walked *slowly* past the *stately* Lord & Taylor *department* store when the sight of a *fashionable, green, low-heeled dress* shoe with the *ultra-chic Ferragamo* label paralyzed her.

Okay, I overdid it a bit, but you get the point. The descriptive words clarify the meaning of the sentence, particularly for the fashion-challenged. As you see, adjectives and adverbs are useful, and you should know how to insert them into your sentences.

TEST ALERT

Both adjectives and adverbs enhance the meaning of your sentences, but these parts of speech aren't interchangeable. Standardized tests capitalize on that fact by asking questions that require you to spot adjectives and adverbs used incorrectly. For example, you may see a sentence containing "real pretty." You need to know that *real* should be *really*. Not to worry: After you've read this chapter, you'll ace this sort of question.

Adding Adjectives

An *adjective* is a descriptive word that changes the meaning of a noun or a pronoun. An adjective adds information on number, color, type, and other qualities to your sentence.

TIP

Where do you find adjectives? In the adjective aisle of the supermarket. Okay, you don't. Most of the time you find them in front of the word they're describing. Keep in mind, however, that adjectives can also roam around a bit. Here's an example:

> George, *sore* and *tired,* pleaded with Lulu to release him from the headlock she had placed on him when he called her *"fragile."*

Sore and *tired* tells you about *George. Fragile* tells you about *her.* (Well, *fragile* tells you what George thinks of *her.* Lulu actually works out with free weights every day and is anything but fragile.) As you can see, these descriptions come after the words they describe, not before.

Adjectives describing nouns

The most common job for an adjective is describing a noun. Consider the adjectives *poisonous, angry,* and *rubber* in these sentences. Then decide which sentence you would most like to hear as you walk through the zoo.

> There is a *poisonous* snake on your shoulder.
>
> There is an *angry, poisonous* snake on your shoulder.
>
> There is a *rubber* snake on your shoulder.

The last one, right? In these three sentences, those little descriptive words certainly make a difference. *Angry, poisonous,* and *rubber* all describe *snake,* and all of these descriptions give you information that you would really like to have. See how diverse and powerful adjectives can be?

POP QUIZ

Find the adjectives in this sentence.

> With a shiny cover and a large screen, the new phone drew huge crowds when it went on display.

Answer: *shiny* (describing *cover*), *large* (describing *screen*), *new* (describing *phone*), *huge* (describing *crowds*).

Adjectives describing pronouns

Adjectives can also describe *pronouns* (words that substitute for nouns). When they're giving you information about pronouns, adjectives usually appear after the pronoun they're describing:

> There's something *strange* on your shoulder. (The adjective *strange* describes the pronoun *something.*)

Everyone *conscious* at the end of Ronald's play made a quick exit. (The adjective *conscious* describes the pronoun *everyone*.)

Anyone *free* must report to the meeting room immediately. (The adjective *free* describes the pronoun *anyone*.)

Attaching adjectives to linking verbs

Adjectives may also follow linking verbs, in which case they describe the subject of the sentence. To find an adjective after a linking verb, ask the question *what*. (See Chapter 5 for more information.)

Just to review for a moment: *Linking verbs* join two ideas, associating one with the other. These verbs are like giant equal signs, equating the subject — which comes before the verb — with another idea after the verb. (See Chapter 2 for a full discussion of linking verbs.)

Sometimes a linking verb joins an adjective (or a couple of adjectives) and a noun:

Lulu's favorite dress is *orange* and *purple*. (The adjectives *orange* and *purple* describe the noun *dress*.)

The afternoon appears *gray* because of the smoke from Roger's cigar. (The adjective *gray* describes the noun *afternoon*.)

George's latest jazz composition sounds *awful*. (The adjective *awful* describes the noun *composition*.)

Articles: Not just for magazines

If you ran a computer program that sorted and counted every word in this book, you'd find that *articles*, a branch on the adjective family tree, are the most common words, even though the article-branch includes only *a*, *an*, and *the*.

Melanie wants *the* answer to question 12, and you'd better be quick about it.

The preceding statement means that Melanie is stuck on problem 12, and Mom won't let her leave until her homework is finished. All Melanie's friends are at the basketball game, and now she's texting, demanding *the* answer to number 12, so she can join them. Now look at the same sentence, with one small change:

Melanie wants *an* answer, and you'd better be quick about it.

This statement means that Melanie simply has to know whether you'll invest in her startup. She asked you a week ago, but if you're not going to send her money, she'll ask someone else. She's lost patience, and she doesn't even care anymore whether you invest or not. She just wants *an* answer.

To sum up: Use *the* when you're speaking specifically and *an* or *a* when you're speaking more generally.

WARNING

A apple? An book? A precedes words that begin with consonant sounds (all the letters except *a, e, i, o,* and *u*). *An* precedes words beginning with the vowel sounds *a, e, i,* and *o*. The letter *u* is a special case. If the word sounds like *you*, choose *a*. If the word sounds like someone kicked you in the stomach — *uh* — choose *an*. Another special case is the letter *h*. If the word starts with a hard *h* sound, as in *horse*, choose *a*. If the word starts with a silent letter *h*, as in *herb*, choose *an*. Here are some examples:

> an almanac (a = vowel)
>
> a belly (b = consonant)
>
> an egg (e = vowel)
>
> a UFO (*U* sounds like *you*)
>
> an unidentified flying object (*u* sounds like *uh*)
>
> a helmet (hard *h*)
>
> an hour (silent *h*)

TIP

Special note: People stuck in the past say *an historic event* because that word, a couple of centuries ago, used to begin with a silent *h*. The rest of us say *a historic event*, matching *a* with the modern pronunciation of *historic*, which includes a hard *h*.

Pop the question: Identifying adjectives

To find adjectives, go to the words they describe — nouns and pronouns. Start with the noun or pronoun and ask three questions. (Not "What's the new hot app?" or "Did you see Will's new profile photo?" This is grammar, not life.) Here are the three questions:

>> How many?

>> Which one?

>> What kind?

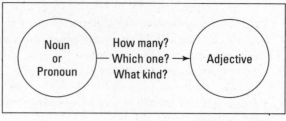

© *John Wiley & Sons, Inc.*

Take a look at this sentence:

George posted three new photos on his favorite website.

You see three nouns: *George, photos,* and *page.* George has led a colorful life, but you can't find the answer to the following questions: How many *Georges?* Which *George?* What kind of *George?* No words in the sentence provide that information, so no adjectives describe *George.*

But try these three questions on *photos* and *website* and you do come up with something: How many *photos?* Answer: *three. Three* is an adjective. Which *photos?* What kind of *photos?* Answer: *new. New* is an adjective. The same goes for *website:* What kind? Answer: *favorite. Favorite* is an adjective.

You may have noticed that *his* answers one of the questions. (Which *website?* Answer: *his website.*) *His* is working as an adjective, but *his* is also a pronoun. Normal people don't have to worry about whether *his* is a pronoun or an adjective. Only English teachers care, and they divide into two camps — the adjective camp and the pronoun camp. Needless to say, each group feels superior to the other. (I'm a noncombatant. As far as I'm concerned, you can call *his* a parakeet for all I care. Just spell it correctly and you're fine.)

Look at another sentence:

The angry reaction thrilled George's rotten, little, hard heart.

This sentence has three nouns. One *(George's)* is possessive. If you ask how many *George's,* which *George's,* or what kind of *George's,* you get no answer. The other two nouns, *reaction* and *heart,* do yield an answer. What kind of *reaction? Angry reaction.* What kind of *heart? Rotten, little, hard heart.* So *angry, rotten, little,* and *hard* are all adjectives.

WARNING

Sometimes writers change nouns into adjectives — improperly! The word *quality,* for example, is a noun meaning *worth, condition,* or *characteristic.* Salespeople and advertising writers often use *quality* as an adjective meaning *good* or *luxurious.* Grammatically, you can't buy a *quality tablet.* You can buy a *high-quality tablet.*

That said, some nouns do function as adjectives, depending upon the sentence they're in. Look at these two sentences, each containing the name of one of my favorite teams:

> I love the New York Liberty. (New York Liberty = WNBA basketball team = noun)

> The Liberty store sells team merchandise. (Liberty = adjective)

If you're not sure whether a particular word may function as an adjective in proper English, check the dictionary.

Stalking the Common Adverb

Adjectives aren't the only descriptive words. Adverbs — words that alter the meaning of a verb, an adjective, or another adverb — are another type of description. Check these out:

> The boss *regretfully* said no to Phil's request for a raise.

> The boss *furiously* said no to Phil's request for a raise.

> The boss *never* said no to Phil's request for a raise.

If you're Phil, you care whether the words *regretfully, furiously,* or *never* are in the sentence. *Regretfully, furiously,* and *never* are all adverbs. Notice how adverbs add meaning in these sentences:

> Lola *sadly* sang George's latest song. (Perhaps Lola is in a bad mood.)

> Lola sang George's latest song *reluctantly*. (Lola doesn't want to sing.)

> Lola *hoarsely* sang George's latest song. (Lola has a cold.)

> Lola sang George's latest song *quickly*. (Lola is in a hurry.)

Pop the question: Finding the adverb

Adverbs mostly describe verbs, giving more information about an action. Nearly all adverbs — enough so that you don't have to worry about the ones that fall through the cracks — answer one of these four questions:

>> How?

>> When?

>> Where?

>> Why?

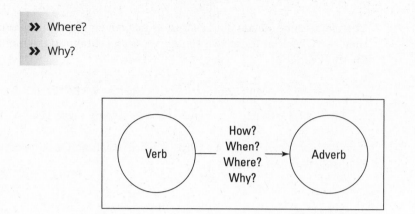

© John Wiley & Sons, Inc.

To find the adverb, go to the verb and pop the question. (See Chapter 2 for information on finding the verbs.) Look at this sentence:

Ella secretly swiped Sandy's slippers yesterday and then happily went home.

You note two verbs: *swiped* and *went*. Take each one separately. *Swiped* how? Answer: *swiped secretly. Secretly* is an adverb. *Swiped* when? Answer: *swiped yesterday. Yesterday* is an adverb. *Swiped* where? No answer. *Swiped* why? No answer.

Go on to the second verb in the sentence. *Went* how? Answer: *went happily. Happily* is an adverb. *Went* when? Answer: *went then. Then* is an adverb. *Went* where? Answer: *went home. Home* is an adverb. *Went* why? Probably to feed the slippers to her new puppy, but you find no answer in the sentence.

Here's another example:

Bill soon softly sighed and delicately slipped away.

You identify two verbs again: *sighed* and *slipped.* First one up: *sighed. Sighed* how? Answer: *sighed softly. Softly* is an adverb. *Sighed* when? Answer: *sighed soon. Soon* is an adverb. *Sighed* where? No answer. *Sighed* why? No answer again. Now for *slipped. Slipped* how? Answer: *slipped delicately. Delicately* is an adverb. *Slipped* where? Answer: *slipped away. Away* is an adverb. *Slipped* when? No answer. *Slipped* why? No answer. The adverbs are *soon, delicately,* and *away.*

TIP

Adverbs can be lots of places in a sentence. If you're trying to find them, rely on the questions *how, when, where,* and *why,* not the location. Similarly, a word may be an adverb in one sentence and something else in another sentence. Check out this example:

Gloria went home in a huff because of that slammed door.

Home is where the heart is, unless you are in George's cabin.

Home plate is the umpire's favorite spot.

In the first example, *home* tells you where Gloria went, so *home* is an adverb in that sentence. In the second example, *home* is a place, so *home* is a noun in that sentence. In the third example, *home* is an adjective, telling you what kind of *plate*.

Final answer: Pop the question and see if you reveal an adverb, adjective, or another part of speech.

Adverbs describing adjectives and other adverbs

Adverbs also describe other descriptions, usually making the description more or less intense. (A description describing a description? Give me a break! But it's true.) Here's an example:

An extremely unhappy Larry collapsed when the stock market crashed.

How *unhappy?* Answer: *extremely unhappy. Extremely* is an adverb describing the adjective *unhappy.*

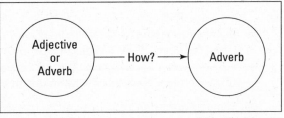

© *John Wiley & Sons, Inc.*

TIP

Sometimes the questions you pose to locate adjectives and adverbs are answered by more than one word in a sentence. In the previous example sentence, if you ask, "Seemed when?" the answer is *when the stock market crashed.* Don't panic. Longer answers may be prepositional phrases (see Chapter 9) or clauses. In the last example sentence, *when the stock market crashed* is a clause (see Chapter 18). Phrases and clauses are just different members of the adjective and adverb families.

Now back to work. Here's another example:

> Once he began to speak, Mary's very talkative pet parrot wouldn't shut up.

How *talkative?* Answer: *very talkative. Very* is an adverb describing the adjective *talkative.*

And another:

> Larry's frog croaked *quite hoarsely.*

This time an adverb is describing another adverb. *Hoarsely* is an adverb because it explains how the frog *croaked.* In other words, *hoarsely* describes the verb *croaked.* How *hoarsely?* Answer: *quite hoarsely. Quite* is an adverb describing the adverb *hoarsely,* which in turn describes the verb *croaked.*

Choosing Between Adjectives and Adverbs

Does it matter whether a word is an adjective or an adverb? Some of the time, no. In your crib, you demanded, "I want a bottle NOW, Mama." You didn't know you were adding an adverb to your sentence. For that matter, you didn't know you were making a sentence! You were just hungry. Now that you're past the crib stage, you should know the difference between these two parts of speech so you can select the form you need. Here are some guidelines:

>> **Many adverbs end in -*ly*.** Strictly is an adverb, and *strict* is an adjective. *Nicely* is an adverb, and *nice* is an adjective. *Generally* is an adverb, and *general* is an adjective. *Lovely* is a . . . gotcha! You were going to say *adverb*, right? Wrong. *Lovely* is an adjective. (That's why I started this paragraph with *many*, not *all*.)

>> **Some adverbs don't end in -*ly*.** *Soon, now, home, fast,* and many other words that don't end in -*ly* can be adverbs, too.

>> **One of the most common adverbs, *not*, doesn't end in -*ly*.** *Not* is an adverb because it reverses the meaning of the verb from positive to negative. Loosely speaking, *not* answers the question *how*. (How are you going to the wedding? Oh, you're *not* going!)

TIP

While I'm speaking of *not*, I should remind you to avoid double negatives. In many languages (Spanish, for example), doubling or tripling the negative adjectives and adverbs or throwing in a negative pronoun or two simply makes your denial stronger. In Spanish, saying, "I did not kill no victim" is okay. In English, however, that sentence is a confession, because if you *did not* kill *no* victim, you killed at least *one* victim. (Other types of double negatives may trip you up. See Chapter 22 for more information.)

TIP

The best way to tell if a word is an adverb is to ask the four adverb questions: *how, when, where,* and *why.* If the word answers one of those questions, it's an adverb.

Identify the adjectives and adverbs in the following sentences.

POP QUIZ

A. Thank you for the presents you gave us yesterday.

B. The lovely perfume you gave us smells like old socks.

C. The presents you kindly gave us are very rotten.

Answers: In sentence A, *yesterday* is an adverb, describing when *you gave* the presents. In sentence B, *lovely* is an adjective describing the noun *perfume. Old* is an adjective describing *socks;* sentence B has no adverbs. In sentence C, the adverb is *kindly* and it describes the verb *gave.* Also in sentence C, the adverb *very* describes the adjective *rotten. Rotten* is an adjective describing *presents.*

Try one more. Find the adjectives and adverbs.

The carefully decorated purse that Bob knitted is already fraying around the edges.

Answers: The adverb *carefully* describes the adjective *decorated.* The verb *is fraying* is described by the adverb *already.*

REMEMBER

Adjectives describe nouns or pronouns, and adverbs describe verbs, adjectives, or other adverbs.

Sorting out "good" and "well"

If I am ever elected emperor of the universe, one of the first things I'm going to do (after I get rid of apostrophes — see Chapter 11) is to drop all irregular forms. Until then, you may want to read about *good* and *well.*

Good is an adjective, and, except when you're talking about health, *well* is an adverb. Take a look at this sentence:

I am *good.*

The adjective *good* in this sentence means *I have the qualities of goodness* or *I am in a good mood.* In informal, conversational English, the sentence may also mean *everything's fine with me, I don't need anything,* or *My health is good.* (The sentence may also be the world's worst pickup line.) Now look at another statement:

> I am *well.*

Well is an adjective here. The sentence means *I am not sick.* One more:

> I play the piano *well.*

This time *well* is an adverb. It describes how I play. In other words, the adverb well describes the verb *play.* The sentence means that I don't have to practice anymore.

POP QUIZ

Which sentence is correct?

A. When asked how he was feeling, Larry smiled at his ex-girlfriends and replied, "Not well."

B. When asked how he was feeling, Larry smiled at his ex-girlfriends and replied, "Not good."

Answer: Sentence A is correct because Larry's ex-girlfriends are inquiring about his health.

Try one more. Which sentence is correct?

A. Egbert did not perform good on the crash test.

B. Egbert did not perform well on the crash test.

Answer: Sentence B is correct because the adverb *well* describes the verb *did perform. Did perform* how? Answer: *did perform well.*

Dealing with "bad" and "badly"

Bad is a bad word, at least in terms of grammar. Confusing *bad* and *badly* is one of the most common errors. Check out these examples:

> I felt badly.
>
> I felt bad.

Badly is an adverb, and *bad* is an adjective. Which one should you use? Well, what are you trying to say? In the first sentence, you went to the park with your mittens on. The bench had a sign on it: "WET PAINT." The sign looked old, so you decided to check. You put your hand on the bench, but the mittens were in the way. You felt *badly* — that is, not very accurately. In the second sentence, you sat on the bench, messing up the back of your coat with dark green stripes. When you saw the stripes, you felt *bad* — that is, you were sad. In everyday speech, of course, you're not likely to express much about *feeling badly*. Few people walk around testing benches, and even fewer talk about their ability to feel something physically. So 99.99 percent of the time you feel *bad* — unless you're in a good mood.

TIP

In conversational English, *I feel badly* is becoming an acceptable way to express regret, as in *I feel badly about setting fire to the chem lab.* In formal English, opt for *I feel bad* — and in either situation, be careful with flammable material!

POP QUIZ

Which sentence is correct?

A. Lola felt bad when she discovered a dent in her motorcycle.

B. Lola felt badly when she discovered a dent in her motorcycle.

Answer: Sentence A is correct. Lola loves her Harley, and every scratch and dent depresses her. Therefore "bad" is an adjective describing Lola (actually, Lola's state of mind). In sentence B, *badly* is an adverb, so it would have to describe Lola's ability to feel. That meaning makes no sense.

Try one more. Which sentence is correct?

A. Lola did bad in her negotiations with the insurance company.

B. Lola did badly in her negotiations with the insurance company.

Answer: Sentence B is correct because the adverb *badly* describes the verb *did. Did* how? Answer: *did badly.* (In other words, PayUp, Inc. denied Lola's claim.)

Adjectives and adverbs that look the same

Odd words here and there (and they are odd) do double duty as both adjectives and adverbs. They look exactly the same, but they take their identity as adjectives or adverbs from the way that they function in the sentence. Take a look at these examples:

> Upon seeing the stop sign, Abby stopped *short.* (adverb)

> Abby did not notice the sign until the last minute because she is too *short* to see over the steering wheel. (adjective)

Lola's advice is *right*: Abby should not drive. (adjective)

Abby turned *right* after her last-minute stop. (adverb)

Abby came to a *hard* decision when she turned in her license. (adjective)

Lola tries *hard* to schedule some time to chauffeur Abby, now that Abby's carless. (adverb)

TIP

The English language has too many adjectives and adverbs to list here. If you're unsure about a particular word, check the dictionary for the correct form.

Which sentence is correct?

POP QUIZ

A. It was real nice of you to send me that bouquet of poison ivy.

B. It was really nice of you to send me that bouquet of poison ivy.

Answer: B. How *nice? Really nice. Real* is an adjective and *really* is an adverb. Adverbs answer the question *how*.

Creating Comparisons with Adjectives and Adverbs

Adjectives and adverbs often show up in comparisons. Is your knowledge of comparisons *more better* or *less worse*? If you chose one of those two alternatives, this section is for you because *more better* and *less worse* are both incorrect. English has two ways of creating comparisons, but you can't use them together and they're not interchangeable.

Ending it with -er or giving it more to adjectives

Some adjectives form comparisons by adding *-er* or *-est* to the basic adjective. Some rely on additional words. Take a close look at the italicized comparisons in these sentences:

Roger's smile is *more evil* than Michael's, but Michael's giggle sounds *cuter*.

Egbert searched for the *least expensive* car, believing that his image is *less important* than having the *biggest* bank account.

Betsy's *most recent* symphony was *less successful* than her *earlier* composition.

Anna's *older* sister is an even *greater* mathematician than Anna herself, though Anna has the edge in geometry.

Lulu's *latest* tattoo is *grosser* than her first, but Lulu, not the *shyest* girl in the class, is looking for the *most extreme* design for her next effort.

What did you notice about the comparisons in the preceding sample sentences? Here's the stripped-down list: *more evil, cuter, least expensive, less important, biggest, most recent, less successful, earlier, older, greater, grosser, latest, shyest, most extreme.*

As you see, some comparisons relied on *-er* or *-est*, and some were expressed by adding *more, most, less,* or *least* to the quality that's being compared. How do you know which is appropriate? (Or, to use a comparison, how do you know which is *better?*) The dictionary is the final authority, and you should consult one if you're in doubt about a particular word. However, there are some general guidelines:

>> Add *-er* and *-est* to most single-syllable adjectives when the comparison is positive (showing that the first item being compared is greater or more intense).

>> If the word already ends in the letter *e,* don't double the *e* by adding *-er* or *-est.* Just add *-r* or *-st.*

>> *-Er* and *-est* endings are not usually appropriate for words ending in *-ly.*

>> *-Er* and *-est* endings don't work for negative comparisons, when the second item being compared is greater or more intense.

Table 10-1 is a chart of some adjectives that describe Lola, with both the *-er* and *-est* forms. *Note:* To understand Lola's personality, you need to know to what (or to whom) she's being compared, so I include a few clues.

TABLE 10-1 ## Single-Word Comparisons with Adjectives

Description of Lola	*-ER* Form	*-EST* Form
able	abler than Lulu	ablest of all the scientists in her lab
bald	balder than an eagle	baldest of the models
cute	cuter than an elf	cutest of all the assassins
edgy	edgier than caffeine	edgiest of the atom splitters
friendly	friendlier than a grizzly bear	friendliest person on the block
glad	gladder than the loser	gladdest of all the lottery winners

TIP

Notice that when the last letter is *y*, you must often change the *y* to *i* before you tack on the ending.

Table 10-2 contains even more descriptions of Lola, this time with *more*, *less*, *most*, and *least* added to the adjective.

TABLE 10-2 ## Two-Word Adjective Comparisons

Description of Lola	*More/Less* Form	*Most/Least* Form
intelligent	more intelligent than her teacher	most intelligent of all the students
knock-kneed	less knock-kneed than an old sailor	least knock-kneed of all the beauty pageant contestants
magnificent	more magnificent than a Picasso	most magnificent of all the ninjas
notorious	more notorious than a princess	most notorious of the florists
queenly	more queenly than Queen Elizabeth	most queenly of all the models
rigid	less rigid than a grammarian	least rigid of the traffic cops

TIP

These two tables give you a clue about another important comparison characteristic. Did you notice that the second column is always a comparison between Lola and *one other* person or thing? The addition of *-er* or *more* or *less* compares two things. In the last column of each chart, Lola is compared to a group with more than two members. When the group is larger than two, *-est* or *most* or *least* creates the comparison and identifies the extreme.

To sum up the rules:

>> Use *-er* or *more/less* when comparing only two things.

>> Use *-est* or *most/least* when singling out the extreme in a group that is larger than two.

>> Never combine two comparison methods, such as *-er* and *more*.

POP QUIZ

Which sentence is correct?

A. Egbert's design for the new refrigerator is simpler than the one his competitor hatched.

B. Egbert's design for a new refrigerator is more simpler than the one his competitor hatched.

Answer: Sentence A is correct. Never combine two forms of comparison. Sentence B hits the penalty box because it combines the *-er* form with the word *more*.

Creating comparisons with adverbs

Placing the correct form of an adverb in a comparison is (mostly) simpler than figuring out how to select the proper adjective form for comparisons. Adverbs nearly always rely on two-word comparisons, employing *less, least, more,* and *most.* Exceptions to this pattern include a few irregular forms (explained in the next section) and some single-syllable adverbs such as *soon, fast,* and others. Have a look at these example sentences:

Ben's company markets its apps *more effectively* than Elena's firm.

Of all the coders in her group, Rebecca works *most rapidly.*

Did you know that the apps on your phone run *less reliably* than advertised?

That fuel, compared with all the others, burns *least efficiently.*

Check out Table 10-3 for some additional examples of adverb comparisons.

TABLE 10-3   **Comparisons with Adverbs**

Description of Tim's Actions	*More/Less* Form	*Most/Least* Form
[sings] beautifully	more beautifully than the opera star	of all the singers in the karaoke bar, [Tim sings] most beautifully
[punches] forcefully	less forcefully than a two-year-old	of all the boxers in the Olympics, [Tim punches] least forcefully
[gives] generously	more generously than his sister	of all the billionaires, [Tim gives] most generously
[speaks] carefully	less carefully than most politicians	of all the candidates, [Tim speaks] least carefully

As with adjectives, the second column of Table 10-3 compares two things, using *more* or *less.* The comparisons in the third column single out the *most* or *least* in a group of more than two.

POP QUIZ

Which sentence is correct?

A. Of all the chefs, Natalie prepared her menus more quickly.

B. Of all the chefs, Natalie cooked least confidently.

Answer: Sentence B is correct. When comparing more than two actions, *most* or *least* is required.

Breaking the Rules: Irregular Comparisons

Whenever English grammar gives you rules that make sense, you know it's time for the irregulars to show up. Not surprisingly, then, you have to create a few common comparisons without *-er, -est, more/less,* or *most/least* — the regular comparisons I explain in the preceding sections.

Good, bad, well

I think of these as the "report card" comparisons because they evaluate quality. The first word of each line provides a description. The second word shows you that description when two elements are beings compared. The last word is for comparisons of three or more.

>> Good, better, best

>> Bad, worse, worst

>> Well, better, best

Time to visit *good, bad,* and *well* when they're on the job:

Although Michael's trumpet solo is *good* and Roger's is *better,* Lulu's trumpet solo is the *best* of all. (adjectives)

Lulu's habit of picking at her tattoo is *bad,* but Ralph's constant sneezing is *worse.* Egbert's tendency to crack jokes is the *worst* habit of all. (adjectives)

Lola sings *well* in the shower, but Max sings *better* in the bathtub. Ralph croons *best* in the hot tub. (adverbs)

POP QUIZ

Answer this question in correct English (and then correct the question itself).

Who's the baddest kid on the playground?

Answer: The *worst* (not *baddest*) kid on the playground is Roger, unless Lola is in one of her moods. The correct question is *Who's the worst kid on the playground?*

Try another. Which sentence is correct?

A. Michael says that he is feeling worse today than yesterday, but his statement must be considered in light of the fact that today is the algebra final.

B. Michael says that he is feeling more bad today than yesterday, but his statement must be considered in light of the fact that today is the algebra final.

Answer: Sentence A is correct. *More bad* is incorrect; use *worse*.

Little, many, much

These are the measuring comparisons, words that tell you about quantity. The first word on each line is the description, the second creates comparisons between two elements, and the last word applies to comparisons of three-plus elements.

>> Little, less, least

>> Many, more, most

>> Much, more, most

Check out these words in action (actually, in sentences, but you know what I mean):

Lulu likes a *little* grape jelly on her pizza, but Egbert prefers *less* exotic toppings. On that menu, Lulu likes chocolate pizza *least*. (*little, less* = adjectives, *least* = adverb)

Roger spies on *many* occasions, but he seldom uncovers *more* secrets than his brother Al. Lola is the *most* successful spy of all. (adjectives)

Anna has *much* interest in mathematics, though she's *more* devoted to her trumpet lessons. Of all the musical mathematicians I know, Anna is the *most* likely to succeed in both careers. (*much* = adjective, *more, most* = adverb)

TIP

Many or *much*? How do you decide which word is needed? Easy. *Many* precedes plurals of countable elements (*many crickets or shoes*, for example) and *much* precedes words that express qualities that may not be counted, though these qualities may sometimes be measured (*much noise or sugar*, for instance).

POP QUIZ

Which sentence is correct?

A. Anna and Michael studied together for the algebra final, but Michael is the least prepared.

B. Anna and Michael studied together for the algebra final, but Michael is less prepared.

Answer: Sentence B is correct. *Less* is the word you want when comparing two elements. Because you're comparing only Anna and Michael, *less* triumphs over *least*, which is a good word when you're comparing Anna, Michael, Lola, and the rest of the study group — in other words, three or more elements.

TIP

Making a comparison with an adjective or an adverb involves more than selecting the proper form. You also need to be sure that your comparison is complete and logical. Turn to Chapter 21 for more information on this topic.

3

Conventional Wisdom: Punctuation and Capitalization

Chapter **11**

Punctuation Law That Should Be Repealed: Apostrophes

Taking a walk recently, I noticed an odd sign:

GRANDMAS PUNCH

Interesting, I thought. *Grandmas punch* whom? Their grandchildren? Surely not! People who refuse to look at one more photo of the adorable tykes? Possibly. I soon realized that the sign was in front of a bar. Ah, I thought. *Grandma's punch* — a drink made from a family recipe. Then I heard a thud, as the apostrophe rule bit the dust yet again.

Apostrophes are curved punctuation marks that hang near certain letters, or, occasionally, numbers. For some reason, even educated people throw apostrophes where they don't belong and leave them out where they're needed. So I favor repealing the apostrophe rule. As New Yorkers say, "Enough already!" Until that happy day when apostrophes disappear, you have to learn how to use them. In this chapter, I show you how apostrophes indicate ownership and shorten words.

The Pen of My Aunt or My Aunt's Pen? Using Apostrophes to Show Possession

Most other languages are smarter than English. To show possession in French, for example, you say

the pen of my aunt (la plume du ma tante)

the fine wines of that bar

the letters of the lovers

and so on. You can say the same thing in English, too, but English has added another option — the apostrophe. Take a look at these same phrases — with the same meaning — using apostrophes:

my *aunt's* pen

that *bar's* fine wines

the *lovers'* letters

TIP

All these phrases include nouns that express ownership. I like to think of the apostrophe as a little hand, holding onto an *s* to indicate ownership or possession. In the first two examples, you notice that the apostrophe shows singular nouns that own something *(aunt's, bar's).* In the third example, the apostrophe indicates that a plural noun *(lovers')* owns something.

Ownership for singles

No, I'm not talking about buying a home all by yourself, with your very own mortgage. I'm talking about using apostrophes to show ownership with singular nouns. Here's the bottom line: To show possession by one owner, add an apostrophe and the letter *s* to the owner:

the *dragon's* burnt fang (the burnt fang belongs to the dragon)

Lulu's pierced eyebrow (the pierced eyebrow belongs to Lulu)

Michael's gold bar (the gold bar belongs to Michael)

TIP

Another way to think about this rule is to see whether the word *of* expresses what you're trying to say. With the *of* method, you note

the sharp claw *of* the crocodile = the *crocodile's* sharp claw

the peanut-stained trunk *of* the elephant = the *elephant's* peanut-stained trunk and so on.

Sometimes, no clear owner appears in the phrase. Such a situation arises mostly when you're talking about time. If you can insert *of* into the sentence, you may need an apostrophe. For an idea of how to apply the "of test," read these phrases:

> one week's house cleaning = one week *of* house cleaning
>
> a year's lawn care = one year *of* lawn care

Here's the bottom line: When you're talking about time, give your sentence the "of test." If it passes, insert an apostrophe.

POP QUIZ

Which sentence is correct?

A. Lulu told Lola that Roger needs a years work on his motorcycle.

B. Lulu told Lola that Roger needs a year's work on his motorcycle.

Answer. Sentence B is correct because Roger needs *a year of work* on that Harley he found in a junkyard.

Sharing the wealth: Plural possessives

You'd be finished figuring out apostrophes now if everything belonged to only one owner. Amazon is close, but even that company hasn't taken over everything (yet). So for now, you need to deal with plural owners. The plurals of most English nouns — anything greater than one — already end with the letter *s*. To show ownership, all you do is add an apostrophe after the *s*. Take a look at these examples:

> ten *gerbils'* tiny toes (the tiny toes belong to ten gerbils)
>
> many *dinosaurs'* petrified tails (the petrified tails belong to a herd of dinosaurs)
>
> a thousand sword swallowers' sliced tonsils (the sliced tonsils belong to a thousand sword swallowers)

TIP

The *of* test works for plurals, too. If you can rephrase the expression using the word *of*, you may need an apostrophe. Remember to add the apostrophe after the letter *s*.

> three *days'* editing work on that chapter = three days *of* editing work
>
> sixteen *years'* creativity from Lulu's tattoo artist = sixteen years *of* creativity
>
> two *degrees'* increase in temperature = two degrees *of* increase in temperature

Which is correct?

A. The coach has only one goal in life: to improve the Yankee's batting.

B. The coach has only one goal in life: to improve the Yankees' batting.

Answer: Sentence A is correct if you're talking about one player. Sentence B is correct if you're talking about 24 players, the entire team.

Try another. Which sentence is correct?

A. The Halloween decorations are decaying, especially the pumpkins teeth. Sam carved all ten jack-o-lanterns, and he can't bear to throw them away.

B. The Halloween decorations are decaying, especially the pumpkins' teeth. Sam carved all ten jack-o-lanterns, and he can't bear to throw them away.

C. The Halloween decorations are decaying, especially the pumpkin's teeth. Sam carved all ten jack-o-lanterns, and he can't bear to throw them away.

Answer: Sentence B is correct. The context of the sentence (*all ten jack-o-lanterns*) reveals that more than one pumpkin is rotting away. In sentence B, *pumpkins'* expresses a plural possessive. In sentence A, *pumpkins* has no apostrophe, though it clearly shows possession. In sentence C, the apostrophe is placed before the *s*, the spot for a single pumpkin.

Irregular plural possessives

At the beginning of this chapter, I mentioned *grandchildren*. That word is plural, but *grandchildren* doesn't end with the letter *s*. In other words, it's an irregular plural. To show ownership for an irregular plural, add an apostrophe and then the letter *s* (*grandchildren's*). Check out these examples:

teeth's cavities (The cavities belong to the teeth.)

children's toys (The toys belong to the children.)

the three blind *mice's* eye doctor (The eye doctor belongs to the three blind mice.)

the *women's* lipstick-stained tissues (The lipstick-stained tissues belongs to the women.)

the *mice's* cheesy odor (The cheesy odor belongs to the mice.)

geese's beaks (The beaks belong to the geese.)

Compound plural possessives

What happens when two single people own something? In real life they go to court and fight. In grammar, they (or you) add one or two apostrophes, depending on the type of ownership. If two people own something together, as a couple, use only one apostrophe.

George and Martha *Washington's* home (The home belongs to the two of them.)

Larry and *Ella's* wedding (The wedding was for both the blushing groom and the frightful bride.)

Lulu and *Lola's* new set of nose rings (The set was too expensive for either one alone, so Lulu and Lola each paid half and agreed to an every-other-week wearing schedule.)

Roger and the superspy's secret (Roger told it to the superspy, so now they're sharing the secret.)

If two people own things separately, as individuals, use two apostrophes:

George's and *Martha's* teeth (He has his set of teeth — false, by the way — and she has her own set.)

Lulu's and *Gary's* new shoes. (She wears size 2, and he wears size 12. Hers are lizard skin with four-inch heels. His are plastic with five-inch heels.)

Egbert's and *Roy's* attitudes toward dieting. (Egbert doesn't worry about cholesterol. Roy monitors every scrap of food he eats.)

Lester's and *Archie's* sleeping habits (You don't want to know. I'll just say that Lester sleeps all night, and Archie sleeps all day.)

Cedric's and *Lola's* fingernails. (He has his; she has her own; both sets are fake and quite long.)

WARNING

Speaking of plurals: Remember that an apostrophe shows ownership. Don't use an apostrophe when you have a plural that is *not* expressing ownership. Here are some examples:

RIGHT: Labels stick to your shoes.

WRONG: Label's stick to your shoes.

ALSO WRONG: Labels' stick to your shoes.

Look at another set:

RIGHT: The gnus grunted when they heard the news.

WRONG: The gnus' grunted when they heard the news.

ALSO WRONG: The gnu's grunted when they heard the news.

To sum up the rule on plurals and apostrophes: If the plural noun is not showing ownership, *don't* use an apostrophe. If the plural noun shows ownership, *do* add an apostrophe after the *s* (for regular plurals). For irregular plurals showing ownership, add *'s.*

TIP

I have to admit that in two special cases, apostrophes do show up in plurals. If you're writing the plural of a lowercase letter, you add an apostrophe and an *s.* To help the reader along, you should italicize the letter but not the apostrophe or the *s.* If you're writing the plural of a word used as a word (not for what it means), italicize the word and add a nonitalicized s (with no apostrophe). If you're writing with a pen, not a computer, italics aren't possible. Pen-writers should place the plural of the word used as a word or the letter in quotation marks and add an apostrophe and an *s.* Take a peek at these examples:

You have too many *g*'s in that word, young lady!

The boss throws "impossible's" into every discussion of my raise.

Up until a few years ago, the plurals of capital letters, numbers, and symbols were also formed with apostrophes (*F*'s, *1960*'s, and &'s, for example). Most writers now omit the apostrophe in these cases (*Fs*, *1960s*, and &s). So far, civilization hasn't crumbled from the shock. Stay tuned!

Possession with Proper Nouns

Companies, stores, and organizations also own things, so these proper nouns — singular or plural — also require apostrophes. Put the apostrophe at the end of the name:

Macy's finest shoes

Microsoft's finest operating system

McGillicuddy, Pinch, and Cinch's finest lawsuit

Grammar, Inc.'s finest apostrophe rule

Special note: Some stores have apostrophes in their names, even without a sense of possession:

Macy's occupies an entire city block.

Macy's is always written with an apostrophe, even when there's no noun after the store name. *Macy's* implies a shortened version of a longer name (perhaps *Macy's Department Store*).

Place apostrophes where they're needed in this paragraph.

Jeff went to Macys Department Store to buy a suit for Lolas party. His shopping list also included a heart for the Valentines Day dinner and a card for his brothers next anniversary. Jeffs shopping spree was successful, in spite of Lulus and Lolas attempts to puncture his tires.

Answer: Jeff went to *Macy's* Department Store to buy a suit for *Lola's* party. His shopping list also included a heart for the *Valentine's* Day dinner and a card for his *brother's* next anniversary. *Jeff's* shopping spree was successful, in spite of *Lulu's* and *Lola's* attempts to puncture his tires. (***Note:*** Lulu and Lola made separate stabs at the tires.)

Ownership with Hyphenated Words

Other special cases of possession involve compound words — son-in-law, mother-of-pearl, and all the other words with *hyphens* (those little horizontal lines). The rule is simple: Put the apostrophe at the end of the word. Never put an apostrophe inside a word. Here are some examples of singular compound nouns:

the *secretary-treasurer's* report on the missing money (The report belongs to the secretary-treasurer.)

the *dogcatcher-in-chief's* cat video (The cat video belongs to the dogcatcher-in-chief.)

my *mother-in-law's* huge elbows (The elbows belong to my mother-in-law.)

The same rule applies to plural compound nouns that are hyphenated. Take a look at these examples:

the *doctors-of-philosophy's* study lounge (The study lounge is owned by all the doctors-of philosophy.)

my *fathers-in-law's* wedding present (The wedding present was from both fathers-in-law.)

Possessive Nouns That End in *S*

Singular nouns that end in *s* present special problems. Let me explain: My last name is Woods. My name is singular, because I am only one person. When students evaluate me, they may write,

> Ms. Woods's grammar lessons can't be beat.

or

> Ms. Woods' grammar lessons can't be beat.

(Okay, they say a lot of other things, too, but I like to think positive. I'll omit the other comments.)

TIP

In informal speech and writing, both of the example sentences are correct. Why are these two options — *Ms. Woods's* and *Ms. Woods'* — acceptable? The answer has to do with sound. If you say the first sentence above, by the time you get to the word *grammar* you're hissing and spitting all over your listener. Not a pleasant idea. The second sentence sounds better. So the grammar police have given in on this one, except in the most formal situations or when the word may be misunderstood. For example, if you don't know that my name is *Woods*, you may think that *Woods' grammar book* is a book belonging to more than one person named *Wood*. If you ignore the saliva factor, you can write *Woods's grammar book* and avoid any confusion, because that format clearly shows a singular, possessive noun, *Woods's*.

To sum up: If the name of a singular owner ends in the letter *s* and you're in an informal situation, you may add only an apostrophe, not an apostrophe and another *s*. But if you like hissing and spitting or if you have to be on your best grammatical behavior, add an apostrophe *and* an *s*.

POP QUIZ

Which sentence is correct?

A. The walrus' tusk gleamed because the walrus brushed it for ten minutes after every meal.

B. The walrus's tusk gleamed because the walrus brushed it for ten minutes after every meal.

Answer: Both are correct, depending upon the situation. Sentence B calls for more saliva, but it satisfies the strictest grammarian. Sentence A breaks the rule, but nowadays breaking that rule is acceptable in informal situations. (Yes, it was a trick question. You know how teachers are.)

Try another set. Which sentence is correct?

A. My whole family got together for Thanksgiving. The Woods' are a large group.

B. My whole family got together for Thanksgiving. The Woods's are a large group.

Answer: Another trick question. Neither is correct. Both sentences call for a plural noun, not a possessive. You want "Woodses," the word, not the family. (Trust me on this one!) No apostrophe should appear because you're not expressing ownership.

Common Apostrophe Errors with Pronouns

English also supplies pronouns — words that take the place of a noun — for ownership. Some possessive pronouns are *my, your, his, her, its, our,* and *their.* Here's a rule so basic — and so often broken — that you should consider taping it to your pinky finger: No possessive pronoun ever has an apostrophe. A few examples of possessive pronouns in action:

> *your* completely unruly child — not your' completely unruly child (also wrong: that completely unruly child of yours')

> *our* extremely well-behaved youngster — not our' extremely well-behaved youngster (also wrong: the extremely well-behaved youngster of ours')

> *their* tendency to fight — not their' tendency to fight (also wrong: the tendency of theirs' to fight)

> *his* call to the police — not his' call to the police

POP QUIZ

Which sentence is correct?

A. Roy insulted Jenny because of their' ancient feud.

B. Roy insulted Jenny's son because of their ancient feud.

C. Roy stole Jennys sword because of their ancient feud.

Answer: Sentence B is correct. In sentence A, *their* should not have an apostrophe because no possessive pronoun ever has an apostrophe. In sentence C, *their* is written correctly, but *Jennys* lacks the apostrophe.

Just one more. Which sentence is correct?

A. Egbert claims that a weeks supply of ham is in the refrigerator.

B. Egbert claims that he can't store any more ham of theirs'.

C. Egbert claims that a day's supply of ham is not enough in case of emergency.

Answer: Sentence C is correct. In sentence A, *a weeks* needs an apostrophe because the phrase means *a week of.* In sentence B, *theirs* is a possessive pronoun, and no possessive pronoun takes an apostrophe. In sentence C, you're talking about one *day,* so adding *'s* is the way to go.

Two possessive pronouns, *whose* and *yours,* are error-magnets. *Whose* shows ownership. It probably wouldn't cause any problems if it didn't sound like another word, *who's. Who's* is a contraction — a shortened form of *who is.* In other words

> The boy *whose* hat was burning was last seen running down the street screaming, "*Who's* in charge of fire fighting in this town?"

and

> *Whose* box of firecrackers is on the radiator? *Who's* going to tell Egbert that his living room looks like the Fourth of July?

Your is a possessive pronoun. This word causes trouble when it tangles with *you're,* which means *you are. Your* shows possession. These two words are not interchangeable. Some examples:

> "*You're* not going to eat that rotten pumpkin," declared Rachel. *(You are not going to eat.)*

> "*Your* refusal to eat the pumpkin means that you will be given week-old sushi instead," commented Dean. (The refusal comes from *you,* so you need a possessive word.)

> "*You're* going to wear that pumpkin if you threaten me," said Lola. *(You are going to wear.)*

> "I'm not afraid of *your* threats!" stated Art. (The threats come from *you,* so you need a possessive word.)

TIP

When you're typing on a smartphone or touchpad, words you may want to use pop up after you've entered only a letter or two. Be especially careful to choose the correct word, because it's likely that the app will give you one version with an apostrophe and one without. For more on electronic media, see Chapter 16.

Shortened Words for Busy People: Contractions

Are you in a hurry? Probably. So like just about everyone in our society, you probably use contractions when you speak. A *contraction* shortens a word by removing one letter or more and substituting an apostrophe in the same spot. For example, chop *wi* out of *I will*, throw in an apostrophe, and you have *I'll*. The resulting word is shorter and faster to say, with only one syllable (sound) instead of two.

Take a look at Table 11-1 for a list of common contractions. Notice that a couple of contractions are irregular. (*Won't*, for example, is short for *will not*.)

TABLE 11-1

Contractions

Phrase	Contraction	Phrase	Contraction
are not	aren't	she is	she's
cannot	can't	that is	that's
could not	couldn't	they are	they're
do not	don't	they will	they'll
does not	doesn't	they would	they'd
did not	didn't	we are	we're
he will	he'll	we will	we'll
he would	he'd	we would	we'd
he is	he's	we have	we've
is not	isn't	what is	what's
it is	it's	who is	who's
I am	I'm	will not	won't
I will	I'll	would not	wouldn't
I would	I'd	you are	you're
I have	I've	you have	you've
she will	she'll	you will	you'll
she would	she'd	you would	you'd

If you'd like to make a contraction that isn't in Table 11-1, check your dictionary to make sure it's legal!

You Coulda Made a Contraction Mistake

If you've gone to the mall — any mall — chances are you've seen a sign like this:

Doughnuts 'N Coffee

or

Broken Grammar Rules

Okay, I doubt you've seen the last one, at least as a sign, but you've seen *'n* as a contraction of *and.* And therefore, you've witnessed broken grammar rules at the mall. I know I'm fighting a losing battle here, and I know I should be worried about much more important issues, like the economy and the environment. Even so, I also care about the grammatical environment, and thus I make a plea to the store owners and sign painters of the English-speaking world. Please don't put *'n* in anything. It's a grunt, not a word. Thank you.

TIP

I explain two common errors that occur when writers use a contraction instead of a possessive pronoun, and vice versa, in "Common Apostrophe Errors with Pronouns" earlier in this chapter. The contraction/pronoun pairs are *who's/whose* and *you're/your.*

Woulda, coulda, shoulda. These three "verbs" are potholes on the road to better grammar. Why? Because they don't exist. Here's the recipe for a grammatical felony. Start with three real verb phrases: *would have, could have,* and *should have.*

And turn them into contractions: *would've, could've,* and *should've.*

Now turn them back into words. But don't turn them back into the words they actually represent. Instead, let your ears be your guide. (It helps if you have a lot of wax in your ears because the sounds don't quite match.) Now you say the following: *would of, could of,* and *should of.*

These three phrases are never correct. Don't use them! Take a look at these examples:

WRONG: If George had asked me to join the spy ring, I would of said, "No way."

RIGHT: If George had asked me to join the spy ring, I would have said, "No way."

ALSO RIGHT: If George had asked me to join the spy ring, I would've said, "No way."

Here's another set:

WRONG: When I heard about the spy ring, I should of told the Central Intelligence Agency.

RIGHT: When I heard about the spy ring, I should have told the Central Intelligence Agency.

ALSO RIGHT: When I heard about the spy ring, I should've told the Central Intelligence Agency.

POP QUIZ

Which is correct?

A. Jane wouldnt go to the laundromat even though her hamper was overflowing.

B. Jane wouldn't go to the laundromat, even though her hamper was overflowing.

Answer: Sentence B is correct. *Wouldn't* is short for *would not.*

TIP

When you're texting, you may be tempted to drop apostrophes altogether. After all, it's annoying to type on a screen the size of a couple of business cards, and there's little chance someone will misunderstand *dont* without the apostrophe (*don't*). Resist the temptation, at least when you're writing to someone who expects to read actual English. Also, be careful when an app presents you with one or two possible words after you type a couple of letters. You can save time by touching the word you want, but do be sure it really *is* the word you want, with or without an apostrophe as required by the meaning of what you're writing.

Chapter **12**

Quotations: More Rules Than the Internal Revenue Service

What's the most annoying answer in English or any other language? *Because I said so.* No logic, or very little, underlies that answer. It's an assertion of power:

KID: Why can't I go to Elena's party? (powerless)

PARENT: Because I said so. (powerful)

A related statement (first runner up in the annoying-answer competition) is *because tradition says so.* Once again, that answer comes from a position of power, in this case from grammarians and editors who decide where and when to insert quotation marks. Reason and common sense govern some of these rules, but not all. Either way, you have to follow them to produce correct, proper English writing. Sadly, the list of rules is even longer than the US tax code. Lucky for you, quotation rules aren't as hard to follow as the regulations set by that beloved government agency, the Internal Revenue Service.

And I Quote

A *quotation* is a written repetition of someone else's words — just one word or a whole statement or passage. *Quotation marks* are small curves — usually a pair but sometimes a single curve — that hang above the line, before and after the quoted words. In Britain, these punctuation marks are known as *inverted commas,* an accurate description of their appearance.

Quotations pop up in almost all writing online or on paper, in articles, novels, essays, blog posts, and so on. To get an idea how to identify a quotation, take a look at the following story:

One day, while Betsy was on her way to a music lesson, she gazed through a shop window at a grand piano. Suddenly, a piano whizzed by her ear. One of the movers had taken a bite of his tuna fish sandwich, allowing the piano to break loose from the ropes hoisting it to the third floor. The piano landed a mere inch away from Betsy. What did Betsy say?

> She said that she was relieved.

This sentence tells you about Betsy and her feelings, but it doesn't give her exact words. It's a general report, not an exact record of the words actually spoken or written. You can write that sentence if you heard Betsy say, "I am relieved." You can also write the same sentence if you heard Betsy say, "Thank goodness it missed me. My knees are shaking! I could have been killed."

As an observer, you can also record Betsy's reaction by writing:

> She said that she was "relieved."

This account of Betsy's reaction is a little more exact. Some of the sentence is general, but the reader knows that Betsy actually said the word "relieved" because it's in quotation marks. The quotation marks are signs for the reader; they mean that the material inside the marks is exactly what was said.

> Betsy said, "I am so relieved that I could cry."

> "I am so relieved that I could cry," Betsy said.

These two sentences quote Betsy. The words enclosed by quotation marks are exactly what Betsy said. The only thing added is an identifying phrase that tells you who said the words (in this case, Betsy). As you see in the example, you can place the identification at the beginning of the sentence or at the end. (You can also idenitfy the speaker in the middle of the sentence. I talk about that situation later in this chapter.) The quotation marks enclose the words that were said or written.

POP QUIZ

Which sentences are quotations? Which sentences are general reports of what was said?

A. Bob doesn't get along with the conductor of the school orchestra, according to Lulu.

B. "I refuse to play anything that was composed before the twenty-first century," declared Bob.

Answer: Sentence A is a general report with none of Bob's exact words. Sentence B quotes Bob's statement in his exact words.

TIP

In the academic world, omitting quotation marks can get you into serious trouble. Without this punctuation, you're not identifying the original source. Teachers call this practice *plagiarism* and consider it a serious crime. Even outside the school walls, you want to be an honest person. Hijacking someone else's words is *not* honest. Plus, when quoted material is identified, the reader knows whom to credit or criticize. Given the exact words, the reader may also decide the meaning and importance of the remarks and not simply form an opinion based on the writer's interpretation.

Punctuating Quotations

If quotation marks were the only punctuation you had to worry about, this chapter would be very short. But quotation marks hang out with other punctuation, including commas, periods, question marks, and other members of the punctuation family. Can't you just picture their holiday dinner table? As in most families, who sits next to whom matters. This section explains where to put your annoying cousins — er, I mean punctuation — in a sentence containing a quotation.

Quotations with speaker tags

A *speaker tag* is what I call the little label (*he said, Mary posted, the senator denies,* and so forth) that identifies the speaker or writer of the quoted words. In this section, I show you how to handle quotations with speaker tags attached.

Speaker tags before or after the quotation

When the speaker tag comes first, put a comma after the speaker tag. The period at the end of the sentence, if there is one, goes *inside* the quotation marks.

> The gang remarked, "Lola's lottery ticket is sure to win."

> Lola replied, "I didn't buy a ticket this week."

When the speaker tag comes last, put a comma *inside* the quotation marks and a period at the end of the sentence.

> "Lola can't win the lottery if she has no ticket," the gang continued.

> "I don't like the odds," explained Lola.

Now you know the first two (of far too many) quotation rules. Keep in mind that it doesn't matter where you put the speaker tag as long as you punctuate the sentence correctly.

POP QUIZ

Which sentence is correct?

A. Alonzo muttered, "I don't want to practice the piano".

B. Alonzo muttered, "I don't want to practice the piano."

Answer: Sentence B is correct, because the period is inside the quotation marks.

Here's another pair. Which sentence is correct?

A. "The equation that Al wrote on the board is incorrect," trilled Anna.

B. "The equation that Al wrote on the board is incorrect", trilled Anna.

Answer: Sentence A is correct, because the comma is inside the quotation marks.

Interrupted quotations

Sometimes a speaker tag lands in the middle of a sentence. To give you an example of this sort of placement, I revisit Betsy, who narrowly missed being squashed by a falling piano. (Her story is in "And I Quote" at the beginning of this chapter.)

> "I think I'll sue," Betsy explained, "for emotional distress."

> "You can't imagine," she added, "what I felt."

"The brush of the piano against my nose," she sighed, "will be with me forever."

"The scent of tuna," she continued, "brings it all back."

In each of these example sentences, the speaker tag interrupts the quotation. Time for more rules for sentences with interrupted quotations:

>> Place a comma *inside* the quotation marks at the end of the first half of a quotation.

>> Insert a comma *after* the speaker tag but *before* the quotation marks that begin the second half of the quotation.

>> If the sentence ends with a period, place the period *inside* the closing quotation marks.

>> The second half of a quotation does *not* begin with a capital letter unless the word is a proper name or the pronoun *I*. (Turn to Chapter 15 for more on capitalization.)

POP QUIZ Which sentence is correct?

A. "After the concert", said Lulu, "the piano player goes out to eat."

B. "After the concert," said Lulu, "The piano player goes out to eat."

Answer: Neither is correct. In sentence A, the comma after *concert* is in the wrong place. It should sit directly after *concert* and before the quotation marks. In sentence B, the second half of the quotation should not begin with a capital letter. Here is the correct sentence:

"After the concert," said Lulu, "the piano player goes out to eat."

TIP Notice that in all the interrupted quotations I supply in this section, the quoted material adds up to only one sentence, even though that sentence is written in two separate parts.

Avoiding run-on sentences with interrupted quotations

When you plop a speaker tag right in the middle of someone's conversation, make sure that you don't create a run-on sentence. A *run-on sentence* is actually two sentences that have been stuck together (that is, *run* together) without a conjunction (a word that joins grammatical elements) or a semicolon. Just because you're quoting is no reason to ignore the rules about joining sentences. Check out this set of examples:

> WRONG: "When you move a piano, you must be careful," squeaked Al, "Betsy could have been killed."

> RIGHT: "When you move a piano, you must be careful," squeaked Al. "Betsy could have been killed."

The quoted material forms two complete sentences:

> SENTENCE 1: When you move a piano, you must be careful.

> SENTENCE 2: Betsy could have been killed.

Because the quoted material forms two complete sentences, you must write two separate sentences. If you cram this quoted material into one sentence, you've got a run-on.

TIP

Remove the speaker tag and check the quoted material. What is left? Enough for half a sentence? That's okay. Quoted material doesn't need to express a complete thought. Enough material for one sentence? Also okay. Enough material for two sentences? Not okay, unless you write two sentences. (For more information on run-on sentences, see Chapter 4.)

POP QUIZ

Which is correct?

A. "A piano hits the ground with tremendous force," explained the physicist. "I would move to the side if I were you."

B. "A piano hits the ground with tremendous force," explained the physicist, "I would move to the side if I were you."

Answer: Sentence A is correct. The quoted material forms two complete sentences and you must quote it that way. Sentence 1 = *A piano hits the ground with tremendous force.* Sentence 2 = *I would move to the side if I were you.*

Here's another. Which is correct?

A. "I insist that you repeal the laws of physics," demanded Lola, "Pianos should not kill people."

B. "I insist that you repeal the laws of physics," demanded Lola. "Pianos should not kill people."

Answer: B is correct. Choice A is a run-on because only a comma follows *Lola.* In B, the two complete thoughts are expressed in two sentences and punctuated correctly.

Quotations without speaker tags

Not all sentences with quotations include speaker tags. The punctuation and capitalization rules for these sentences are a little different. Check out these examples:

> According to the blurb on the book jacket, Anna's history of geometry is said to be "thrilling and unbelievable" by all who read it.

> Michael said that the book "wasn't as exciting as watching paint dry" but "useful" as a paperweight. Anna threw a pie in his face.

> Michael's lawyer is planning a lawsuit for "serious injury to face and ego."

The rules for quotations without speaker tags actually make sense. The quotations in this sort of sentence aren't set apart. They're tucked into the sentence. Treat them accordingly:

> » If the quotation doesn't have a speaker tag, the first word of the quotation is not capitalized. The exception, of course, is proper names or the pronoun *I*.

> » No comma separates the quotation from the rest of the sentence if the quotation doesn't have a speaker tag, unless you need a comma for some other reason. (Chapter 13 explains when commas are appropriate.)

See what I mean about making sense? You don't want to put a random capital letter in the middle of the sentence, which is where quotations without speaker tags usually end up. Also, omitting the comma preserves the flow of the sentence.

TIP

Notice that quotations without speaker tags tend to be short — a few words rather than an entire statement. If you're reporting a lengthy statement, you're probably better off with a speaker tag and the complete quotation. If you want to extract only a few, relevant words from someone's speech, you can probably do without a speaker tag.

POP QUIZ

Which is correct?

A. Egbert said that the latest nutritional research was "Suspect" because the laboratory was "Unfair."

B. Egbert said that the latest nutritional research was, "suspect" because the laboratory was, "unfair."

C. Egbert said that the latest nutritional research was "suspect" because the laboratory was "unfair."

Sentence C is correct. In sentence A, *suspect* and *unfair* should not be capitalized. In sentence B, no comma should be placed after *was.*

Quotations with question marks

Remember Betsy's piano from the section "And I Quote" earlier in this chapter? When the piano nearly squashed Betsy, she said a few more things. (Not all of them are printable, but I'll ignore those remarks.) Here are her other comments:

> "How can you eat a tuna sandwich while lifting a piano?" Betsy asked as she eyed his lunch.

> "May I have a bite?" she continued.

Let me put it another way:

> As she eyed his lunch Betsy asked, "How can you eat a tuna sandwich while lifting a piano?"

> She continued, "May I have a bite?"

What do you notice about these two sets of quotations? That's right! The quoted words are questions. (Okay, I didn't actually hear your answer, but I'm assuming that because you were smart enough to buy this book, you're smart enough to notice these things.) The rule is simple: If you quote a question, put the question mark *inside* the quotation marks.

This rule makes good sense; it distinguishes a quoted question from a quotation tucked inside a question. Time to look at one more part of Betsy's encounter with the falling piano. The piano mover answered Betsy, but no one could understand his words. (He had a mouthful of tuna.) I wonder what he said.

> Did he say, "I can't give you a bite of my sandwich because I ate it all"?

> Did he really declare, "It was just a piano"?

The quoted words in these example sentences are not questions. However, each entire sentence is a question. When the quoted words aren't a question but the entire sentence is a question, the question mark goes *outside* the quotation marks.

To sum up the rules on question marks:

>> If the quoted words are a question, put the question mark *inside* the quotation marks.

>> If the entire sentence is a question, put the question mark *outside* the quotation marks.

Some of you detail-oriented (actually, picky) people may want to know what to do when the quotation and the sentence are both questions. In this case, put the question mark *inside* the quotation marks.

Here's an example of this rule:

> Did the mover really ask, "Is that lady for real?"

No matter what, don't use two question marks:

> WRONG: Did Betsy ask, "What's the number of a good lawyer?"?
> RIGHT: Did Betsy ask, "What's the number of a good lawyer?"

POP QUIZ

Which sentence is correct?

A. Did Lulu say, "I wish a piano would drop near me so that I could sue?"

B. Did Lulu say, "I wish a piano would drop near me so that I could sue"?

Answer: Sentence B is correct. Because the quoted words are not a question and the entire sentence is a question, the question mark goes outside the quotation marks.

Quotations with exclamation points

Exclamation points follow the same general rules as question marks. In other words, if the entire sentence is an exclamation, but the quoted words aren't, put the exclamation point *outside* the quotation marks. If the quoted words are an exclamation, put the exclamation point *inside* the quotation marks.

Here are some sample sentences with exclamation points:

> Gene said, "I can't believe you got a tattoo!" (The quoted words are an exclamation but the entire sentence is not.)
> I simply cannot believe that Gene actually said, "No, thank you"! (Now the entire sentence is an exclamation but the quoted words are not.)

For those of you who like to dot every *i* and cross every *t*: If both the sentence and the quotation are exclamations, put the exclamation point *inside* the quotation marks.

Take a look at this example:

> I cannot believe that Gene actually said, "No way would I run for president!"

No matter what, don't use two exclamation points:

> WRONG: I refuse to believe that Gene said, "In your dreams!"!

> RIGHT: I refuse to believe that Gene said, "In your dreams!"

Quotations with semicolons

Every hundred years or so you may write a sentence that has both a quotation and a semicolon. (In Chapter 4, I explain semicolons in detail.) When writing a sentence that includes a quotation and a semicolon, put the semicolon *outside* the quotation marks, as in this example:

> Cedric thinks that vending-machine snacks are a food group; "I can't imagine eating anything else," he said.

and

> Cedric said, "I can't imagine eating anything but vending-machine snacks"; he must have the IQ of a sea slug.

Okay, maybe that last sentence was a bit nasty. I apologize to sea slugs everywhere.

Quotations inside quotations

Now the topic of quotations becomes a little complicated. Sometimes you need to place a quotation inside a quotation. Consider this situation:

Al is hoping to make a billion dollars selling his app, QuoPro, which punctuates quotations automatically. He's angry at Archie, who coded some parts of QuoPro, because he thinks that Archie made some semicolon errors. Al wants Archie to rewrite the program. Archie is outraged by the demand because he believes that his semicolons are exactly where they should be. You're writing a story, quoting Archie, who is quoting Al. How do you punctuate this quotation?

> Archie says, "Al had the nerve to tell me, 'Your semicolon should be outside the quotation mark.'"

A sentence like this has to be sorted out. Without any punctuation, here's what Al said:

> Your semicolon should be outside the quotation mark.

Without any punctuation, here are all the words that Archie said:

Al had the nerve to tell me your semicolon should be outside the quotation mark.

Al's words are a quotation inside another quotation. So Al's words are enclosed in single-quotation marks, and Archie's are enclosed (in the usual way) in double quotation marks. In other words, surround a quotation inside another quotation with single quotation marks.

Another example: Lola says, "I'm thinking of piercing my tongue." Lulu tells Lola's mom about Lola's plan, adding a comment as she does so. Here's the complete statement:

Lulu declares, "As a strong opponent of piercing, I am sorry to report that Lola told me, 'I'm thinking of piercing my tongue.'"

Lola's words are inside single quotation marks and Lulu's complete statement is in double quotation marks.

TIP

Commas and periods follow the same rules in both double and single quotations.

WARNING

The Revolutionary War ended more than a couple of centuries ago, but the United States and Great Britain have not stopped fighting about grammar rules. Everything I've told you about quotation rules is true for punctuating American English. But the reverse is often true for British English. British writers frequently use single quotation marks when they're quoting, and double marks for a quotation inside another quotation. Thus a British book might punctuate Lulu's comment in this way:

Lulu says, 'As a strong opponent of piercing, I am sorry to tell you that Lola told me, "I'm thinking of piercing my tongue."'

What should you, a puzzled grammarian, do when you're quoting? Follow the custom of the country you're in.

POP QUIZ

Which sentence is correct (in the U.S.)?

A. Angel complained, "He said to me, 'You are a devil.'"

B. Angel complained, "He said to me, "You are a devil."

Answer: Sentence A is correct. You must enclose *You are a devil* in single quotation marks and the larger statement *He said to me you are a devil* in double quotation marks. The period at the end of the sentence goes inside both marks.

Who Said That? Identifying Speaker Changes

In a conversation, people take turns speaking. Take a look at this extremely mature discussion:

> "You sat on my tuna fish sandwich," Michael said. "It's flatter than a pancake, and I hate pancakes."
>
> "No, I didn't sit on your sandwich," Ella said. "I sat ten feet away from your lunch bag."
>
> "Did too," Michael said.
>
> "Did not!" Ella said.

Notice that every time the speaker changes, a new paragraph is formed. By starting a new paragraph every time the speaker changes, the conversation is easy to follow; the reader always knows who is talking. Here's another version of the tuna fight:

> "You sat on my tuna fish sandwich," Michael said. "It's flatter than a pancake, and I hate pancakes."
>
> "No, I didn't sit on your sandwich," Ella said. "I sat ten feet away from your lunch bag."
>
> "Did too."
>
> "Did not!"

Although the speaker tags are left out after the first exchange, you can still figure out who is speaking because of the paragraph breaks. Every change of speaker is signaled by a new paragraph.

TIP

The new-speaker/new-paragraph rule applies even if the argument deteriorates into single-word statements such as *yes* or *no* or some other single-word statements. (I won't specify because this is a family-friendly book.)

POP QUIZ

Who said what? Label each statement, using the paragraph clues.

> "Are you in favor of piano-tossing?" asked Roger curiously.
>
> "Not really," replied Cedric. "I like my pianos to have all four feet on the floor."
>
> "But there's something about music in the air that appeals to me."

"There's something about no broken bones, no concussions, and no flattened bodies that appeals to me."

"You really have no artistic instinct!"

Answer: Here's the passage again, with the speakers' names inserted. (Note the punctuation.)

"Are you in favor of piano-tossing?" asked Roger curiously.

"Not really," replied Cedric. "I like my pianos to have all four feet on the floor."

Roger continued, "But there's something about music in the air that appeals to me."

Cedric countered, "There's something about no broken bones, no concussions, and no flattened bodies that appeals to me."

"You really have no artistic instinct!" shouted Roger.

TIP

If you're quoting someone who's very longwinded, you may want to leave out some extra words. No problem, as long as you don't change the meaning of the quotation. Simply replace the missing words with an *ellipsis* (three spaced dots). If you're cutting out more than one sentence, insert four spaced dots — one is the period, and the other three are for the ellipsis. If you need to add a word to a quotation to clarify meaning, put *brackets* — these symbols [ ] — around the addition. Here's what I mean:

ORIGINAL STATEMENT: "I must practice the piano, the whole piano, and nothing but the piano in order to keep my notes sharp."

STATEMENT WITH WORDS OMITTED: "I must practice . . . in order to keep my notes sharp." (The ellipsis takes the place of *the piano, the whole piano, and nothing but the piano.*)

ORIGINAL STATEMENT: "He doesn't like flat-screen televisions either."

STATEMENT WITH CLARIFICATION: "He [Ollie] doesn't like flat-screen televisions either."

Germ-Free Quotations: Using Sanitizing Quotation Marks

Sanitizing quotation marks (also known as *apologetic quotation marks*) tell the reader that you don't completely approve of the words inside the quotation marks. You often see sanitizing quotation marks enclosing slang, highly informal speech that falls outside standard English. (For more information on slang, see Chapter 1.) Check out this example:

> Mack's friends considered his burritos "delish" and thought "ka-ching" when Mack submitted the recipe to the Best New Chef contest.

The writer knows that "delish" and "ka-ching" aren't correct, but those words show the ideas (but not the exact remarks) of Mack's friends.

WARNING

Don't overuse sanitizing quotation marks. Think of them as plutonium; a little goes a long way. Or, to sanitize that statement, a little goes a "long" way. Annoying, right?

TIP

A useful little word is *sic. Sic* (a Latin word that literally mean "thus"), indicates that you're quoting exactly what was said or written, even though you know something is wrong. In other words, you put a little distance between yourself and the error by showing the reader that the person you're quoting made the mistake, not you. For example, if you're quoting from the works of Dan Quayle, former Vice President of the United States (and a *very* poor speller) you may write

"I would like a potatoe [sic] for supper."

> "Potato," of course, is the correct spelling.

Punctuating Titles: When to Use Quotation Marks

In your writing, sometimes you may need to include the title of a magazine, the headline of a newspaper article, the title of a song or movie, and so on. When punctuating these magazine titles, headlines, and song or movie titles, follow these rules:

1. **Quotation marks enclose titles of smaller works or parts of a whole.**

and

2. **Italics or underlining sets off titles of larger works or complete works.**

In other words, use quotation marks for the titles of

>> Poems

>> Stories

>> Essays

>> Songs

>> Chapter titles

>> Individual episodes of a podcast

>> Magazine or newspaper articles

>> Individual episodes of a television series

>> Page of a website

Use italic or underlining for the titles of

>> Collections of poetry, stories, or essays

>> Titles of books

>> Titles of CDs or tapes or records (Do they still make records?)

>> Magazines or newspapers

>> Television and radio shows

>> Podcasts (the series)

>> Plays

>> The name of an entire website

Here are some examples:

>> "A Thousand Excuses for Missing the Tax Deadline" (a newspaper article) in *The Ticker Tape Journal* (a newspaper)

>> "Ode to Taxes Uncalculated" (a poem) in *The Tax Poems* (a book of poetry)

>> "I Got the W2 Blues" (a song title) on *Me and My Taxes* (a CD containing many songs)

>> "On the Art of Deductions" (a podcast) in *Getting Rich and Staying Rich* (a series of podcasts)

>> "Small Business Expenses" (an individual episode) on *The IRS Report* (a television series)

>> *April 15th* (a play)

>> "Deductions Unlimited" (a page in a website) in *Beat the IRS* (name of a website)

TIP

You may be wondering which letters you should capitalize in a title. For information on capitalization, see Chapter 15.

Add quotation marks and italics to the following paragraph.

POP QUIZ

Gloria slumped slowly into her chair as the teacher read The Homework Manifesto aloud in class. Gloria's essay, expressing her heartfelt dislike of any and all assignments, was never intended for her teacher's eyes. Gloria had hidden the essay inside the cover of her textbook, The Land and People of Continents You Never Heard Of. Sadly, the textbook company, which also publishes The Most Boring Mathematics Possible, had recently switched to thinner paper, and the essay was clearly visible. The teacher ripped the essay from Gloria's frightened hands. Gloria had not been so embarrassed since the publication of her poem I Hate Homework in the school magazine, Happy Thoughts.

Answer: Put "The Homework Manifesto" and "I Hate Homework" in quotation marks because they're titles of an essay and a poem. Italicize *The Land and People of Continents You Never Heard Of* and *The Most Boring Mathematics Possible* and *Happy Thoughts,* because they're titles of books and a magazine.

WARNING

When a title is alone on a line — on a title page or simply at the top of page one of a paper — don't use italic or quotation marks. Don't underline the title either. The centering calls attention to the title. Nothing else is needed. One exception: If part of the title is the name of another work, treat that part as you would any other title. For example, suppose you've written a brilliant essay about Gloria's poem, "I Hate Homework." The title page contains this line, centered:

Freudian Imagery in "I Hate Homework"

If your brilliant essay is about the magazine *Happy Thoughts,* the title page includes this line (also centered):

The Decline of the School Magazine: A Case Study of *Happy Thoughts*

Chapter **13**

The Pause That Refreshes: Commas

Aloud, commas are the sounds of silence — short pauses that contrast with the longer pause at the end of each sentence. Commas are signals for your reader. Stop here, they say, but not for too long. Commas also cut parts of your sentence away from the whole, separating something from whatever's around it in order to change the meaning of the sentence. When you're speaking, you do the same thing with your tone of voice and the timing of your breaths.

The rules concerning commas aren't very hard, once you grasp the underlying logic. In this chapter, I guide you through that logic so you know where to put commas in common situations.

Distinguishing Items: Commas in Series

Imagine that you text a shopping list to your roommate Charlie, who's at the store shopping for your birthday party. (If you're curious about texting and grammar rules, turn to Chapter 16.) Everything's on one line.

> flashlight batteries butter cookies ice cream cake

How many things does Charlie have to buy? Perhaps only three:

> flashlight batteries
>
> butter cookies
>
> ice cream cake

Or five:

> flashlight
>
> batteries
>
> butter cookies
>
> ice cream
>
> cake

How does Charlie know? He doesn't, unless you use commas. Here's what Charlie actually needs to buy — all four items:

> flashlight batteries, butter cookies, ice cream, cake

To put it in a sentence:

> Charlie has to buy flashlight batteries, butter cookies, ice cream, and cake.

The commas between these items are signals. When you read the list aloud, the commas emerge as breaths:

> Charlie has to buy flashlight batteries [breath] butter cookies [breath] ice cream [breath] and cake.

TIP

You need commas between each item on the list, with one important exception. The comma in front of the word *and* is often optional. Why? Because when you say *and*, you've already separated the last two items. You must insert the comma if your reader may misunderstand the meaning. Suppose you see this sentence:

> Jenny made the podcast with her sisters, Anne and Elizabeth.

How many people worked on the podcast with Jenny? Possibly two: Anne (Jenny's sister) and Elizabeth (Jenny's other sister). Possibly four or more: Jenny's sisters (Helen and Kelly) and Anne and Elizabeth. In this sort of sentence, that last comma makes all the difference:

> Jenny made the podcast with her sisters, Anne, and Elizabeth.

Now the reader knows for sure that *Anne* and *Elizabeth* are part of a list that begins with *two sisters*, not the names of the *two sisters* added as extra information.

WARNING

Never put a comma in front of the first item on the list.

> WRONG: Charlie has to buy, flashlight batteries, butter cookies, ice cream and cake.
>
> RIGHT: Charlie has to buy flashlight batteries, butter cookies, ice cream and cake.
>
> ALSO RIGHT: Charlie has to buy flashlight batteries, butter cookies, ice cream, and cake.
>
> ALSO RIGHT, BUT NOT A GOOD IDEA: Charlie has to buy flashlight batteries and butter cookies and ice cream and cake.

You don't need commas at all in the last sentence because the word *and* does the job. Grammatically, that sentence is fine. In reality, if you write a sentence with three *ands*, your reader will think you sound like a little kid.

TIP

When you're texting, commas can be a pain to insert because you sometimes have to switch screens to find one. You can skip the commas if you want and instead separate the items, line by line, by pressing "enter" after each. Be warned, though, that some apps remove extra spaces automatically. Your job is to be sure the person reading the text will not misunderstand what you mean. For more about electronic media, turn to Chapter 16.

POP QUIZ

Punctuate the following sentence.

> Belle requested a jelly doughnut a silk dress four sports cars and a racehorse in exchange for the rights to the computer code she had written.

Answer: Belle requested a jelly doughnut, a silk dress, four sports cars, and a race-horse in exchange for the rights to the computer code she had written. *Note:* You may omit the comma before the *and* because the meaning of the sentence is clear.

Using "Comma Sense" to Add Information to Your Sentence

Your writing relies on nouns and verbs to get your point across. But if you're like most people, you also enrich your sentences with descriptions. In grammar terminology, you add adjectives and adverbs, participles and clauses, and an occasional appositive. Before you hyperventilate, let me explain that you don't have to know any of those terms in order to write — and punctuate — a good sentence. You just have to keep a couple of key ideas in your head. In this section, I explain how to place commas so that your writing expresses what you mean.

Separating a list of descriptions

Writers often string together a bunch of single-word descriptions, *adjectives,* in grammar lingo. (For more information on adjectives, turn to Chapter 10.) If you have a set of descriptions, you probably have a set of commas also. Take a look at the following sentences:

"What do you think of me?" Belle asked Jill in an idle moment.

Jill took a deep breath, "I think you are a sniffling, smelly, pimply, frizzy-haired monster."

"Thank you," said Belle, who was trying out for the part of the witch in the school play. "Do you think I should paint my teeth black too?"

Notice the commas in Jill's answer. Four descriptions are listed: *sniffling, smelly, pimply, frizzy-haired.*

A comma separates each of the descriptions from the next, but there is no comma between the last description (*frizzy-haired*) and the word that it's describing (*monster*).

Here's a little more of Belle and Jill's conversation:

"So do I get the part?" asked Belle.

"Maybe," answered Jill. "I have four sniffling, smelly, pimply, frizzy-haired monsters waiting to audition. I'll let you know."

Now look closely at Jill's answer. This time there are five descriptions of the word *monster: four, sniffling, smelly, pimply, frizzy-haired.*

There are commas after *sniffling, smelly,* and *pimply.* As previously stated, no comma follows *frizzy-haired* because you shouldn't put a comma between the last description and the word that it describes. But why is there no comma after *four?* Here's why: *sniffling, smelly, pimply,* and *frizzy-haired* are more or less equal in importance in the sentence. They have different meanings, but they all do the same job — telling you how disgusting Belle's costume is. *Four* is in a different category. It gives you different information, telling you how many monsters are waiting, not how they look. Therefore, it's not jumbled into the rest of the list.

TIP

Numbers aren't separated from other descriptions or from the word(s) that they describe. Don't put a comma after a number. Also, don't use commas to separate other descriptions from words that indicate number or amount — *many, more, few, less,* and so forth. More descriptive words that you shouldn't separate from other descriptions or from the words that they describe include *other, another, this, that, these, those.* Examine these correctly punctuated sentences:

> Sixteen smelly, bedraggled, stained hats were lined up on the shelf marked, "WITCH COSTUME."

> Additional stinky, mud-splattered, toeless shoes sat on the shelf marked, "GOBLIN SHOES."

> No drippy, disgusting, artificial wounds were in stock.

> This green, glossy, licorice-flavored lipstick belongs in the witch's makeup kit.

> Those shiny, battery-powered, factory-sealed witches' wands are great.

POP QUIZ

Punctuate this sentence.

> Jill was worried about some items she must have for a musical number: one hundred scraggly fluorescent flowing beards.

Answer: Jill was worried about some items she must have for a musical number: one hundred scraggly, fluorescent, flowing beards.

Note: Don't put a comma after a number (*one hundred*) or after the last description (*flowing*).

In your writing, you may create other sentences in which the descriptions should not be separated by commas. For example, sometimes a few descriptive words create one larger description in which one word is clearly more important than the rest. Technically the list of descriptions may provide two or three separate facts about the word that you're describing, but in practice, they don't deserve equal attention. Take a look at this example:

> Jill just bought that funny little French hat.

You already know that you should not separate *that* from *funny* with a comma. But what about *funny, little,* and *French*? If you write

> Jill just bought that funny, little, French hat.

you're giving equal weight to each of the three descriptions. Do you really want to emphasize all three qualities? Probably not. In fact, you're probably not making a big deal out of the fact that the hat is *funny* and *little.* Instead, you're emphasizing that the hat is *French.* So you don't need to put commas between the other descriptions.

TIP

Sentences like the example require judgment calls. Use this rule as a guide: If the items in a description are not of equal importance, don't separate them with commas.

Essential or extra? Commas tell the tale

The descriptions in a sentence may be longer than one word. You may have a subject–verb expression (which grammarians call a *clause*) or a verb form (in technical terms, a *participle*). No matter what they're called, these longer descriptions follow one simple rule: If a description is essential to the meaning of the sentence, don't put commas around it. If the description provides extra, nonessential information, set it off with commas.

TEST ALERT

If you expect to darken little ovals with a #2 pencil (and by the way, what's wrong with a #1 or a #3 pencil?), spend a little extra time in this section and the next, "Commas with appositive influence." Standardized tests such as the SAT and the ACT gauge your knowledge of essential and nonessential commas.

Consider this situation:

In her quest to reform Larry's government, Ella made this statement:

> Taxes, which are a hardship for the people, are not acceptable.

Lou, who is a member of Larry's Parliament, declared himself in complete agreement with Ella's statement. However, his version had no commas:

> Taxes which are a hardship for the people are not acceptable.

Do the commas really matter? Yes. They matter a lot. Here's the deal. If the description *which are a hardship for the people* is set off from the rest of the sentence by commas, the description is extra — not essential to the meaning of the sentence. You can cross it out and the sentence still means the same thing. If commas do not set off the description, however, the description is essential to the meaning of the sentence. It may not be removed without altering what you are saying. Can you now see the difference between Ella's statement and Lou's? Here's the expanded version of each statement:

> ELLA'S EXPANDED STATEMENT: The government should not impose taxes. We can run the government perfectly well by selling postage stamps to foreign tourists. I suggest a tasteful portrait of the royal bride (me) on a new stamp.

Because Ella's original sentence includes commas, the description *which are a hardship for the people* is extra information. You can omit it from the sentence. Thus Ella is against all taxes.

> LOU'S EXPANDED STATEMENT: The government is against any taxes which are a hardship for the people. No one wants to place a burden on the working families of our great nation. However, the new tax on texts is not a hardship; it pays my salary. This particular tax is acceptable.

Lou's proposal is much less extreme than Ella's. Without commas the description is a necessary part of the sentence. It gives the reader essential information about the meaning of *taxes*. Lou opposes only some taxes — those he believes are a burden. He isn't against all taxes. This description doesn't simply add a reason, as Ella's does. Instead it identifies which taxes Lou opposes.

TIP

The pronouns *which* and *that* may help you decide whether or not you need commas. *That* generally introduces information that the sentence can't do without — essential information that isn't set off by commas. The pronoun *which*, on the other hand, often introduces nonessential information that may be surrounded by commas. Keep in mind, however, that these distinctions are not true 100 percent of the time. Sometimes *which* introduces a description that is essential and therefore needs no commas. On rare occasions, the pronoun *that* introduces nonessential material.

Check out these additional examples, with the description in italics:

> SENTENCE: The students *who are planning a sit-in tomorrow* want to be paid for doing homework.

> PUNCTUATION ANALYSIS: The description is not set off by commas, so you may not omit it.

WHAT THE SENTENCE MEANS: Some of the students — those planning a sit-in — want to be paid for doing homework. Not all the students want to be paid. The rest are perfectly content to do math problems for free.

SENTENCE: The senators, planning to revolt, have given the network exclusive streaming rights to their demonstration.

PUNCTUATION ANALYSIS: The commas indicate that the description is extra, nonessential information.

WHAT THE SENTENCE MEANS: All the senators are involved. They're quite upset, and all expect to earn a lot of money from Netflix.

POP QUIZ

Which sentence means that you can't fly to Cincinnati for your cousin's wedding?

A. The pilots who are going on strike demand that organic snacks be served in the cockpit.

B. The pilots, who are going on strike, demand that organic snacks be served in the cockpit.

Answer: Sentence B talks about *all* the pilots. They all demand organic snacks in the cockpit, and they're all going on strike. The description between the commas adds that little bit of information. In sentence A, only the pilots who like organic snacks are going on strike.

TIP

The word "because" generally introduces a reason. At the beginning of a sentence, the "because" statement acts as an introductory remark and is always set off by a comma.

Because the tattoo was on sale, Lulu whipped out her credit card and rolled up her sleeve.

At the end of a sentence, the "because" statement is sometimes set off by commas, in which case it may be lifted out of the sentence without changing the meaning. Without commas, it's essential to the meaning. Take a look at these two statements:

WITH COMMAS: Lulu didn't get that tattoo, because it was in bad taste.

MEANING: No tattoos for Lulu! The "because" information is extra, explaining why Lulu passed on the design.

WITHOUT COMMAS: Lulu didn't get that tattoo because it was in bad taste.

MEANING: Lulu got the tattoo, but not because it was in bad taste. She got it for another reason (perhaps a sale). The fact that the tattoo grossed out everyone who saw it was just an extra added attraction to Lulu, who enjoys looking strange.

Commas with appositive influence

If you're seeing double when you read a sentence, you've probably encountered an *appositive*. Strictly speaking, appositives aren't descriptions, though they do give you information about something else in the sentence. Appositives are nouns or pronouns that are exactly the same as the noun or pronoun preceding them in the sentence. Some appositives are set off by commas, and some aren't. The rule concerning commas and appositives: If you're sure that your readers will know what you're talking about before they get to the appositive, set off the appositive with commas. If you're not sure your readers will know exactly what you're talking about by the time they arrive at the appositive, you should not use commas. (This rule is a variation of the rule that I explain in the preceding section.)

Note the difference between these two sentences:

Michael's play *Dinner at the Diner* won the Drama Critics' "Most Boring Plot Award."

Dinner at the Diner, Michael's play, won the Drama Critics' "Most Boring Plot Award."

In the first example sentence, *Dinner at the Diner* is the appositive of *Michael's play.* When you get to *play,* you don't know which of Michael's plays is being discussed. The appositive supplies the name. Hence, the appositive is essential and isn't set off by commas. In the second example sentence, *Michael's play* is the appositive of *Dinner at the Diner.* Because *Dinner at the Diner* comes first, the reader already knows the name of the play. The fact that Michael wrote the play is extra information and must therefore be surrounded by commas.

Here are a two more examples. In each sentence, *Mary* is the appositive of *sister*:

Lulu has five sisters, but her sister Mary is definitely her favorite.

Because Lulu has five sisters, you don't know which sister is being discussed until you have the name. *Mary* identifies the sister and shouldn't be placed between commas.

Roger has only one sibling. His sister, Mary, does not approve of Roger's wife.

Because Roger has only one sibling, the reader knows that he has only one sister. Thus the words *his sister* pinpoint the person being discussed in the sentence. The name is extra information, not identifying information, and is set off by commas.

Which sentence is correct?

A. Lola's spouse, Lou, doesn't approve of Lola's pierced eyebrow.

B. Lola's spouse Lou doesn't approve of Lola's pierced eyebrow.

Answer: Sentence A is correct. Lola has only one spouse, so the name is extra, not identifying information.

You Talkin' to Me? Direct Address

When writing a message to someone, you need to separate the person's name from the rest of the sentence with a comma. Otherwise, your reader may misread the intention of the message. Take a look at the following note that Michael left on the door:

> Roger wants to kill Wendy. I locked him in this room.

You think: Wendy is in danger. That's a shame. Oh well, I guess I'm safe. However, when you unlock the door and sit down for a cup of tea, Roger jumps up and starts chasing you around the room. You escape and run screaming to Michael. "Why didn't you tell me that Roger was violent!" Michael pleads guilty to a grammatical crime. He forgot to put in the comma in his note to Wendy. Here's what he meant:

> Roger wants to kill, Wendy. I locked him in this room.

It was your bad luck to read a note intended for Wendy. In grammarspeak, *Wendy* is in a *direct-address* sentence. Because the writer was directing his comments to Wendy, her name should be cut her off from the rest of the sentence with a comma. Direct address is also possible at the beginning or in the middle of a sentence:

> Wendy, Roger wants to kill, so I locked him in this room.

> Roger wants to kill, Wendy, so I locked him in this room.

Which sentence is correct?

A. The teacher called, Emma, but I answered.

B. The teacher called Emma, but I answered.

Answer: It depends. If you're talking to Emma, telling her that Mr. Mean phoned your house to report missing homework but you, not your mom, picked up the phone, then sentence A is correct. However, if you're explaining that the teacher screamed to Emma, "Bring your homework up here *this minute!*" and instead you replied, "Mr. Mean, Emma asked me to tell you that the computer crashed and erased her homework," sentence B is correct.

TIP

When you're texting, you don't need the name of the person who will read your message because your words will pop up only on that person's phone or computer. Some people like to begin with "Hi, Wendy" or something similar, to create a softer tone. Proper grammar requires a comma between the greeting (*Hi*) and the name (*Wendy*). But proper grammar often eases up when you're using electronic communication. No one is likely to misunderstand *Hi Wendy,* so unless the reader loves punctuation rules, you can safely do without a comma. For more on electronic media and grammar, check out Chapter 16.

Using Commas in Addresses and Dates

Commas are good, all-purpose separators. They won't keep you and your worst enemy apart, but they do a fine job on addresses and dates — especially when items that are usually placed on individual lines are put next to each other on the same line.

Addressing addresses

Where are you from? Jill is from Mars. Belle is from a small town called Venus. Here's her (fictional) address, the way you see it on an envelope:

Ms. Belle Planet

223 Center Street

Venus, New York 10001

In the body of a letter, you can insert an address in "envelope form" like this:

Please send a dozen rockets to the following address:

Ms. Belle Planet

223 Center Street

Venus, New York 10001

TIP

The introductory words (*Please send a dozen rockets to the following address*) end with a colon (:) if they express a complete unit of thought. If the introductory words leave you hanging (*Please send a dozen rockets to,* for example), don't use a colon.

If you put Belle's address into a sentence, you have to separate each item of the address, as you see here:

Belle Planet lives at 223 Center Street, Venus, New York 10001.

Here's the address (envelope style) for her best friend Jill:

Jill Willis

53 Asimov Court

Mars, California 90210

And now the sentence version:

Jill Willis lives at 53 Asimov Court, Mars, California 90210.

TIP

Notice that the house number and street are not separated by a comma, nor are the state and zip code.

If the sentence continues, you must separate the last item in the address from the rest of the sentence with another comma:

Belle Planet lives at 223 Center Street, Venus, New York 10001, but she is thinking of moving to Mars in order to be closer to her friend Jill.

If there is no street address — just a city and a state — put a comma between the city and the state. If the sentence continues after the state name, place a comma after the state.

Belle Planet lives in Venus, New York, but she is thinking of moving to Mars.

Commas also separate countries from the city/state/province:

Roger lives in Edinburgh, Scotland, near a large body of water. His brother Michael just built a house in Zilda, Wisconsin.

POP QUIZ

Punctuate the following sentence.

Police believe that Scott ran away from his home at 77 Main Street Zilda Wisconsin because his parents reduced his screen time to 45 hours per week.

Answer: Police believe that Scott ran away from his home at 77 Main Street, Zilda, Wisconsin, because his parents reduced his screen time to 45 hours per week.

Punctuating dates

Confession time: The rules for placing commas in dates aren't very stable these days. What was once carved into stone (and I mean that literally) is now sometimes viewed as old-fashioned. To make matters even more complicated, writers from different areas (science, literature, and the like) favor different systems. In this section, I show you the traditional form and some variations. If you're writing for business or school, the traditional form should get you through. If you're up for publication, check with your editor about the publisher's preferred style.

If the date is alone on a line (perhaps at the top of a letter), these formats are fine:

September 28, 2060 or Sept. 28, 2060 (traditional)

9/28/60 (informal)

28 September 2060 (modern in the United States, traditional in many other countries)

When dates appear in a sentence, the format changes depending upon (a) how traditional you want to be and (b) how much information you want to give. Take a look at the commas — or the lack of commas — in these sentences:

On September 28, 2060, Lulu ate far too much candy. (Traditional: Commas separate the day and year and the year from the rest of the sentence.)

In October, 2060, Lulu gave up sugary snacks. (Traditional: A comma separates the month from the year and the year from the rest of the sentence.)

Lulu pigs out every October 31st. (Timeless: Both the traditional and modern camp omit commas in this format.)

In October 2060 Lulu suffered from severe indigestion. (Modern: No commas appear.)

Lulu visited a nutritionist on 20 October 2060. (Modern: No commas appear.)

POP QUIZ

Punctuate this sentence, rearranging parts of the date as needed:

Lola testified under oath that on December 18 2016 she saw Lulu place a carton of gummy bears under the counter without paying for it.

Traditional Answer: Lola testified under oath that on December 18, 2016, she saw Lulu place a carton of gummy bears under the counter without paying for it.

Modern Answer: Lola testified under oath that on 18 December 2016 she saw Lulu place a carton of gummy bears under the counter without paying for it.

Getting Started: The Introductory Comma

Some sentences plunge into the main idea immediately, and others take a moment (actually, one or more words) to get into gear. Commas help readers figure out what's going on by separating introductory words from the rest of the sentence. This section explains the guidelines.

Words not connected to the meaning of the sentence

Yes, this section introduces a comma rule. No, it's not optional. Have you figured out the rule yet? Reread the first two sentences of this paragraph. A comma separates words that aren't part of the sentence but instead comment on the meaning of the sentence. That's the rule. If you omit these words, the sentence still means the same thing. Common introductory words include *yes, no, well, oh*, and *okay*. Read these examples twice, once with the introductory words and once without. See how the meaning stays the same?

Yes, you are allowed to chew hard candy during class, but don't complain to me if you break a tooth.

Oh, I didn't know that you needed your intestines today.

To sum up the rule on introductory words, use commas to separate them from the rest of the sentence, or omit them entirely.

Phrases and clauses

Longer descriptions, what grammarians call *phrases* and *clauses*, sometimes serve as introductory elements. Don't worry about the terminology. Just think about the meaning. In these example sentences, the introductory element is italicized:

Scrolling through her newsfeed, Lola stopped only when she glimpsed a motorcycle.

Whenever she can, Lola works on her Harley.

At midnight last Wednesday, Lola went out for a ride.

As you see, commas separate the introductory words and help the reader "hear" the sentence in the right way by adding a pause before the main idea. If the introductory element is very short, though, you can usually skip the comma:

At midnight Lola is seldom at home.

In Part 4, I go into detail about phrases and clauses and how they can spice up your sentences.

Which sentence is correct?

A. Well Ella plays the piano forcefully when she is in the mood.

B. When she is in the mood Ella plays the piano forcefully.

C. Yes, Ella plays the piano forcefully when she is in the mood.

Answer: Sentence C is correct. If you omit the first word, the sentence means exactly the same thing. *Yes* is an introductory word that a comma should separate from the rest of the sentence. In sentence A, there is no comma after *well*. In sentence B, the introductory element *When she is in the mood* should be separated from the rest of the sentence by a comma.

Punctuating Independently

When you join two complete sentences with the conjunctions (joining words) *and*, *or*, *but*, *nor*, *yet*, *so*, or *for*, place a comma before the conjunction. Some examples include:

Agnes robbed the bank, and then she went out for a hamburger.

James spies, but apart from that lapse he is not a bad fellow.

Sam bribed the judges, for he is determined to qualify for the national tournament.

If the two complete sentences are short, you may omit the comma:

Max won and you lost.

For more information on conjunctions and complete sentences, see Chapter 4.

WARNING

Some sentences have one subject (whom or what you're talking about) and two verbs joined by *and*, *but*, *or*, and *nor*. Don't put commas between the two verbs. You aren't joining two complete sentences, just two words or groups of words. Here are some examples:

WRONG: Ella wrote a statement for the media, and then screamed at her press agent for an hour.

WHY IT IS WRONG: The sentence has one subject *(Ella)* and two verbs *(wrote, screamed)*. You aren't joining two complete sentences, so you shouldn't place a comma before *and*. Either way, Ella should learn to control her temper.

RIGHT: Ella wrote a statement for the media and then screamed at her press agent for an hour.

POP QUIZ

Which sentence is correct?

A. Al slits envelopes with his teeth, but Dorothy opens the mail with a knife.

B. Al answers every letter on the day he receives it but doesn't pay any bills.

Answer: Both sentences are correct. In sentence A, the conjunction *but* joins two complete sentences. A comma must precede the conjunction *but*. In sentence B, *but* joins two verbs *(answers, does pay)*. No comma precedes the conjunction.

Chapter **14**

Useful Little Marks: Dashes, Hyphens, and Colons

I n a classic episode of an old detective show, the hero's sidekick writes a book with no punctuation whatsoever. The author explains that he's going to put in "all that stuff" later. Many writers sympathize with the sidekick. Who has time to worry about punctuation when the fire of creativity burns? But the truth is that the three little marks I explain in this chapter — dashes, hyphens, and colons — go a long way toward getting your point across.

Inserting Information with Dashes

Long dashes — what grammarians call "em dashes" — are dramatic. Those long straight lines draw your eye and hold your attention. But long dashes aren't just show-offs. They insert information into a sentence and introduce lists. Short dashes — technically, "en dashes" — aren't as showy as their wider cousins, but they're still useful. Short dashes show a range or connect words when the word *to* or *and* is implied.

Long dashes

A long dash's primary job is to tell the reader that you've jumped tracks onto a new (though related) subject, just for a moment. Here are some examples:

> After we buy toenail clippers — the dinosaur in that exhibit could use a trim, you know — we'll stop at the cafe.

> With a tail as long as a basketball court, the dinosaur — delivered to the museum only an hour before the grand opening — is the star of the exhibit.

The information inside the dashes is slightly off-topic. Take it out, and the sentence makes sense. The material inside the dashes relates to the information in the rest of the sentence, but it acts as an interruption to the main point that you're making.

A dash's second job is to move the reader from general to specific, often by supplying a definition. Check out the following examples:

> I think I have everything I need for the first day of camp — bug spray, hair spray, sun block, and DVD player.

Everything I need is general; *bug spray, hair spray, sun block, and DVD player* are the specifics.

> Louie said that he would perform the *chew-chew* — the ritual unwrapping of the season's first piece of chewing gum.

The definition of *chew-chew* is *the ritual unwrapping of the season's first piece of chewing gum.*

WARNING

Long dashes may be fun to write, but they're not always fun to read. For a little change of pace, dash a new idea into your sentence. Just don't dash in too often or your reader will be tempted to dash away.

Short dashes

If you master this punctuation mark, you deserve an official grammarian's badge — sure to improve your profile on dating apps! Short dashes show a range:

> From May–September, the editors prune commas from literature written over the winter.

Short dashes also show up when you're omitting the word *to* between two elements:

The New York–Philadelphia train is always on time.

Finally, a short dash links two or more equal elements when *and* is implied:

The catcher–pitcher relationship is crucial to the success of the Yankees. (Sorry, can't resist rooting for my favorite team.)

WARNING

Don't confuse short dashes with hyphens, an even shorter punctuation mark that I cover in the next section. Also, don't send a short dash to do a long dash's job. One common mistake is to join two complete sentences with a short dash, as in this example:

Don't worry about Lola–she'll impress your friends.

Here's the corrected sentence:

Don't worry about Lola — she'll impress your friends.

TIP

If you're typing on a phone keyboard, you may not have the option of inserting either a long or a short dash. If the message is formal and grammar matters, don't substitute a hyphen. Reword your message instead:

Don't worry about Lola. She'll impress your friends.

For more about texting and grammar, see Chapter 16.

H-y-p-h-e-n-a-t-i-n-g Made Easy

Think of a hyphen as a dash that's been on a diet. Occasionally — perhaps when you're writing with a pen or pencil — you may need a hyphen to show that a word continues on a different line. You also need these short, horizontal lines to separate parts of compound words, to write certain numbers, and to create one description from two words. This section provides you with a guide to the care and feeding of the humble hyphen.

Understanding the great divide

If you're writing on an electronic device, you seldom have to worry about hyphens that break a word at the end of a line. Most of the time, the word processing program moves the entire word to a new line if it doesn't fit within the margins. But when you're writing by hand, you may need to divide a word at the end of a line to avoid a long blank space along the right-hand margin. If you have to divide a word, follow these simple rules:

>> Place the hyphen between the *syllables,* or sounds, of a word. (If you're not sure where the syllable breaks are in a word, check the dictionary.)

>> Don't leave only one letter of a divided word on a line. If you have a choice, divide the word more or less in the middle.

>> Don't divide words that have only one syllable.

TIP

Web addresses can be very long. Don't divide them with a hyphen. Either place the web address on its own line or, if you absolutely have to divide, chop the address at a period or slash mark.

Using hyphens for compound words

Hyphens also separate parts of compound words, such as *ex-wife, pro-choice, mother-in-law,* and so forth. When you type or write these words, don't put a space before or after the hyphen.

For some time, the trend (yes, language follows fads) has been toward fewer punctuation marks, and that trend has accelerated now that so many people are trying to express themselves in 140 characters. Thus, many words that used to be hyphenated compounds are now written as single words. *Semi-colon,* for instance, has morphed into *semicolon.* Until recently, I sent *e-mails,* but now I write *emails.* As always, the dictionary is your friend when you're figuring out whether a particular expression is a compound, a single word, or two separate words.

THE BRITISH SYSTEM

The practice of dividing a word between syllables is American. In Britain, words are often divided according to the derivation (family tree) of the word, not according to sound. For example, in the American system, *democracy* is divided into four parts — *de-moc-ra-cy* — because that's how it sounds. In the British system, the same word is divided into two parts — *demo-cracy* — because the word is derived from two ancient Greek forms, *demos (people)* and *kratia (power).* Let the dictionary of the country you're in be the final authority on dividing words.

TIP

One cap or two? The answer is complicated. All the parts of a person's title are capitalized, except for prepositions and articles (*Secretary-Treasurer, Commander-in-Chief,* and so forth). Don't capitalize the prefix *ex-* (as in *ex-President Carter, ex-Attorney-General Holder*). Words that are capitalized for some other reason (perhaps because they're part of a book title or a headline) follow a different rule. Always capitalize the first half. Capitalize the second half of the compound if it's a noun, or if the second half of the compound is equal in importance to the first half: *Secretary-General Lola, President-elect Lulu.* (For more information on capitalization, see Chapter 15.)

Hyphens also show up when a single word might be misunderstood. I once received an email from a student. "I resent the draft," she wrote. I spent ten minutes worrying about her feelings before I realized that she sent the draft of a paper twice because the email didn't go through the first time. To avoid misinterpretation, she should have written *re-sent.* Similarly, a hyphen-free statement can provide two different interpretations — never a good idea. Imagine that you're writing about baseball and use the phrase "first base coach." You may be talking about the first guy to coach at a base during a baseball game — the "first base-coach" who rode a horse to the game. Or, you may be discussing the guy who's standing next to first base now, giving advice to players — the "first-base coach." The hyphen clarifies your intended meaning.

Placing hyphens in numbers

Decisions about whether to write a numeral or a word are questions of style, not of grammar. The authority figure in your life — teacher, boss, parole officer, whatever — will tell you what he or she prefers. In general, larger numbers are usually represented by numerals:

> Roger has been arrested 683 times, counting last night.

However, on various occasions you may need to write the word, not the numeral. If the number falls at the beginning of a sentence, for example, you must use words because in formal English, no sentence may begin with a numeral. You may also need to write about a fractional amount. Here's how to hyphenate:

>> Hyphenate all the numbers from twenty-one to ninety-nine.

>> Hyphenate all fractions used as descriptions (*three-quarters full,* for example).

>> Don't hyphenate fractions used as nouns (*three quarters of the money; one third of all registered voters*).

Utilizing the well-placed hyphen

If two words create a single description, put a hyphen between them if the description comes before the word that it's describing. For example:

a *well-placed* hyphen — BUT — the hyphen is *well placed*.

Don't hyphenate two-word descriptions if the first word ends in *-ly*:

nicely drawn rectangle

completely ridiculous grammar rule

Place hyphens where they're needed.

Lulu was recently elected secretary treasurer of her club, the All Star Athletes of Antarctica. Lulu ran on an anti ice platform that was accepted by two thirds of the members.

Answer: Here's the paragraph with the hyphens inserted, along with explanations in parentheses:

Lulu was recently elected secretary-treasurer (hyphen needed for compound title) of her club, the All-Star (hyphen needed for two-word description) Athletes of Antarctica. Lulu ran on an anti-ice (hyphen needed for two-word description) platform that was accepted by two thirds (no hyphen for fractions not used as descriptions) of the members.

Creating a Stopping Point: Colons

A colon is one dot on top of another (:). It appears when a simple comma isn't strong enough. (It also shows up in the typed emoticons that people write in their emails.) In this section, I look at the colon in a few of its natural habitats: business communications, lists, and quotations.

Addressing a business letter or email

Colons appear in business letters, memos, and emails, as you see in the following examples.

From: I.M. Incharj imincharj@company.net

Re: Employment Status

Mr. Ganglia:

You are getting on my nerves. You're fired.

Sincerely,

I.M. Incharj

To Whom It May Concern:

Everyone in the division is fired also.

Sincerely,

I.M. Incharj

TIP

The colon makes a business communication (email, memo, or letter) more formal. The opposite of a business letter is what English teachers call a *friendly letter*, even if it says something like "I hate you." When you write a friendly letter, put a comma after the name of the person who will receive the letter.

Introducing lists

When you insert a short list of items into a sentence, you don't need a colon. (For more information on how to use commas in lists, see Chapter 13.) When you're inserting a long list into a sentence, however, you may sometimes introduce the list with a colon. Think of the colon as a gulp of air that readies the reader for a good-sized list. The colon precedes the first item. Here are some sentences using colons to introduce lists:

General Parker needed quite a few things: a horse, an army, a suit of armor, a few million arrows, a map, and a battle plan.

Roger sent each spy away with several items: printouts from an espionage website, the Wikipedia entry on Mata Hari, a burner cellphone, and a poison pill.

WARNING

If you put a colon in front of a list, check the beginning of the sentence — the part before the colon. Can it stand alone? If so, no problem. If not, problem — maybe. Here's the deal. Many style manuals (lists of rules for particular publications) frown on colons following an incomplete introductory thought. If your list begins with something like "Buy what you need for" the list elements complete that thought, and a colon gets in the way. To be on the safe side, be sure you have a complete sentence before a colon that comes before a list. Take a look at these examples:

PUNCTUATION PROBLEM: The drawbacks of Parker's battle plan are: no understanding of enemy troop movements, a lack of shelter and food for the troops, and a faulty trigger for the retreat signal. (The words before the colon — *The problems with Parker's battle plan are* — don't form a complete thought.)

BETTER PUNCTUATION: The problems with Parker's battle plan are numerous: no understanding of enemy troop movements, a lack of shelter and food for the troops, and a faulty trigger for the retreat signal. (Now the words before the colon — *The problems with Parker's battle plan are numerous* — form a complete thought.)

For more information on complete sentences, see Chapter 4.

Introducing long quotations

The rule concerning colons with quotations is fairly easy. If the quotation is short, introduce it with a comma. If the quotation is long, introduce it with a colon. Take a look at the following two examples for comparison.

What did Lola say at the meeting? Not much, so a comma does the job.

Lola stated, "I have no comment on the squirrel incident."

What did General Parker say at the press conference? Too much, so a colon is better.

Parker explained: "The media has been entirely too critical of my preparations for war. Despite the fact that I have spent the last ten years and two million gold coins perfecting new and improved armor, I have been told that I am unready to fight."

TIP

When you write a paper for school, you may insert some short quotations (up to three lines) into the text. If a quotation is longer than three lines, you should double-indent and single-space the quoted material so that it looks like a separate block of print. Such quotations are called *block quotations.* Introduce the block quotation with a colon, and don't use quotation marks. (The blocking shows that you're quoting, so you don't need the marks.) Here's an example:

> In his essay entitled, "Why Homework is Useless," Smith makes the following point:
>
> > Studies show that students who have no time to rest are not as efficient as those who do. When a thousand teens were surveyed, they all indicated that sleeping, listening to music, talking on the phone, and playing Pokemon were more valuable than schoolwork.

If you're writing about poetry, you may use the same block format:

> The post-modern imagery of this stanza is in stark contrast to the imagery of the Romantic period:
>
> > Roses are red,
> > Violets are blue,
> > Egbert is sweet,
> > And stupid, too.

TIP

Colons sometimes show up inside sentences, joining one complete sentence to another. A colon may be used this way only when the second sentence explains the meaning of the first sentence, as in this example:

> Lola has refused to accept the nomination: She believes the media will investigate every aspect of her life.

The second half of the sentence explains why Lola doesn't want to run for president. Actually, it explains why almost no Americans want to run for president. Notice that I've capitalized the first word after the colon. Some writers prefer lowercase for that spot. This decision is a matter of style, not grammar. Check with the authority figure in charge of your writing (teacher, boss, warden, and so on) about the preferred style.

SLASHING YOUR SENTENCES

A forward slanting line, the *vergule* in grammar lingo (and the *slash* to ordinary people) shows up in URL addresses. It's also useful to present two alternatives, but if you insert slashes into your sentences, consider them the hottest chili peppers imaginable. How many chili peppers do you want in your meal? That's the number of slashes you should place in your writing. Very, very few.

Here's an example of the slash in action:

> Job applicants must bring photos/examples of their work to the interview.

What should you bring to impress your potential boss? Either a photo of the mural you painted on the side of your house or the house itself. The slash shows the two possible choices.

Slashes also separate lines of poetry when you're quoting them inside a paragraph:

> The effort of mountain climbing contributes to the imagery in Lulu's poem, "Everest or Nothing": "and then the harsh/breath of the mountain/meets the harsh/breath of the climber/I am/ the climber."

The slashes tell you that Lulu's poem looks like this:

> and then the harsh
>
> breath of the mountain
>
> meets the harsh
>
> breath of the climber
>
> I am
>
> the climber.

Chapter **15**

CAPITAL LETTERS

Pads are popular, but not always with English teachers, because, well, take a look at the first letter of this sentence. It's in *lowercase* — what kindergarteners call "small letters." Every sentence must begin with a capital letter, according to *The Official Rule Book for Capital Letters* (which doesn't exist). Why? Partly to help the reader separate sentences, but mostly because it's a tradition, and capitalization is mostly about tradition. That said, I should mention that the major style-setters in the world of grammar sometimes disagree about what should be capitalized and what shouldn't. In this chapter, I explain commonly accepted practices, and I point out some areas of disagreement.

Knowing What's Up with Uppercase

Fortunately, the rules for *uppercase*, or capital letters, are easy. You already know one:

» **Begin every sentence with a capital letter**. Yes, the iPad (and the iMac and the *i* everything) break the rule, but a company is allowed to name itself, and Apple picked a lowercase *i*. Unless your sentence begins with a similar name, start with a capital letter. What's that you asked? What about sentences that begin with a numeral? Caught you! You're not supposed to begin a sentence with a numeral. If a number is needed in that spot, you have to write the word and capitalize it. So if you're a star pitcher and the Yankees make an offer, don't send this text:

$10,000,000 per game is not enough.

Instead, type one of these messages:

A mere $10,000,000 per game is not enough.

Ten million dollars per game is not enough.

TIP

Traditionally, the first letter of each line of a poem is capitalized, even if it isn't the beginning of a sentence. However, poets, like computer companies, enjoy trashing (sorry, I meant *reinterpreting*) rules. In poetry, anything goes — including capitalization rules.

» **Capitalize *I*.** I have no idea why the personal pronoun *I* — the word you use to refer to yourself — must be capitalized. The reason probably has something to do with psychology, but I'm not a shrink. I'm a grammarian. So go for caps when you write *I*, and save lowercase for other pronouns (*he, she, us, them,* and so on).

» **Capitalize names.** This rule applies when you're using an actual name, not a category. Write about *Elizabeth*, not *elizabeth*, when you're discussing the cutest kid ever (my granddaughter). She's a *girl*, not a *Girl*, because *girl* is a category, not a name. Elizabeth lives in *Washington*, not *washington* (her *state*, not *State*, because *state* is a general category, not a name). You also capitalize brand names (*Sony*, for example) unless the company itself uses lowercase letters (such as *iPad*, as I point out earlier in this chapter).

» **Capitalize words that refer to the deity.** Believers generally capitalize the name of the being or beings they worship. Respectful writers do so also, even when writing about a religion other than their own. Traditionally, writers also capitalized pronouns referring to a deity, as in this line from a famous hymn:

God works in mysterious ways *His* wonders to perform.

Modern style manuals usually call for lowercase pronouns (*h* for *his* in the preceding example). Traditional style capitalizes mythological gods only when giving their names:

The ancient Greeks built temples in honor of *Zeus* and other *gods*.

» **Begin most quotations with a capital letter.** When quotation marks appear, so do capitals — most of the time. (For exceptions to this rule, turn to Chapter 13.)

That's it for the basics. For the picky stuff, keep reading.

Capitalizing (or Not) References to People

If human beings were called only by their names, life would be much simpler, at least in terms of capital letters. But most people pick up a few titles and some relatives as they journey through life. In this section, I tell you what to capitalize when you're referring to people.

Sorting out titles

Allow me to introduce myself. I'm *Ms.* Woods, *Chief Grammarian* Woods, and *Apostrophe-Hater-in-Chief* Woods (see Chapter 11). All these titles start with capital letters because they're attached to the front of my name. In a sense, they've become part of my name.

Allow me to introduce my friend Egbert. He's *Mr.* Egbert Henhuff, *director of poultry* at a nearby farm. Next year *Director of Poultry* Henhuff plans to run for *state senator,* unless he cracks under the pressure of a major campaign, in which case he'll run for *sheriff.*

Now what's going on with the capitals? The title *Mr.* is capitalized because it's attached to Egbert's last name. Other titles — *state senator* and *sheriff* — are not. In general, lowercase titles are not connected to a name.

Notice that *Director of Poultry* is capitalized when it precedes Egbert's last name but not capitalized when it follows Egbert's name. *Director of Poultry Henhuff* functions as a unit. If you were talking to Egbert, you might address him as *Director of Poultry Henhuff.* So the first *Director of Poultry* in the paragraph above functions as part of the name. When the title follows the name, it gives the reader more information about Egbert, but it no longer acts as part of Egbert's name. Hence, the second *director of poultry* in the previous paragraph is in lowercase.

WARNING

No self-respecting rule allows itself be taken for granted, so this capitalization rule has an exception or two, just to make sure that you're paying attention. Some style manuals, but not all, tell you to capitalize very important titles even when they appear without the name of the person who holds them. What's very important? Definitely these:

>> President of the United States

>> Secretary General of the United Nations

>> Chief Justice of the Supreme Court

>> Vice President of the United States

>> Prime Minister of Great Britain

Here's an example of one of these titles, President of the United States, in action:

> The President of the United States addressed the nation tonight. In his address, the President called for the repeal of all illogical grammar rules.

Of course, there's some leeway with the rule on titles, with the boss or editor or teacher making the final decision. (When in doubt, check with the authority in question.) The following titles are often, but not always, in lowercase when they appear without a name:

» representative

» ambassador

» consul

» justice

» cabinet secretary

» judge

» mayor

Nameless titles that are even lower on the importance ladder are strictly lowercase:

» assistant secretary

» dogcatcher-in-chief

» officer

» sergeant

TIP

When capitalizing a hyphenated title, capitalize both words *(Chief Justice)* or neither *(assistant secretary)*. One exception (sigh) to the rule is for *exes* and *elects*:

» ex-President

» President-elect

Writing about family relationships

It's not true that Elizabeth's *grandma* was imprisoned for illegal sentence structure. I know for a fact that *Uncle Bart* took the blame, although his *brother* Alfred tried desperately to convince *Grandma* to make a full confession. "My *son* deserves to do time," said *Grandma,* "because he dropped a verb when he was little and got away with it."

What do you notice about the family titles in the preceding paragraph? Some of them are capitalized, and some are not. The rules for capitalizing the titles of family members are simple. If you're labeling a relative, don't capitalize. (I'm talking about kinship — *aunt, sister, son,* and so on — not appearance or personality flaws — *chubby, sweet, dishonest,* and so on.) If the titles take the place of names (as in *Uncle Bart* and *Grandma*), capitalize them. For example:

> Lulu's *stepsister* Sarah poured a cup of ink into every load of wash that Lulu did. (*stepsister* = label)

> Sarah told *Mother* about the gallon of paint thinner that Lulu had dripped over Sarah's favorite rose bush. (*Mother* = name)

> I was surprised when my *father* took no action; fortunately, *Aunt Aggie* stepped in with a pail of bleach for Lulu. (*father* — label; *Aunt Aggie* — name)

TIP

If you can substitute a real name — Mabel or Jonas, for example — in the sentence, you probably need a capital letter:

> I told *Father* that he needed to shave off his handlebar moustache and put it on his bicycle. (original sentence)

> I told *Jonas* that he needed to shave off his handlebar moustache and put it on his bicycle. (The substitution sounds fine, so capitalize *Father.*)

If the substitution sounds strange, you probably need lowercase:

> I told my *grandmother* not to shave off her moustache. (original sentence)

> I told my *Mabel* not to shave off her moustache. (The substitution doesn't work because you don't generally say *my Mabel.* Use lowercase for *grandmother.*)

TIP

The word *my* and other possessive pronouns (*your, his, her, our, their*) often indicate that you should lowercase the title. (For more information on possessive pronouns, see Chapter 8.)

POP QUIZ

Which sentence is correct?

A. Ever since he heard that housework requires effort, Archie helps mother around the house as little as possible.

B. Ever since he heard that housework requires effort, Archie helps Mother around the house as little as possible.

Answer: Sentence B is correct. *Mother* is used as a name, not a label, so you must capitalize it. (Try the *Mabel* test; it works!)

Tackling race and ethnicity

If you come from Tasmania, you're Tasmanian. If you come from New York, you're a New Yorker. (Don't ask me about Connecticut; I've never been able to get an answer, though I've asked everyone I know from that state.) Those examples of capitalization are easy. But what about race and ethnicity? Like everyone else, grammarians struggle to overcome the legacy of a racist society and its language. Here are some guidelines concerning capitalization and race:

>> White and Black (or white and black) are acceptable descriptions, with lowercase being a bit more popular. Whichever you choose, be consistent. Don't capitalize one and not the other. Always capitalize *Asian* because the term is derived from the name of a continent.

>> European American, Asian American, African American (and the less popular Afro-American) are all in capitals.

>> Mexican American, Polish American, and other descriptions of national origin are written with capital letters because the terms are derived from country names.

>> To hyphenate or not to hyphenate, that is the question. *Afro-American* is generally written with a hyphen. As for terms such as Asian American, Mexican American, African American, and the like, the answer depends on your politics. Without the hyphen, *American* is the primary word, described by the word that precedes it. So without the hyphen, you emphasize the identity of *American*. With the hyphen, both words are equal, so both parts of the identity have equal importance.

Capitalizing Geography: Directions, Places, and Languages

Even if nothing more than your imagination leaves the living room, you still need to know the rules for capitalizing the names of places, languages, geographical features, regions, and directions. Here's a complete guide to capitalizing geography.

Directions and areas of a country

My pet parakeets don't migrate for the winter, but if they did, where would they go — south or South? It depends. The direction of flight is *south* (lowercase). The area of the country where it's easy to get a tan is the *South* (uppercase). Got it? From New York City you drive *west* to visit the *West* (or the *Midwest*).

The names of other, smaller areas are often capitalized too. Plopped in the center of New York City is Central Park, which the West Side and the East Side flank. Chicago has a South Side and London has Bloomsbury. Note the capital letters for the names of these areas.

Capitalizing geographic features

Capitalize locations within a country when the proper name is given (the name of a city or region, such as the *Mississippi River, the Congo,* or *Los Angeles,* for example).

Is *the* part of the name? Usually not, even when it's hard to imagine the name without it. In general, don't capitalize *the*.

When the name doesn't appear, use lowercase for geographical features (*mountain, valley, gorge,* or *beach,* for instance).

In general, you should capitalize the names of countries and languages. One exception to this rule: common objects with a country, area, or nationality as part of the name (*french fries, scotch whiskey, venetian blinds,* and so forth). By attaching itself to a common object, the name takes on a new meaning. It no longer refers to the country or language. Instead, the reader simply thinks of an everyday object. If you're not sure whether or not to capitalize the geographical part of a common item, check the dictionary.

Correct the capitalization in this paragraph.

> When Alex sent his little brother Abner to Italy, Abner vowed to visit mount Vesuvius. Alex asked Abner to bring back some venetian blinds, but Abner returned empty-handed. "Let's go out for chinese food," said Abner when he returned. "Some sesame noodles will cheer me up."

Here is the answer, with explanations in parentheses:

> When Alex sent his little brother Abner to Italy (correct — country name), Abner vowed to visit Mount Vesuvius (capitalize the entire name of the mountain). Alex asked Abner to bring back some venetian blinds (correct — lowercase for the

name of a common object), but Abner returned empty-handed. "Let's go out for Chinese food (because this isn't the name of one specific item, such as french fries, capitals are better)," said Abner when he returned. "Some sesame noodles will cheer me up."

Marking Seasons and Other Times

Read this paragraph, paying special attention to the italicized words and letters:

Lou hates the *summer* because of all the tourists who invade his coastal town. He's been known to roar something about *"winter's* peaceful *mornings,"* even though he seldom wakes up before *3 p.m.* and never before *noon.*

After reading the preceding example, you can probably figure out this rule without me. Write the seasons of the year in lowercase, as well as the times of day.

TIP

Some books tell you to capitalize the abbreviations for morning and afternoon (A.M. and P.M.) and some specify lowercase (a.m. and p.m.). So no matter what you do, half your readers will think you're right (the good news) and half will think you're wrong (the bad news). Your best bet is to check with the authority overseeing your writing. If you're the authority, do what you wish. Also, because it's sometimes a pain to insert periods into messages typed on tiny screens, omitting this punctuation mark has become more acceptable (AM, PM). Just be careful not to confuse the reader with *am* (a form of the verb *be)* and the abbreviation for morning (*a.m.).* For more information on grammar and electronic communication, read Chapter 16.

Schooling: Courses, Years, and Subjects

As every student knows, school is complicated. So is the rule concerning the capitalization of school-related terms. Don't capitalize subjects and subject areas (*history, science, physics, phys ed,* for example) unless the name refers to a language (*Spanish, Latin, English,* and so on). Capitalize the titles of courses (*Economics 101, Math for Poets, Paper Clips in American History,* and the like).

The years in school, while interminable and incredibly important, are not capitalized (*seventh grader, freshman, sophomore,* for instance).

Correct the capitalization in this paragraph.

Hurrying to Chemistry class, Jack slipped on the stairs on the very first day of his Senior year. He wanted to see his sweetheart, Freshman Lila Jones, who had enrolled in history of the ancient world with Professor Krater. Lila, deep in the study of history, didn't see Jack's accident.

Answer: Here's the correct version, with the reasons in parentheses:

Hurrying to chemistry (don't capitalize subjects) class, Jack slipped on the stairs on the very first day of his senior year (never capitalize years in school). He wanted to see his sweetheart, freshman (never capitalize years in school) Lila Jones, who had enrolled in History of the Ancient World (capitalize course titles) with Professor Krater. Lila, deep in the study of history (this one is correct — lowercase for subject areas), didn't see Jack's accident.

Writing Capitals in Titles

Titles of articles, books, websites, blog posts, and other writings require capital letters. Two systems of capitalization are acceptable, roughly divided by content. If the work falls into the general interest or humanities (literature, art, history, and so forth) slot, you probably want *headline style*. Scientists opt for *sentence style*, which also sometimes pops up in publications devoted to other types of content. If you're not sure where your work belongs, check with the relevant authority figure. No supervisor? Pick the system you like the best. In this section, I explain both.

Headline style

Most newspaper and magazine articles, as well as creative works, employ headline style. You can find examples by looking at — how surprising — headlines. Here are the rules, which I illustrate with a title of a book, *I Am Not a Monster.* (This isn't a real book, by the way.)

» Capitalize *I* and *Monster*. *I* is always uppercase and *Monster* is an important word. Also, *I* is the first word of the title, and the first word of the title is always capitalized.

» Capitalize *Am* because it's a verb, and verbs are at the heart of the title's meaning. (See Chapter 2.)

» Capitalize *Not* because it changes the meaning of the verb and thus has an important job to do in the sentence.

» Lowercase the only word left — *a*. Never capitalize articles (*a, an,* and *the*) unless they're the first words in the title.

Do you see the general principles that I've applied? Here is a summary of the rules for all sorts of titles:

>> Capitalize the first word in the title.

>> Capitalize verbs and other important words.

>> Lowercase unimportant words — articles (*a*, *an*, *the*), conjunctions (words that connect, such as *and, or, nor,* and the like), and prepositions (*of, with, by,* and other words that express a relationship between two elements in the sentence).

TIP

Some grammarians capitalize long prepositions — those with more than four letters. Others tell you to lowercase all prepositions, even the huge ones — *concerning, according to,* and so on. (See Chapter 9 for a list of common prepositions.) Your best bet is to check with your immediate authority (editor, boss, teacher, and so on) to make sure that you write in the style to which he or she is accustomed.

WARNING

When writing the title of a magazine or newspaper, should you capitalize the word *the*? Probably not. Modern style manuals generally lowercase *the*, even when the publication itself uses a capital *T*, unless the title is alone on the line or is the first word of a sentence.

POP QUIZ

Which words should you capitalize in these titles?

the importance of being prepared

romeo and lulu

slouching toward homework

Answers:

The Importance of Being Prepared (*The* is the first word of the title. *Importance, Being,* and *Prepared* are important words. Lowercase *of* because it's not an important word.)

Romeo and Lulu (*Romeo* is the first word of the title and is also a name. Similarly, *Lulu* is a name. Lowercase *and* because it's not an important word.)

Slouching Toward Homework (*Slouching* is the first word of the title. *Homework* is important. *Toward* can go either way. It's a preposition — a relationship word — and thus may be lowercase, at least according to some grammarians. It's also a long word, which makes it suitable for capitalization in the opinion of other grammarians.)

Sentence style

Scientists are practical people, don't you think? They've simplified the rules of capitalization for works in their field, such as this article (which doesn't actually exist):

> Oxygen saturation in freshwater: A comparative study of Kelton Lake and Walden Pond

Can you figure out the rules? Here they are, in all their glory:

>> **Capitalize the first word of the title**. In this book, that's *Oxygen*.

>> **Capitalize the first word of the subtitle**. Here, that word is *A*.

>> **Capitalize proper names.** *Kelton Lake* and *Walden Pond* name specific places and are therefore capitalized.

>> Lowercase everything else.

Don't you love science? At least when you're capitalizing?

Concerning Historic Capitals: Events and Eras

What's the lowdown — and what's up? — with history? Read this paragraph, paying special attention to the italicized words and phrases:

> Jane entered her time machine and set the dial for the *Middle Ages*. Because of a tiny problem with the power supply, Jane instead ended up right in the middle of the *Industrial Revolution*. Fortunately for Jane, the *Industrial Revolution* did not involve a real *war*. Jane still shudders when she remembers her brief stint in the *Civil War*. She is simply not cut out to be a fighter, especially not a fighter in the *nineteenth century*. On the next *Fourth of July*, Jane plans to fly the bullet-ridden flag she brought back from the *Battle of Gettysburg*.

The story of Jane's adventures should make the rules concerning the capitalization of historic events and eras easy. Capitalize the names of specific time periods and events but not general words. Hence

>> Capitals: Middle Ages, Industrial Revolution, Civil War, Fourth of July, Battle of Gettysburg

>> Lowercase: war, nineteenth century

Some grammarians capitalize *Nineteenth Century* because they see it as a specific time period. Others say that you should lowercase numbered centuries. I prefer to lowercase the century. As always, ask for the preference of the publication or authority figure overseeing your work.

Correct the capitalization in this paragraph.

> Jane has never met Marie Antoinette, but Jane is quite interested in the French revolution. With her trusty time-travel machine, Jane tried to arrive in the Eighteenth Century, just in time for Bastille Day. However, once again she missed her target and landed in the middle of the first crusade.

Answer, with explanations in parentheses:

> Jane has never met Marie Antoinette, but Jane is quite interested in the French Revolution. (Capitalize the name of a war.) With her trusty time-travel machine, Jane tried to arrive in the eighteenth century, (Optional, but most grammarians write numbered centuries in lower case.) just in time for Bastille Day. (Correct. Capitalize the names of important days.) However, once again she missed her target and landed in the middle of the First Crusade. (Capitalize the name of the war.)

?4U: Cn U AbbreV8?

Do you like the shortened title of this section? At 18 characters, it's much shorter than the 36 characters needed for the full-length version: *Question for You: Can You Abbreviate?* With this abbreviation, you save time. Plus, you save space, an advantage when you're limited to say, 140 characters, as you are in tweets.

But abbreviations have a downside. The first time you saw *e.g.,* did you know that it meant *for example?* If so, fine. If not, you probably didn't understand what the author was trying to say. Second, abbreviations clash with formal writing. Formal writing implies thought and care, not haste. (Yes, I know things are different when you're thumbing in a message, a post, or a tweet. Check out Chapter 16 for more on electronic media and grammar.)

Sometimes, however, you do want to abbreviate. Here's how to do so correctly:

>> Capitalize abbreviations for titles and end the abbreviation with a period. For example, *Mrs.* Snodgrass, *Rev.* Tawkalot, *Sen.* Veto, Jeremiah Jones, *Jr.,* and *St.* Lucy.

>> Capitalize geographic abbreviations when they're part of a name but not when they're a general category. Put a period at the end of the abbreviation:

Appalachian *Mts.* or Amazon *R.*, for example. On a map you may write *mt.* (mountain).

» The United States Postal Service has devised a list of two-letter state abbreviations. Don't put periods in these abbreviations. Examples: *AZ* (Arizona), *CO* (Colorado), *WY* (Wyoming), and so on.

» Write most measurements in lowercase and end the abbreviation with a period (*yds.* for *yards* or *lbs.* for *pounds*). Metric abbreviations are written without periods (*km* for *kilometer* or *g* for *gram*).

WARNING

Don't confuse abbreviations with acronyms. Abbreviations chop some letters out of a single word. Acronyms are new words made from the first letters of each word in a multiword title. Some common acronyms include the following:

NATO: North Atlantic Treaty Organization

OPEC: Organization of Petroleum Exporting Countries

AIDS: Acquired Immune Deficiency Syndrome

WARNING

Want to drive your teacher crazy? Write a formal essay with &, w/, w/o, or b/c. (For the abbreviation–deprived, & means *and*, w/ means *with*, w/o means *without*, b/c means *because*.) These symbols are fine for your notes but not for your finished product. Similarly, save *brb* (*be right back*), *lol* (*laugh out loud*), and other texting abbreviations for your friends, not for authority figures. (For more on texting and electronic media, turn to Chapter 16.)

POP QUIZ

Correct Legghorn's homework.

Yesterday (Tues.) I went in the a.m. to CO. I saw Mr. Dean, who told me that the EPA had outlawed his favorite pesticide. I have three gal. in the basement, & I'll have to discard it.

Answer:

Yesterday (Tuesday) I went in the morning to Colorado. I saw Mr. Dean, who told me that the EPA had outlawed his favorite pesticide. I have three gallons in the basement, and I'll have to discard it.

Explanation: Don't abbreviate in homework assignments except for titles (*Mr. Dean*) and easily understood acronyms (*EPA*, or *Environmental Protection Agency*). If you're writing about an acronym that your reader may not understand, write the whole thing out the first time you use it and place the acronym in parentheses. Thereafter, the acronym alone is fine. Also, if this had been a note to a friend, the abbreviations would have been perfectly acceptable.

Chapter **16**

Rules of Thumb: Adapting Grammar to Electronic Media

When people first started writing down their thoughts thousands of years ago, critics warned that memory and concentration would deteriorate. Ditto for internet research and word-processed prose, many centuries later. Even today, as texts and tweets pour forth, headlines predict terrible consequences: "People are too dependent on machines!" "Brains are shrinking!" "Grammar is dead!"

I don't know anything about brain science, but I can say for sure that grammar is definitely *not* dead. In fact, some studies show that teens who text "ru l8t?" (translation: "Are you late?") and similar messages actually do better on standard grammar exams than those who don't. The theory is that teens adapt language to suit the medium they're using. Whatever your age, you should do the same, because technology isn't going away. In this chapter, I explain the most commonly accepted grammar guidelines for twenty-first-century electronic media, including texts, tweets, social media posts, blog posts, and presentation slides.

Thumb Wrestling with Grammar: Texts, Tweets, and Instant Messages

Will you stay and read this section now, or will you *BRB?* If that last "word" is a mystery to you, I'm guessing that your thumbs are rested and relaxed because you haven't been using them to type on a cell phone, tablet, or similar device. In other words, you're not into tweeting (issuing 140-character statements) or texting (sending short notes) or instant messaging (having a real-time, written "chat" via computer). But if you easily decoded "BRB" as "be right back" and you thumb much of your communication with the outside world, this section is for you.

TIP

The distinction between traditional email (isn't it amazing that a medium only a couple of decades old is already "traditional"?) and text messages is blurry; often both arrive on and depart from the same device, usually a cell phone or tablet. In this section, I deal with messages that are generally short and frequently written without benefit of a desk, coffee cart, family photos, and other accessories that accompany a traditional work space. The next section, "Emailing Your Way to Good Grammar," explains how to adapt your grammar when you're writing longer messages, presumably on a laptop or desktop computer under more pleasant, less rushed conditions.

Choosing formal or informal language

In Chapter 1, I discuss making your language suit your purpose, audience, and message by changing levels of formality. The same tiered structure applies to electronic media also:

>> **Friendspeak** is my term for deliberately informal English. Friendspeak, in electronic media, includes abbreviations (*imho* = in my humble opinion, *g2g* = got to go, and so forth) and emoticons (smiley faces, flowing tears, splashing sobs, and other picture-communications). Punctuation, in friendspeak, both decreases and increases. Messages often omit periods and commas but pile on exclamation points or question marks (or a combination of the two) to show strong feeling. The old rules go out the window (and don't come back) for punctuation in friendspeak.

>> **Conversational English** is casual language between friends and acquaintances. In texts, tweets, and social media posts, conversational English drops words and some punctuation, and adds other punctuation to show enthusiasm, anger, and other feelings. Conversational English is usually the language of choice for captions or memes accompanying photos or other illustrations on social media sites.

>> **Formal English** respects all the rules and conventions of grammar that educated people hold dear. In professional situations — tweets representing a company or publication, for example — formal English is still the best and safest choice.

I've seen texts and tweets written in all three of these general categories, and under the right circumstances, I think all of them work well. (As a grammarian, however, I have to use proper English in all circumstances — in flashmobs, during arguments with my husband, for conversations with telemarketers, and — well, *everywhere*. Normal people have more leeway.) Now it's time for specifics on deciding which level of formality is best. Apply these guidelines:

>> Consider the identity of the person receiving the message. If you're dealing with someone who can practically read your mind, formal English isn't necessary. Abbreviations and half-sentences are probably fine, and you don't need to worry about capitalization and punctuation — mostly.

TIP

Friendspeak has some rules of its own when it comes to punctuation. One survey of texters showed that young people viewed a period at the end of a sentence as a sign of anger; to them, that punctuation mark ended the conversation abruptly, not grammatically. Periods within a sentence add emphasis: *Best. Sign. Ever.* The punctuation in this statement is the equivalent of a finger-poke in the face, one after each word.

>> The less friendly the relationship, the more correct your language and grammar should be. If you're writing to someone you've met once or twice, don't chop out letters or words unless you know that the recipient appreciates informality. Stick to the normal rules for capitalization and punctuation unless you're sure that the message-receiver is comfortable with nonstandard English.

>> Power matters also. If you're the boss, you make the rules. Your subordinates aren't going to point out that you lowercased a word that should be in caps — not if they want to keep working for you! But if your message is going up the chain of command, choose formal English.

TIP

With the possible exception of people who wear tie-dyed t-shirts and love beads because they're stuck in the "cool" sixties, most teachers favor formal English. Follow grammar rules when you write to anyone in the academic world. This advice isn't only for students. I once received this message from a parent who was stuck at work and late for our conference: *w8 4 me.* I did "wait for" her, but not happily. It wasn't the time or inconvenience that bothered me. It was the fact that she hadn't taken a minute to type out some actual words.

>> Think about the impression you're trying to make. If you're writing to a potential client, formal language may show respect and care. On the other hand, if you've got an antsy client — the type who wants the work done yesterday, if not sooner — a few dropped words or characters may give the

impression that you're speeding along on the client's behalf, too busy for such niceties as commas and periods.

TIP

>> Save abbreviations such as "ttyl" *(talk to you later),* lol *(laugh out loud,* indicating a joke), and "ctn" *(can't talk now)* for someone who is your "bff" *(best friend forever).* However, some abbreviations are acceptable in business or academic writing. For example, you may begin a message with "FYI" *(for your information)* and ask for a reply "ASAP" *(as soon as possible).* If the abbreviation appears in a dictionary, it's probably okay unless you're writing in an extremely formal situation.

PICTURE THIS

Many writing systems started off as pictures carved in stone or scratched on clay. For example, early Egyptian hieroglyphs (picture symbols) used a pair of legs for the word "walk" and a little bird for "duck." But drawings are time-consuming, especially when you're carving them in stone. Gradually, picture symbols came to represent sounds, becoming letters that combined to form words.

Now, though, electronic media is taking communication back in time. Maybe because you can't hear someone's tone of voice when you're reading, or maybe because short messages can easily be misunderstood, someone came up with *emoticons* and *emoji* (the Japanese-invented forms). First a colon and a parenthesis made a smiley face like this :) or a frown like this :(and then a semicolon and a parenthesis winked out like this ;). Pretty soon, apps appeared to transform and expand writers' options. These days you can "like" something with an image of a thumb pointing upward, express love with a heart, show strength with a flexed bicep, and so forth.

Emoticons and emoji aren't subject to grammar rules, but they do open up a world of problems. If your reader's device doesn't have the proper app, the emoticon may appear as a small square, communicating nothing. Plus, not every reader understands how to use these little pictures. (Did the ancient Egyptians have the same problem?) If you post that your dog is sick, and someone hits the thumbs-up button, does that show support for you? Or happiness that the little monster isn't perky enough to bite your ankle? Also, when an emoticon appears on a tiny screen, the message may be unclear. Put a Thanksgiving turkey leg in your message, and your reader may picture your holiday dinner — or mistake the image for a "Rosie the Riveter" muscled, human arm. Imagine your reader's response to the accompanying message "I ate too much of this!" The only sensible approach is to use emoticons to write to friends who are likely to enjoy and decode them properly. For anything serious, opt for actual words.

WARNING

No matter who the recipient is, you have to get your point across. Check out the next section for some tips on writing understandable messages.

Getting creative within character limits

The screens and keyboards of tablets and smartphones can be as tiny as a low-calorie cookie, so sending or reading a long letter isn't comfortable. Plus, depending upon the device and cost structure of your carrier, you may pay extra if you're not concise. Some formats, such as tweets, have a character limit. (A *character*, in this context, is a letter, a space, or a punctuation mark. They all count toward your limit, not just the number of words.) The conclusion is obvious: Make your messages as short as possible in order to avoid eye and finger fatigue.

TIP

One advantage of limited formats is that the writer has to zero in on the most important idea, not wander around verbally, wasting readers' time. This skill may carry over into all sorts of writing. As you compose, say, a tweet, identify the main point you want to make. Check that you haven't stated the obvious or repeated yourself. You find some hints here on writing concisely. In Chapter 21, I add more.

Compressing your thoughts into the smallest space doesn't get you off the hook when it comes to grammar, however. Remember one rule, no matter what you're writing with, on, or to:

Be clear!

Your reader has to understand what you mean, or your message is a failure. Period, end of story. With that principle in mind, check out these guidelines:

Dropping words

Because every character counts, you may at times break the "complete sentence" rule when you're texting. The most common cut is the subject of a sentence. (See Chapter 3 for more information on subjects.) For example, you may type

Left meeting early. No progress.

to someone who knows that despite having an early dinner date, you attended a session of that learned (and imaginary) society, Grammarians for Punctuation Reform. However, don't omit a subject unless you're absolutely sure that no confusion may result. For instance, suppose you and a colleague spoke about the meeting and identified the key figure in the pro-apostrophe group. His support for punctuation reform is guaranteed to convince everyone else. His disapproval means that any proposal is dead on arrival. Upon receiving the previous text message, will your colleague know who left the meeting early? Perhaps she will think you left because the situation was going nowhere and you'd rather be nibbling an appetizer. Or she may believe that the apostrophe expert skipped out, leading you to conclude that nothing was going to change. In such a situation, it's better to type

> Danby left meeting early. No progress.

or

> I left the meeting early. No progress.

so your colleague understands what happened.

TIP

Articles (*a, an, the*) and conjunctions (words that join, such as *and, or, but,* and so forth) can often be omitted. Just be aware that the resulting message sounds rushed and at times strange. Can you imagine typing, "I went to bar"? Somehow *the* makes a big difference.

Dropping punctuation and capital letters

Some handhelds automatically correct your typing by inserting capital letters and a period after you've typed two spaces. Others don't, and I realize that capital letters may be a pain to type when you're on the go. Nevertheless, I'm in favor of that little extra effort. Ditto for periods. Yes, some people text

> saw helen after the meeting

and civilization hasn't crumbled, at least not grammatically. But don't you like this version better?

> Saw Helen after the meeting.

Or

> I saw Helen after the meeting.

Okay, maybe you don't. But some people, including me, do. Why take a chance on offending your reader?

WARNING

Dropping a comma or a period usually isn't crucial. However, don't skip anything that adds meaning, such as question marks. Take a look at these two text messages:

> Dinner at 7

> Dinner at 7?

Obviously, they express two different ideas. The first assumes attendance, and the second is an invitation. Still another temptation is to drop prepositions, such as *at:*

Dinner 7

Does that text mean seven people are coming for dinner? Or that you and the person receiving the message are dining at seven o'clock? Before you hit send, think about possible misinterpretations.

Making a text and checking it twice

Type carefully, and reread what you typed before sending the message. Some people easily decode mistyped words as they read (*teh* is most likely a mistyped *the,* for example). But errors such as this one show a lack of thought and care — not the best message for your reader. Do you want to risk having your wrods — oops, I mean *words* — turn into a puzzle? It's worth an extra secod of your time. Er, that's *second.*

Also think twice before tapping on a word that the device suggests. Smartphones, for example, are programmed to look for the most likely word after you type in only one or two letters, refining the choices based on what other people have written. Sometimes the device proposes an entire word before you hit even a single letter, because the computer program links that word with the one preceding it. If I type *loo,* for example, the phone suggests *look, looking,* and *looks.* Once I hit *looking,* the phone suggests *forward.* These shortcuts are terrific, but you have to be careful. It's far too easy to hit the wrong spot on the screen — what some people call "fat finger" mistakes.

Autocorrect — a program that is supposed to find errors and fix them without your input — can also be a problem. I recently texted my husband that I was "heading home on CPW," referring to a street named Central Park West. He received this text "heading home on a cow." He knew I was on a bus, not an animal, because not many herds of cattle roam around New York City, where I live. He didn't know where I was, though, because he couldn't make a logical connection between "cow" and "Central Park West." And at least that's an innocent substitution. Some autocorrects aren't. A quick internet search for "auto correct fails" will show you exactly how bad things can get. (Hint — really, really bad. X-Rated! Be careful!)

Speech-to-text programs, which convert what you say to your phone into written words on the screen, have improved quite a bit in recent years. Unfortunately, improvement isn't perfection. Check your text to see if you need to fix anything before you hit send.

Wireless messages often include a little phrase saying something like "sent from a ____ " (fill in the name of your device). I've heard a number of arguments about this phrase. One side believes that readers accept mistakes when they see it because they know that texts and instant messages are written quickly, without proofreading. The other side believes that if you're writing, you should write with care. You can probably guess my stance. I don't give get-out-of-grammar-jail-free cards!

Emailing Your Way to Good Grammar

In this section, I talk about electronic messages that can be considerably longer than the usual text message. (Yes, I know that emails can be short also. When a student asks to be excused from homework, usually in a *very* long message, I reply with a one-word email: "No.") Here I discuss emails that are a little more structured than text-messages — closer to a traditional, paper-printed letter than to a 140-character message (the current limit for "tweets" — short messages sent via Twitter). I take you through the parts of the email, explaining the best format to use when you're writing to someone who expects good grammar.

The heading

Atop every email is a little box with a heading, which includes a "From," "To," and "Subject" line. You don't have to worry about the proper format of the "To" and "From" boxes. The "To" contains the name connected with the email address of the recipient, and the email program automatically slots your name into the "From" line. Some programs display the email addresses in the "from" and "to" line automatically; others hide them unless you click to see them.

The subject line is the "title" of your email. Most people follow standard, headline-style capitalization rules for the subject line. (See Chapter 15 for a complete explanation of how to capitalize a title.) If you're not worried about formality, feel free to ignore the rules for caps.

Emails without a subject line may never reach the eyes of the intended reader. Unless you know the recipient will read anything and everything you send, give a hint in the subject line. Also, don't send a blank email because you assume that the subject line carries all the information. Instead of admiring your time-saving techniques, people receiving that sort of email are more likely to think "computer glitch" and hit the Delete button without understanding what you were trying to communicate.

The greeting

Time being a precious resource, many email writers skip the greeting and go directly to the message. No problem, unless you happen to be writing to traditionalists, who prefer the time-honored formats, or egotists, who love seeing their names in print. A message without a greeting may seem informal (okay for friends) or cold (not okay for potential customers). If you do include a greeting (in English-teacher terminology, a *salutation*), you have several choices. These are all acceptable greetings, complete with punctuation:

> **Dear Ms. Snodgrass,** or **Dear Ms. Snodgrass:** The one with the comma is less formal. Begin the message on the following line.
>
> **To Whom It May Concern:** This one always has a colon. It's ultra-formal and old-fashioned — some would say stuffy. Use with care! If you do choose this option, begin the message on the following line.
>
> **Hi, Lola.** or **Hi, Ms. Snodgrass.** Use these forms for friends and acquaintances. Begin the message right after the period, not on the next line. Some people omit the comma. That's not an earth-shattering mistake, but it's not technically correct either. *Lola* and *Ms. Snodgrass* are being addressed here, so strict punctuation rules specify that a comma separate them from *hi*.
>
> **Hi, Lola!** This one is for friends only. Begin the message right after the exclamation point. Drop the comma if you're not worried about punctuation rules, as I explain in the preceding bullet point.
>
> **Lola,** Informal messages need nothing more than the name. The message begins on the following line.
>
> **Ms. Snodgrass,** This greeting can be a bit stern, as if you couldn't be bothered with the *Dear*. Start the message one line below this greeting.
>
> **Hi, Everyone.** or **Hi, Everyone!** Use these when you write to a group of friends or colleagues. Begin the message on the same line.

The body

The body contains what you want to communicate — words, links to websites, photos or videos, whatever. If you're a traditionalist, your emails probably mimic paper, mailed-in-envelopes letters. I should probably say, "try to mimic" because what you see when you're typing isn't necessarily what the reader sees on his or her screen. Some email programs automatically delete spaces between paragraphs when they zap the message to wherever it's going. Plus, different operating systems don't always play nicely together, though this problem is decreasing. A quotation mark may show up as a strange symbol (@ or a box, perhaps), and margins may wander in and out. Sigh. If you really care about how the document looks, you can attach the message as a text file. That last maneuver isn't perfect because not every bit of formatting may come through properly. But most of your document will probably look the way you want it to. The only surefire method to preserve formatting is to send your message as a Portable Document Format (.pdf) file, which is a "picture" of your document.

Regardless of method, follow the grammar rules outlined in the rest of *English Grammar For Dummies*, matching your level of formality to the identity of the person you're writing to. (See "Choosing formal or informal language" in this chapter for more information.)

The closing

If you haven't bothered with a greeting (which I explain earlier in this section), don't worry about a closing either, unless you want to "sign" your name at the end of the message. If you like a big send-off, try one of these:

> **Best,** (short for "best regards" and good for formal and informal emails)
>
> **Sincerely,** (formal)
>
> **See you soon,** (informal)
>
> **Hope to hear from you,** (somewhere between formal and informal)
>
> **Regards,** (formal and a little old-fashioned)

TIP

All the preceding closings contain commas. You can also close your message simply by typing your name (*Lola* or *Ms. Snodgrass*) or with your initials (*LS* for "Lola Snodgrass"), in which case no commas are needed.

Handling Grammar on the Internet

Is your passion peanut butter and marshmallow sandwiches? Films of the 1990s? Astrophysics? If something revs you up, chances are you're blogging or posting something about it on Facebook or another social-networking site. As you explain to your readers the merits of chunky versus smooth or the symbolism of Indiana Jones' hat or the significance of dark matter, should you worry about grammar? Yes! And no, too. Confused? Read on.

Blogging for fun and (sometimes) profit

Do you follow any blogs as you surf the internet? For those who don't, let me explain that a *blog* is a series of posts on a single subject — any subject. My own blog, for example, is www.grammarianinthecity.com. I post signs that I find on my walks around New York City and make snarky comments about the grammar or language I see there. Generally, blogs allow readers to post comments (I do), so each post becomes an extended conversation.

Some blogs are just for fun, and some become money-makers. A few years ago, Julie Powell turned her blog about cooking her way through Julia Child's *Mastering the Art of French Cooking* into a book and then a movie, *Julie and Julia.* Even if you aren't aiming for these achievements in your blog, you should pay attention to structure, tone — and yes, grammar. Depending on your intended audience, you may want to choose either conversational or formal English. I like to pretend I'm chatting with my friends when I post, so I opt for conversational English. Someone posting on a professional website may wish to follow every grammar rule ever invented.

Of course, lots of bloggers are perfectly comfortable typing "cuz" instead of "because." Some bloggers avoid proper grammar as if it were a contagious disease, and their readers may not mind at all. In fact, they may see Standard English as rigid and inauthentic. So the most important question is the identity of the readers. Who are they, and what impression do you want to make on them? Do you want them to see you as friends sitting in the living room with shoes off and feet up? Break a few grammar rules, and you're there. Do you want readers to accept your authority — to see you as someone who truly understands the care and feeding of boa constrictors or the impact of your transportation method on the environment? Then you should probably put on your game face and pull out your best grammar.

TIP

Comments on blog posts can garner a lot of attention, too, because it's easy to repost a comment or share it on many other websites. If you're commenting, match the level of formality of your writing to what you see in the original posts or other comments that you respect and enjoy. Also think about how your readers will react — not just to what you say but also to how you say it.

Blogs are as varied as the people who create them. Some blogs place a title on each entry (see Chapter 15 for help with capitalizing titles), and some don't bother. Whatever level of grammar you choose, remember that communication is a two-way street. You've got readers, not mind readers. Be sure that your intended audience can decode your message.

Navigating social networks

Facebook, Twitter, Instagram, and other social networking sites allow you to interact with 349,450 (or any number) of your closest friends and to connect with members who have similar interests. Each social networking site is a little different from the others, but all generally include a "profile," in which you cover basic biographical information, post fake photos — okay, sometimes they're real — and indicate your areas of interest. You can update your profile as often as you want, and you may share and comment on others' posts as well, link your profile to a blog or another page on the site, start an action campaign, invite a friend to join you at an event, and do many other things that connect you to other people. (That's why they're called "social networks.")

Social networks used to be, well, purely social. Thus the language in them reflected the writer at his or her most casual. (Pause for a grammatical shudder.) Because they've become so popular, companies, politicians, and celebrities now use social networks to get their messages out to a wide range of people. Writing to strangers — and writing to sell — usually raises the level of formality. Proper grammar may not take a starring role, but it's not completely absent.

As with all writing, think about your audience, your message, and yourself. How do you want readers to see you? Too cool for school? Smart enough to be a professor? When you know the context, you can decide how correct you need to be.

TIP

This is life, not grammar, but I can't resist telling you that social networks can be dangerous places. I'm not talking about crazy stalkers (though they do exist); I'm talking about the fact that teachers, potential employers, and date-worthy acquaintances may look at your profile unless you've limited access to it. If you've blogged about hacking into a teacher's email, going to work with an epic hangover, or insulting an ex-friend, you may not get the recommendation, the job, or the date you're hoping for. Plus, even when you take an ill-considered post down, it still exists somewhere in the internet archive. Repeat after me: The internet is forever. When you're online, be careful!

PowerPoint to the People

When you have to present information to business colleagues or classmates, you may be a bit nervous. In the old days, you'd probably work from index cards and illustrations printed on actual pieces of paper. (That's one reason why the "good old days" weren't always good, by the way.) Now you've got presentation software to help you organize and illustrate your ideas and research. PowerPoint, Prezi, Keynote, and similar computer programs give you the ability to create a series of slides containing text and visuals — charts, graphs, diagrams, photos and the like. The information is organized and accessible. All you have to do is speak a little about each slide as it flashes in front of the audience. Oh, and follow some simple grammar rules. (You knew there was a catch, right?) In this section, I tell you everything you need to know about proper presentation slides.

TIP

If you're not making an oral presentation, you may still find useful material in this section. The format for bullet points remains the same whether those points are on a ten-foot screen or a standard sheet of paper. Check out "Biting the bulleted list" in this section for more information.

Writing titles

Your presentation should have a title, and so may individual slides: *The Care and Feeding of Fleas*, *Foods That Fleas Fear*, *Nesting Material*, and so on. Guidelines for presentation titles include the following:

>> **Place the title alone on a slide or on a line.** The title needs to stand out. When you're typing a standard paragraph, the title may be italicized or placed in quotation marks. On a presentation slide, however, neither italics nor quotation marks are needed. Why? Because the title's position calls attention to it, so you don't need anything else, in terms of grammar, at least. (Check out Chapter 12 for title-punctuation guidelines.) If you want the title to fade in, fade out, swirl around, or dance to the latest techno song, go ahead. The laws of taste are not mine to make. Just be sure that your message isn't lost in a sea of special effects.

>> **Generally, don't place punctuation at the end of a title.** If the title is a complete sentence, it's probably too long. Cut it down! For example, you can change

> Fleas crave many types of food.

to

> Foods Fleas Crave

>> **If the title is a question, you need a question mark.** Continuing the example from the previous bullet point, you may write,

> What Foods Do Fleas Crave?

>> **Follow the standard capitalization rules for titles.** Headline style, in which the important words are capitalized and unimportant words are in lowercase, is best for general-interest and business material. Sentence style, which capitalizes only the first word of the title and subtitle and any proper names, is the one you want for scientific material. I explain both systems in detail in Chapter 15.

TIP

With your sharp eyes, you probably noticed that the title of some sections (including this one) don't follow the rules of capitalization I set forth in Chapter 15. *For Dummies* style calls for standard caps for chapter and section titles but a variation for subsections — capital letters for the first word only. If your presentation has subsections, you can differentiate larger and smaller units in the same way.

Biting the bulleted list

Bullets are an important punctuation mark. Their job is to introduce each item in a list. The bullets in *For Dummies* books are little arrows, but other publishers and writers favor dark circles, little stars, arrows, and similar symbols. A bulleted list has two parts — the introduction and the bullet texts.

Bullet introductions

If the introduction to your bullet list is a complete thought, end it with a colon, as in these sample introductions:

Fleas divert themselves with many exercises:

Fleas' favorite pastimes are varied:

If the introduction to a bullet list is not a complete thought, don't place any punctuation mark at the end of the introduction. Check out these examples:

Fleas love to play with

Fleas' pet peeves are

WARNING

If the introduction line ends with a linking verb as in the second example above, no punctuation follows the verb. See Chapter 2 for more information on linking verbs.

These guidelines make sense. If the introduction is not a complete sentence, the bullets finish the thought. So why would you interrupt with a period? If the introduction is a sentence, the colon indicates that more information is coming. (Turn to Chapter 14 for more about colons.)

If the introduction line begins a series of quotations, place a comma at the end, as in these examples,

Simon Flea always says,

The flea trainer explains,

TIP

In *English Grammar For Dummies*, and all *For Dummies* books, bulleted lists are introduced and punctuated properly. Keep your eyes open to see the rules in action.

Bullet texts

The text for each bullet point is usually fairly short — sometimes just one or two words, and sometimes a bit more. Follow these guidelines in writing bullet points:

>> If the text is a complete sentence, begin with a capital letter and end with a period. Of course, if the sentence is a question, end with a question mark. You may also end a bullet statement with an exclamation point, but in a business or academic setting, this punctuation may be too casual.

>> If the text isn't a complete sentence, don't use any endmarks. You may capitalize the first word of each bullet point, but most people prefer lower case, especially if the introduction line isn't a complete sentence. Whatever style you choose, be consistent. Don't leave half of your bullet points capitalized and half lowercased.

>> Each bullet point on a slide or in a list should have the same grammatical identity. If the first bullet point is a complete sentence, all the bullet points should be complete sentences. If you've begun one bullet point with a noun, begin all of them with nouns. Here's a "before and after" bullet list, illustrating a common mistake and its correction:

INCORRECT

o table tennis

o playing air guitar

o to swing from a trapeze

CORRECT

o table tennis

o air guitar

o trapeze swinging

This grammatical principle is called *parallelism.* (For more information on parallelism, check out Chapter 20.)

WARNING

Many presentations, especially in the academic world, require a slide listing sources (books, websites, articles, films, and so forth). Sources are formatted differently from just about everything else on the planet. I explain all the rules in *Research Papers For Dummies* (Wiley, 2002) and *Punctuation: Simplified and Applied* (Webster's New World, 2005). If you don't want to beautify my royalty statement, feel free to check out any of the many websites devoted to source citation, including www.mla.org and www.apa.org.

4

Polishing Without Wax: The Finer Points of Grammar and Style

Find out how to strengthen verbs, the heart of every sentence.

Work on choosing specific, interesting verbs and delve into the complexity of verb mood and voice.

Discover the advantages of varied sentence patterns that create more interesting, mature sentences.

Learn how to make your sentence elements parallel.

Examine how small elements of writing — the placement of descriptions or the selection of pronouns, for example — can muddy your meaning or make it crystal clear.

Conquer grammar demons: misunderstood or frequently confused words and improper usage.

Chapter **17**

Fine-Tuning Verbs

D o verbs hit a traffic jam when they're taking a trip off your tongue (or your pen or keyboard)? Are you constantly editing yourself to avoid verb problems? In Chapter 6, I cover the basics of choosing the correct verb in easy situations. Here I hit the hard stuff — verb decisions that puzzle most people. To fine-tune your verb skills, read on.

Giving Voice to Verbs

Verbs can have two voices. No, not the growl you hear in questions like "What do you think you're doing, young lady?" or the honey that flows through romantic exchanges like "You're beautiful!" A verb's voice can be either *active* or *passive*. Take a look at these two examples:

> "The window *was broken* yesterday," reported Ben, quietly slipping his baseball bat under the sofa.

> "I *broke* the window yesterday," reported Ben, regretfully handing his baseball bat to his mother.

How do the two versions differ? Grammatically, Ben's statement in the first sentence focuses on the receiver of the action, the *window*, which received the action of *breaking*. The verb is *passive* because the subject is not the person or thing doing the action. Instead, it's the person or thing receiving the action. In sentence two, the verb is in active voice because the subject (*I*) performed the action (*broke*). When the subject is acting or being, the verb is *active*.

To find the subject of a sentence, locate the verb and ask *who?* or *what?* before the verb. For more information on subjects, see Chapter 3.

Here are some active and passive verbs:

> Lulu *gives* a free-tattoo coupon to Lola. (active)
>
> Lola *is convinced* by Lulu to get a tattoo. (passive)
>
> Roger *urges* Lulu to visit the tattoo parlor too. (active)
>
> Lulu *is tattooed* by Lola. (passive)

Label the verbs in these sentences as active or passive.

A. The omelet was made with egg whites, and the yolks were discarded.

B. Egbert slobbers when he eats.

Answer: Sentence A is passive (*was made, were discarded*), and sentence B is active (*slobbers, eats*).

Try one more. Which is active and which is passive?

A. The nail was hammered into that sign by Roger.

B. Roger is building a tank for his pet lizards.

Answer: Sentence A is passive (*was hammered*), and sentence B is active (*is building*).

Actively Seeking a Better Voice

Unless you're trying to hide something, or unless you truly don't know the facts, you should make your writing as specific as possible. Specifics reside in active voice. Compare these pairs of sentences:

> The president of the Omelet-Lovers' Club *was murdered* yesterday. (The cops are still looking for the villain who picked up the hammer and crushed the president's skull like an eggshell.)

Sir Francis Bacon murdered the president of the Omelet-Lovers' Club yesterday. (Bacon will soon move into a maximum-security cell.)

It *is recommended* that the furnace not be cleaned until next year. (Someone wants to save money, but no one is taking responsibility for this action. If the furnace breaks when the thermometer hits 20 below because too much glop is inside, no one's name comes up for blame.)

The superintendent *recommends* that the furnace not be cleaned until next year. (Now the building's residents may threaten the superintendent every time the furnace breaks.)

Do you notice how these active-verb sentences provide extra information? In the first pair of example sentences, the reader or listener knows the name of the murderer. In the second pair, the reader or listener knows who recommends postponing maintenance of the furnace. Knowing (in life as well as in grammar) is usually better than not knowing, and active voice — which generally provides more facts — is usually better than passive voice.

Active voice is also better than passive because active voice tends to use fewer words to say the same thing. Compare the following sentences:

Lulu was failed by the teacher because the grammar book was torn up by Lulu before it was ever opened. (20 words)

The teacher failed Lulu because Lulu tore up the grammar book before opening it. (14 words)

Okay, six words don't make the difference between a 900-page novel and a 3-page story, but those words do add up. If you're writing a letter or an essay, switching from passive to active voice may save you one-third of your words — and therefore one-third of the reader's energy and patience.

WARNING

Right about now you may be remembering a past homework assignment: the teacher asked for 500 words on *Hamlet* and you had only one teeny idea about the play. You may have thought that padding was a good idea! Wrong. Your teacher (or boss) can see that you've buried only one teeny idea in those piles of paragraphs. Besides losing points for knowing too little, you're likely to lose points for wasting the reader's time. The solution? Write in active voice and don't pad your writing.

TEST ALERT

Some questions on the SAT and ACT ask you to "revise" a sentence by choosing the best of four possible versions. Fairly often, the correct answer changes the passive verb of the original to active voice.

Having pointed out all the good aspects of active voice, I am honor-bound to point out that many fine writers opt for passive verbs and still manage to produce artistic and grammatically correct sentences. Both active and passive verbs can work for you. Just be aware of the effect on your writing and go with the one that suits what you're trying to say.

Which sentence works better?

A. The omelet was made with whipped egg whites and chopped ham, but the yolks were discarded.

B. Egbert made an omelet of whipped egg whites and chopped ham but discarded the yolks.

Answer: Sentence B, which employs active voice (*made, discarded*) is preferable to Sentence A, which has passive verbs (*was made, were discarded*). Not only is Sentence B one word shorter, but it also provides more information (the name of the cook).

Try another: Choose the better sentence.

A. The Omelet Contest was run so poorly that some entries were labeled "dangerous" by the health officer.

B. Sal Monella ran the Omelet Contest so poorly that the health officer labeled some entries "dangerous."

Answer: Sentence B wins! Its active verb (*ran*) creates a stronger sentence than the passive verb (*was run*) of Sentence A. Also, Sentence B supplies the name of the contest official who forgot to refrigerate the cooking supplies.

Getting Your Verbs in the Proper Mood

Are you in the *mood* for more information about verbs? Or, to reword the question, what mood is your verb in? I can imagine your reaction: What? Verbs have moods? Aren't *tense* (see Chapter 6) and *voice* (discussed in the preceding section) enough? Let me react to your imagined reaction: Yes, verbs have moods — three, to be exact. You probably don't have to worry about two of those moods, the *indicative* and the *imperative,* because most likely you use them correctly already. It's the third — the *subjunctive* — that causes problems. In this section, I run through the easy moods and then spend more time on the difficult one.

Stating the facts: Indicative

Almost all verbs are in indicative mood. *Indicative* is the everyday, this-is-what-I'm-saying mood, good for questions and statements. The verbs in the two sentences you just read, along with the verbs in the sentence you're reading right now, are in the indicative mood.

Think of indicative verbs as the permanent cast of a TV show. They are always around and are familiar to everyone.

The indicative verbs are italicized in the following sentences:

> Betsy *displayed* her musical range when she *played* a Bach concerto and a hip-hop song in the same concert.

> Larry *will be* the principal tenant of the honeymoon hotel as soon as Ella *agrees* to marry him.

> Egbert often *dreams* about his family farm.

Commanding your attention: Imperative

Don't worry about imperatives. Just use them! The verbs in the first two sentences of this section are in the imperative mood. *Imperative verbs* give commands. Most imperative verbs don't have a written (or spoken) subject. Instead, the subject in an imperative (command) sentence is *you-understood*. The word *you* usually does not appear before the imperative verb. The reader or listener simply understands that *you* is implied.

Here's a command: Read these examples of imperative verbs, italicized in the following sentences:

> *Eat* a balanced diet.

> *Climb* every mountain.

> *Calculate* the odds.

> No matter what happens, *hit* the road.

> *Fake* a sincere smile to impress the voters.

Think of imperative verbs as recurring guest stars on a sitcom, the characters who show up every three or four episodes just to add a little flavor to the mix.

There's almost nothing you can do wrong in creating an imperative sentence, so this topic is a free pass. *Go* fishing, or if you're in the mood to torture yourself, *move* on to the subjunctive. (The italicized verbs are in the imperative mood.)

Discovering the possibilities: Subjunctive

Headache time! The subjunctive mood is rare, but it draws errors the way honey attracts flies. The most common use of a subjunctive verb — and an error-magnet — is to state something that is contrary to fact.

Subjunctive verbs make only a few cameo appearances. Like a pampered super-star, a subjunctive shows up only when the situation is exactly right.

Using subjunctives with "were"

Tevye, the main character in the musical *Fiddler on the Roof,* sings "If I Were a Rich Man" with the sadness of a man who knows that he'll never be anything but poor. Tevye's song is about a *condition contrary to fact* — something that is not true. Take note of the verb in the title: *were.* Normally (that is to say, in an indicative sentence) the subject–verb pair would be *I was.* But Tevye sings *If I were* because he isn't a rich man. The verb *were* is in subjunctive mood.

Unless someone is going to quiz you on it, don't worry about the terminology. Just know that if you're expressing a condition contrary to fact, you need the verb *were* for present and future ideas. (Past tense is different. I discuss the past subjunctive form in "Forming subjunctives with 'had'" later in this section.) Here are some examples of present and future tense:

SUBJUNCTIVE: If Roger *were* an honorable spy, he would not reveal the secret computer code.

WHY IT'S SUBJUNCTIVE: Roger is not an honorable spy, and he's going to blab the secret.

WHAT THE NORMAL SUBJECT–VERB PAIR WOULD BE: Roger was.

SUBJUNCTIVE: If Anna *were* less talented in mathematics, she would have taken fewer algebra courses.

WHY IT'S SUBJUNCTIVE: Anna's a math genius, the kind of student who always says that the test was "totally hard" and then wrecks the curve with a 96.

WHAT THE NORMAL SUBJECT–VERB PAIR WOULD BE: Anna was.

To sum up, in subjunctive sentences, *were* is usually all you need. Here are a few details about subjunctive for present or future statements of conditions contrary to fact:

>> Use *were* for all subjects in the part of the sentence that expresses what is not true. (If she *were* entranced by Max's explanation.)

>> For the other part of the sentence, use the helping verb *would*. (Lola *would stare* at him in silence.)

>> Never use the helping verb *would* in the untrue part of the sentence. For example:

> WRONG: If I would have been president, I would ask the Martian colony to secede.

> RIGHT: If I were president, I would ask the Martian colony to secede.

> WRONG: Daniel acted as though he would have been grammarian-in-chief.

> RIGHT: Daniel acted as though he were grammarian-in-chief.

POP QUIZ

Which sentence is correct?

A. Ella would be happier if she would have been in the Marines.

B. Ella would be happier if she were in the Marines.

Answer: Sentence B is correct. The *if* part of the sentence contains a subjunctive verb *(were)* because it expresses something that is not true. The *if* part of the sentence should never contain the helping verb *would*.

TIP

As though may sometimes sub for *if* in a condition-contrary-to-fact sentence. Check out the following:

> SUBJUNCTIVE: Egbert hurtled through the hall *as though* a giant metal device were intent on scrambling him.

> WHY IT'S SUBJUNCTIVE: Egbert is not being pursued by giant egg-beaters. He is actually hurtling through the hall because he is on a skateboard with one bad wheel.

> WHAT THE NORMAL SUBJECT–VERB PAIR WOULD BE: Giant metal device was.

Forming subjunctives with "had"

Subjunctives also pop up from time to time with the helping verb *had.* For past tense sentences, the *had* belongs in the part of the sentence that is contrary to fact. The contrary-to-fact (that is, the lie) part of the sentence may begin with *if,* or the *if* may be understood.

Just for comparison, in non-subjunctive sentences, the past tense is expressed by a single-word, past tense verb. The *had* form, in a non-subjunctive sentence, is used only to show one action happening before another. (See Chapter 6 for more information.) Here are a few examples of the past subjunctive:

SUBJUNCTIVE WITH THE WORD *IF:* If Lola *had known* about the secret computer code, she would not have thrown the flash drive away.

SUBJUNCTIVE WITHOUT THE WORD *IF: Had* Lola *known* about the secret computer code, she would not have thrown the flash drive away.

WHY IT'S SUBJUNCTIVE: Lola knew nothing about the secret code; Roger told her he was working on a new video game.

WHAT THE NORMAL SUBJECT–VERB PAIR WOULD BE: Lola knew.

SUBJUNCTIVE WITH THE WORD *IF:* If Larry *had married* less often, he would have enjoyed this ceremony more.

SUBJUNCTIVE WITHOUT THE WORD *IF: Had* Larry *married* less often, he would have enjoyed this ceremony more.

WHY IT'S SUBJUNCTIVE: Larry has been married more times than he can count.

WHAT THE NORMAL SUBJECT–VERB PAIR WOULD BE: Larry married.

POP QUIZ

Which sentence is correct?

A. If Betsy would have played the tuba, the gang would have listened to her CD more often.

B. If Betsy had played the tuba, the gang would have listened to her CD more often.

Answer: Sentence B is correct. Betsy played the piano, not the tuba, so subjunctive is appropriate. The word *would* is never part of an *if* statement.

Adding Meaning with Strong Verbs

Though *English Grammar For Dummies* focuses on grammar, I can't resist throwing in a few hints about style. You can get a lot of mileage out of strong verbs — those that add meaning and detail to your sentence. You can also water down your writing with blah, weak verbs. In this section, I show you how to select verbs that can bench-press with the best.

"There is" a problem with boring verbs

In my writing class, I always ask the students to describe a standard school chair. Inevitably, I read sentences like these:

> There is a curved seat.
>
> There are five slats on the back.
>
> There is a school identification mark on the bottom of the chair.

Nothing's wrong with these sentences. They're all grammatically correct, and they're all accurate. But I bet they made you yawn. *There is* and *there are*, as well as their cousins — *there was, there will be, there has been*, and others — are standard (and therefore boring) expressions. How about swapping them for something stronger? Here you go:

> The seat curves to fit your bottom.
>
> Five slats support your back.
>
> The school stamps an identification mark on the bottom of each chair.

Don't you think the second set of sentences is more interesting? You get more information, and the verbs — *curves, support,* and *stamps* — catch the reader's eye.

TEST ALERT

In a writing sample for the SAT or other standardized test, graders watch for sophisticated usage. They want to see that you can manipulate language. *There is/ are* sentences aren't very sophisticated, though they can sometimes be useful. When you find yourself constructing a sentence this way, pause. Can you come up with a more interesting verb?

Does your writing "have" a problem?

If they're overused, forms of the verb *to have* can also put your reader to sleep faster than a sedative. (The Grammarians Code obliges me to point out that *to have* is an infinitive — the grandpappy that gives its name to a verb family but never functions as a verb in a sentence. Chapter 19 tells you more than you ever wanted to know about how infinitives *do* function in a sentence.) Now, back to verb choices. Sometimes nothing works better than *to have,* and of course you need some forms of this verb to indicate tense — the time of the action or state of being. (To learn about verb tense, read Chapter 6.) But too often *has, had,* or *have* ends up in a sentence because the writer is too tired to think of something more creative. Try changing

> The chair has a shiny surface.
>
> The slats have rounded edges as big as my finger.

to

> The chair shone under the fluorescent light.
>
> The rounded edges fit my finger perfectly.

Okay, I added some information to the second set, but you see my point. *Shone* and *fit* are more interesting than *has* and *have.* Plus, after you plop in a good verb, other ideas follow, and the whole sentence improves.

Don't just "say" and "walk" away

To say and *to walk* are fine, upstanding members of the verb community, but they don't give you much information. Why *say* when you can *declare, scream, whisper, hint, bellow, assert, remark* or do any one of the zillions of alternatives available to you when you're describing communication? For movement, consider *stroll, saunter, plod, strut, rush, speed, zig-zag,* and — well, you get the point by now. Look for verbs that go beyond the basics, that add shades of meaning to your sentence. Here are some before-and-after sentence sets to illustrate how more specific verbs pep up your sentences:

> BEFORE: Heidi said she was tired of climbing mountains.
>
> AFTER: Heidi contended that she was tired of climbing mountains. (Now you know that she's speaking with someone who may not believe her.)
>
> ANOTHER AFTER: Heidi murmured that she was tired of climbing mountains. (Here Heidi's a bit shy or perhaps fearful.)
>
> ONE MORE AFTER: Heidi roared that she was tired of climbing mountains. (In this sentence, no one is going to mess with Heidi — not without a struggle!)

BEFORE: Heidi's hiking partner walked away from her.

AFTER: Heidi's hiking partner edged away from her. (The partner knows that Heidi's in one of her moods and trouble is on the way.)

ALSO AFTER: Heidi's hiking partner stomped away from her. (Now the partner is angry.)

THE LAST AFTER: Heidi's hiking partner wandered away from her. (The partner isn't paying attention.)

TIP

Your word-processing program probably has a built-in *thesaurus* — a reference app that lists synonyms for most verbs. You can also buy a thesaurus in book form. If you're looking over your writing and need some spicier verbs, a thesaurus can suggest some alternatives. Be cautious: Verbs, like all words, may be similar but not exactly the same. The list for *stroll* includes *ramble* and *promenade*. You may *ramble* (or *amble*, another verb on this list) without a fixed destination or purpose. If you *promenade*, you're probably also in recreational mode, but this time you have an audience. Bottom line: Don't insert a verb or any other verb into your sentence unless you're sure you know what it means.

Chapter **18**

No Santas but Plenty of Clauses

S ay I give you a new car. What do you do? Open the hood and check the engine, or hop in and drive away? The engine-checkers and the drive-awayers are sub-groups of car owners. The engine-checkers have to know what's going on inside the machine. The other group doesn't care about fuel injection and spark plugs. They just want the car to run.

You can also divide speakers of English into two groups. Some people want to understand what's going on inside the sentence, but most just want to communicate. In this chapter, I provide some information for each — the lift-up-the-hood-of-the-sentence group and the drive-English-to-where-I-need-to-go clan. The first part of this chapter digs into the structure of the sentence, defining clauses. Then I show you how manipulating clauses can change the meaning and effect of a sentence.

Understanding the Basics of Clause and Effect

No matter what food you put between two pieces of bread, you've got a sandwich. That's the definition of *sandwich*: bread plus filling. Clauses have a simple definition, too: subject plus verb. Any subject-verb combination creates a clause. The reverse is also true: no subject or no verb = no clause. You can throw in some extras (descriptions, lettuce, tomato . . . whatever), but the basic subject-verb combination is key. Some sentences have one clause, in which case the whole sentence is the clause, and some have more than one.

TIP

Be sure to check your sentences for completeness. In formal English, each sentence should contain at least one complete thought, expressed in a way that can stand alone. In grammarspeak, each sentence must contain at least one independent clause. (Check out "Getting the goods on subordinate and independent clauses" later in this chapter. For more information on complete sentences, see Chapter 4.)

Here are a few examples of one-clause sentences:

Has Sherlock cracked the Case of the Missing Chicken? (subject = *Sherlock*, verb = *has cracked*)

Lulu crossed the Alps on foot in the dead of winter. (subject = *Lulu*, verb = *crossed*)

Sid and his parents have reached an agreement about his chores. (subjects = *Sid and his parents*, verb = *have reached*)

Al swam for 15 minutes and rowed for an hour before nightfall. (subject = *Al*, verbs = *swam, rowed*)

Notice that some of the clauses have two subjects and some have two verbs, but each expresses one main idea. Here are a few examples of sentences with more than one clause:

SENTENCE: Michael struggled out from under the blankets, and then he dashed after the enemy agent.

CLAUSE 1: Michael struggled out from under the blankets (subject = *Michael*, verb = *struggled*)

CLAUSE 2: then he dashed after the enemy agent (subject = *he*, verb = *dashed*)

SENTENCE: After Cedric had developed the secret microfilm, Barbara sent it to whatever federal agency catches spies.

CLAUSE 1: After Cedric had developed the secret microfilm (subject = *Cedric*, verb = *had developed*)

CLAUSE 2: Barbara sent it to whatever federal agency catches spies (subject = *Barbara*, verb = *sent*)

CLAUSE 3: whatever federal agency catches spies (subject = *agency*, verb = *catches*)

With your sharp eyes, I'm sure you noticed something odd about the last example. Clause #3 is actually part of clause #2. It's not a misprint. Sometimes one clause is entangled in another. (This topic is deep in the pathless forests of grammar! Get out now, while you still can!)

Here's one more example that's really complicated:

> SENTENCE: Whoever ate the secret microfilm is in big trouble.
>
> CLAUSE #1: Whoever ate the secret microfilm (subject = *whoever,* verb = *ate*)
>
> CLAUSE #2: Whoever ate the secret microfilm is in big trouble. (subject = *whoever ate the secret microfilm,* verb = *is*)

Yes, one clause is the subject of another clause. Good grief! What a system. For those who truly love grammar: The subject clause is a noun clause. See "Knowing the three legal jobs for subordinate clauses" later in this chapter for more information.

How many clauses can you find in this sentence?

> The car that Eugene normally drives broke when he accidentally dropped his phone into the motor.

Answer: Three clauses are tucked into this sentence. Did you find them all? Clause #1 = The car broke. Clause #2 = that Eugene normally drives. Clause #3 = when he accidentally dropped his phone into the motor.

Getting the goods on subordinate and independent clauses

Some clauses are like mature grown-ups. They have their own house or apartment, pay their own expenses, and wash the dishes frequently enough to ward off a visit from the health inspector. These clauses have made a success of life; they're *independent.*

Other clauses are like the brother-in-law character in a million jokes. They still live at home, or they crash on someone's couch. They're always mooching a free meal, and they never visit a Parental Unit without a bag of dirty laundry. These clauses are not mature; they can't support themselves. They're *dependent.* These clauses may be called *dependent clauses* or *subordinate clauses.* (The terms are interchangeable.)

Following are two sets of clauses. Both have subject-verb pairs, but the first set makes sense alone and the second doesn't. The first set consists of independent clauses, and the second of subordinate clauses.

Independent clauses:

> Elena blasted Bobby with a radar gun.
>
> Bobby was going 50 m.p.h.
>
> The cougar could not keep up.
>
> Did Bobby award the trophy?

Subordinate clauses:

> After she had complained to the race officials
>
> Because Bobby had installed an illegal motor on his skateboard
>
> Which Tom bought from an overcrowded zoo
>
> Whoever ran the fastest

Independent clauses are okay by themselves, but writing too many in a row makes your paragraph choppy and monotonous. Subordinate clauses, however, are not okay by themselves because they don't make sense alone. To become complete, they have to tack themselves onto independent clauses. Subordinate clauses add life and interest to the sentence (just as the guy crashing on your couch adds a little zip to the household). But don't leave them alone, because disaster will strike. A subordinate clause all by itself is a grammatical felony — a sentence fragment.

TEST ALERT

Standardized test-makers are hooked on complete sentences. Steer clear of fragments and run-ons (see Chapter 4 for more information) when you're taking one of these exams.

TIP

The best sentences combine different elements in all sorts of patterns. (See Chapter 19 for more on this topic.) In the following example, I join the independent clauses and subordinate clauses to create longer, more interesting sentences:

> After she had complained to the race officials, Elena blasted Bobby with a radar gun.
>
> Because Bobby had installed an illegal motor on his skateboard, he was going 50 m.p.h.
>
> The cougar, which Tom bought from an overcrowded zoo, could not keep up.
>
> Did Bobby award the trophy to whoever ran the fastest?

Combine the ideas in each of these sets into one sentence.

Set A:

> Betsy screamed at the piano mover.
>
> The mover dropped the piano on the delicate foot of the violinist.

Set B:

> Anna solved a quadratic equation.
>
> The equation had been troubling the math major.

Set C:

> Michael gave special trophies.
>
> Some people wanted those trophies.
>
> Those people got the trophies.

Answer: Several combinations are possible. Here are three:

A. Betsy screamed at the piano mover who dropped the piano on the delicate foot of the violinist.

B. Anna solved a quadratic equation that had been troubling the math major.

C. Michael gave special trophies to whoever wanted them.

Knowing the three legal jobs for subordinate clauses

Okay, subordinate clauses can't stand alone. What can they do? They have three main purposes in life, as you see in the following sections.

Describing nouns and pronouns

Yup, subordinate clauses can describe nouns and pronouns. That is, the subordinate clause may give your listener or reader more information about a noun or pronoun in the sentence. Here are some examples, with the subordinate clause in italic:

> The book *that Michael wrote* is on the best seller list. *(that Michael wrote* describes the noun *book)*

Anyone *who knows Michael well* will read the book. *(who knows Michael well describes the pronoun anyone)*

The book includes some information *that will prove embarrassing to Michael's friends.* *(that will prove embarrassing to Michael's friends describes the noun information)*

You don't need to know this fact, so skip to the next paragraph. Still here? Okay then. Subordinate clauses that describe nouns or pronouns are called *adjectival clauses* or *adjective clauses.* Happy now?

Describing verbs, adjectives, or adverbs

Subordinate clauses can also describe verbs, adjectives, or adverbs. The subordinate clauses tell you *how, when, where,* or *why.* Some examples, with the subordinate clause in italic, are as follows:

Because Michael censored himself, the book contains nothing about the wire tap. *(Because Michael censored himself describes the verb contains)*

We will probably find out more *when the movie version is released.* *(when the movie version is released describes the verb will find)*

The government may prohibit sales of the book *wherever international tensions make it dangerous.* *(wherever international tensions make it dangerous describes the verb may prohibit)*

Michael is so stubborn *that he may sue the government.* *(that he may sue the government describes the adverb so)*

More grammar terminology, in case you're having a very dull day: Subordinate clauses that describe verbs are called *adverbial clauses* or *adverb clauses.* Subordinate clauses that describe adjectives or adverbs (mostly in comparisons) are also *adverbial clauses.* Adverbial clauses do the same job as single-word adverbs. They describe verbs, adjectives, or other adverbs.

Acting as subjects, objects, or subject complements inside another clause

This one is a bit more complicated: Subordinate clauses may do any job that a noun does in a sentence. Subordinate clauses sometimes act as subjects, objects, or subject complements inside another clause. Here are some examples, with the subordinate clause in italics:

When the book was written is a real mystery. *(When the book was written is the subject of the verb is)*

No one knows *whom Michael hired to write his book.* *(whom Michael hired to write his book is the object of the verb knows)*

Michael signed copies for whoever bought at least five books. (*whoever bought at least five books* is the object of the preposition *for*)

The problem is *that your homework is late.* (*that your homework is late* is the subject complement)

Stop now or risk learning more useless grammar terms. Noun *clauses* are subordinate clauses that perform the same functions as nouns — subjects, objects, appositives, and so on.

Check out the italicized clause in each sentence. Subordinate or independent? You decide.

A. *Even though Michael hit a home run,* our team lost by more than 50 runs.

B. *Max danced for a while,* but then he said that his head was splitting and sat down.

Answer: In sentence A, the italicized clause is subordinate. In sentence B, the italicized clause is independent.

Untangling subordinate and independent clauses

You have to untangle one clause from another only occasionally — when deciding which pronoun or verb you need or whether commas are appropriate. (See the next section, "Deciding when to untangle clauses," for more information.) When you do have to untangle them, follow these simple steps:

1. Find the subject-verb pairs.

2. Use your reading comprehension skills to determine whether the subject-verb pairs belong to the same thought or to different thoughts.

3. If the pairs belong to different thoughts, they're probably in different clauses.

4. If the pairs belong to the same thought, they're probably in the same clause.

Another method also relies on reading comprehension skills. Think about the ideas in the sentence and untangle the thoughts. By doing so, you've probably also untangled the clauses.

Check out these examples:

SENTENCE: The acting award that Lola received comes with a hefty check.

SUBJECT–VERB PAIRS: *award comes, Lola received*

UNTANGLED IDEAS: 1.) The award comes with a hefty check 2.) Lola received the award.

CLAUSES: 1.) *The acting award comes with a hefty check.* (Independent clause) 2.) *that Lola received* (subordinate clause)

SENTENCE: When Lulu tattoos clients, they stay tattooed.

SUBJECT–VERB PAIRS: *Lulu tattoos, they stay*

UNTANGLED IDEAS: 1.) Lulu tattoos clients 2.) they stay tattooed

CLAUSES: 1.) *When Lulu tattoos clients* (subordinate clause) 2.) *they stay tattooed* (independent clause)

POP QUIZ

Untangle this sentence into separate clauses.

Lola's last motorcycle, which she bought second-hand, was once Elvis's property.

Answer: Clause #1 is *Lola's last motorcycle was once Elvis's property.* Clause #2 is *which she bought second-hand.*

Try another. Untangle the following sentence.

No one knows when Anna sleeps.

Answer: Clause #1 is *no one knows.* Clause #2 is *when Anna sleeps.*

Deciding when to untangle clauses

Why would you want to untangle clauses? Not just because you have nothing better to do. (If you have that much free time, please stop by to clean out my closets.) You should untangle clauses when you're choosing pronouns, verbs, and punctuation. Read on for the whole story.

When you're picking a pronoun

When you're deciding whether you need a subject or an object pronoun, check the clause that contains the word. Don't worry about what the entire clause is doing in the sentence. Untangle the clause and ignore everything else. Then decide which pronoun you need for that particular clause.

Many of the decisions about pronouns concern *who* and *whom*. (For tricks to help you make the *who/whom* choice, see Chapter 8. For a general discussion of pronoun usage, turn to Chapter 7.)

Here's one untangling example, with the pronoun problem in parentheses:

SENTENCE: Ella wasn't sure (who/whom) would want a used engagement ring.

UNTANGLED INTO CLAUSES: Clause #1: *Ella wasn't sure.* Clause #2: *(who/whom) would want a used engagement ring.*

RELEVANT CLAUSE: *(who/whom) would want a used engagement ring.*

CORRECT PRONOUN: *who* (subject of *would want*)

When you're deciding on the correct verb

When you're deciding subject-verb agreement in one clause, the other clauses are distractions. (By agreement, I mean matching singular subjects with singular verbs and plural subjects with plural verbs.) If you're writing (not speaking), I recommend that you cross out or cover the other clauses with your finger. Check the clause that worries you. Decide the subject-verb agreement issue, and then erase the crossing-out line or remove your hand. (For more information on subject-verb agreement, see Chapter 7.)

Here are two untangling examples, with the verb choices in parentheses:

SENTENCE: Larry, whose brides are always thrilled to marry into the royal family, (needs/need) no introduction.

UNTANGLED INTO CLAUSES: Clause #1= *Larry (needs/need) no introduction.* Clause #2= *whose brides are always thrilled to marry into the royal family.*

RELEVANT CLAUSE: *Larry (needs/need) no introduction.*

CORRECT VERB: *needs* (Larry = singular, *needs* = singular)

SENTENCE: That ring, which Larry recovers after each divorce and reuses for each new engagement, *has/have* received a recycling award.

UNTANGLED INTO CLAUSES: Clause #1 = *That ring has/have received a recycling award.* Clause #2 = *which Larry recovers after each divorce and reuses for each new engagement.*

RELEVANT CLAUSE: *The ring has/have received a recycling award.*

CORRECT VERB: *has* (*ring* = singular, *has* = singular)

When you're figuring out where to put commas

Sometimes you have to untangle clauses in order to decide whether or not you need commas. Go through the same untangling steps that I discuss earlier in the chapter (see "Untangling subordinate and independent clauses") and then flip to Chapter 13 to see how to use commas correctly.

Putting your subordinate clauses in the right place

Finding the correct place to put your subordinate clauses is simple. Clauses acting as subjects or objects nearly always fall in the proper place automatically. Don't worry about them!

Put the subordinate clause that describes a noun or pronoun near the word that it describes. Here are a few examples of proper placement of clauses that describe nouns and pronouns:

> Larry's wedding coordinator, *who planned the last eight ceremonies,* is hiring more staff. (The italicized clause describes the noun *coordinator.*)

> The coordinator took care of every detail; he even baked the cakes *that Larry's guests enjoyed.* (The italicized clause describes the noun *cakes.*)

> Anyone *who is on a diet* should stay away from Larry's weddings. (The italicized clause describes the pronoun *who.*)

If the subordinate clause describes the verb, it may land at the front of the sentence or at the rear. On rare occasions, the clause settles down in the middle of the sentence. Here are some examples:

> *Although Anna understood the equation,* she chose to put a question mark on her answer sheet. (The italicized clause describes the verb *chose.*)

> She wrote the question mark *because she wanted to make a statement about the mysteries of life.* (The italicized clause describes the verb *wrote.*)

> Anna failed the test; but *until her mother found out about the question mark,* Anna was not distressed. (The italicized clause describes the verb *was.*)

For lots more detail on placing all sorts of descriptions in their proper places, see Chapter 21.

TIP

An unbelievably obscure punctuation rule that no normal people follow calls for a semicolon in front of a conjunction — a word that may join two clauses — when a comma appears elsewhere in the sentence. Conjunctions that fall into this category are *and, but, or, nor,* and *for.* (For more information on comma placement, see Chapter 13.) As someone who's never going to be anything but a nerd, I followed that rule in the preceding sample sentence. Because of the comma after *mark,* I placed a semicolon in front of the conjunction *but.* You should know that if you follow this rule, most of your readers will think that you've made an error. However, a few die-hard grammarians will break into tears of gratitude because someone else knows how to use a semicolon correctly. (Excuse me for a moment while I wipe my eyes.)

Choosing content for your subordinate clauses

What to put in a clause depends upon the writer's purpose. Generally, the most important idea belongs in the independent clause. Subordinate clauses are for less crucial information. Check out these examples:

> IMPORTANT IDEA: Godzilla ate my mother.
>
> LESS IMPORTANT IDEA: My mother was wearing a green dress.
>
> GOOD SENTENCE: Godzilla ate my mother, who was wearing a green dress.
>
> NOT-SO-GOOD SENTENCE: My mother was wearing a green dress when Godzilla ate her.

> IMPORTANT IDEA: Aga just won a trillion dollars.
>
> LESS IMPORTANT IDEA: His name means "ancient bettor" in an obscure language.
>
> GOOD SENTENCE: Aga, whose name means "ancient bettor" in an obscure language, just won a trillion dollars.
>
> NOT-SO-GOOD SENTENCE: Aga, who just won a trillion dollars, says that his name means "ancient bettor" in an obscure language.

Of course, some writers stray from this pattern to make a comic point or to emphasize a character trait. Suppose you're writing about someone who, to put it mildly, tends to be self-absorbed. A sentence like the following one emphasizes that trait:

> While the stock price tanked and sales plummeted, the CEO examined his photo on the company website.

The wreck of the company isn't a big deal for this negligent CEO, and its placement in the subordinate clause reinforces that fact.

TIP

Regardless of what you place in a subordinate clause, be sure to connect it to the sentence properly. For more discussion on joining independent and subordinate clauses, see Chapter 4.

POP QUIZ

Combine these ideas into a single sentence containing at least one independent and one subordinate clause.

> IDEA #1: an archaeologist made a major discovery
>
> IDEA #2: she was listening to classic rock on the radio
>
> IDEA #3: the ancient betting parlor was filled with discarded lottery tickets

Answer: Several combinations are possible. Here are two:

> While listening to classic rock on the radio, the archaeologist made a major discovery, an ancient betting parlor filled with discarded lottery tickets.

In this version, the subordinate clause is *While listening to classic rock on the radio.* The independent clause is *the archaeologist made a major discovery, an ancient betting parlor filled with discarded lottery tickets.* This version emphasizes the discovery. The *classic rock* information is interesting but not particularly important.

> As she made a major discovery, an ancient betting parlor filled with discarded lottery tickets, the archaeologist listened to classic rock.

Now the subordinate clause is *As she made a major discovery, an ancient betting parlor filled with discarded lottery tickets.* The independent clause is *the archaeologist listened to classic rock.* Placing the musical information in the independent clauses raises its importance. This version might appear in an essay about the role of music in the workplace, archaeologists' daily routines, or the musical tastes of this particular archaeologist.

Chapter **19**

Spicing Up Sentence Patterns

I f you're a chef, you need to understand spices — small additions that pep up a blah recipe. You can cook without spices (and, judging from some meals I've had lately, you probably do if you work in an airline or school kitchen) but the food won't taste as good. In this chapter I explain *verbals*, some spicy grammatical elements that give a little zing to your writing. I also show you how to use verbals to create more interesting sentences and how to pep up your writing by playing around with sentence patterns.

Getting Verbal

Ah, variety. Wouldn't the world be boring if everyone and everything were the same? Ah, harmony. Isn't it wonderful when different backgrounds join forces to create a new, improved blend?

In grammar, the new, improved blend of two parts of speech is a *verbal.* Verbals are extremely useful hybrids. In this section, I give you the defining characteristics of each of the three types of verbals, and then I show you how to add them to your writing.

Appreciating gerunds

The noun and the verb get married, move into a little house with rosebushes in the yard and an apple pie in the oven. Pretty soon the patter of little syllables appears. The children of this happy marriage are *gerunds.* Gerunds inherit some characteristics from their mother, the verb:

» They end in *-ing* and look like verbs — *swimming, dripping, being, dancing, bribing,* and so on.

» They may be described by words or phrases that usually describe verbs — swimming *swiftly,* dripping *noisily,* being *in the moment,* dancing *to the rhythm of a great new song,* bribing *yesterday,* and so on.

» The type of clause that usually describes verbs may also describe gerunds — swimming *after the race ends,* dripping *when the cap is not tightened,* being *wherever you should be,* dancing *although you are tired,* bribing *whenever you want something.*

» They may have objects or subject complements — swimming *laps,* dripping *drops of glue,* being *president,* dancing *the tango,* bribing *umpires,* and so on.

From their father, the noun, gerunds inherit only two characteristics, but one is a biggie:

» BIGGIE: They act as nouns in the sentence. Therefore, gerunds may be subjects, objects, and anything else that a noun can be.

» NON-BIGGIE: Words that usually describe nouns or pronouns — adjectives — may also describe gerunds — *my* swimming, *noisy* dripping, *illegal* bribing, and so on. (Is there any legal bribing?)

In these examples, I italicized the gerund and all the words associated with it (the *gerund phrase,* in grammarspeak):

Swimming the Atlantic Ocean was not exactly what Ella had in mind when she married Larry. *(swimming the Atlantic Ocean = subject of the verb was)*

Anna, a neat person in every possible way, hates *my dripping ice cream on the rug.* *(my dripping ice cream on the rug = direct object of the verb hates)*

The importance of *being earnest in one's playwriting* cannot be over-emphasized. *(being earnest in one's playwriting = object of the preposition of)*

After *slapping Roger on the nose,* Michael took off at about 100 m.p.h. *(slapping Roger on the nose = object of the preposition after)*

Betsy gave *bribing the umpire* serious consideration when her team lost its 450th game in a row. *(bribing the umpire = indirect object of the verb gave)*

TIP

You often need a possessive pronoun in front of a gerund, if the action expressed by the gerund is what you want to focus on. Here's what I mean:

WRONG: Sheila loves him shopping for just the right present.

WHY IT'S WRONG: In this sentence, the important idea — what Sheila loves, is the attempt to get the perfect gift. The emphasis should be on *shopping,* not on *him.*

RIGHT: Sheila loves his shopping for just the right present.

WHY IT'S RIGHT: The possessive pronoun *his* leads the reader or listener onward to the next idea — the *shopping.* The emphasis is on that activity, not on *him.*

For more information on pronouns and gerunds, turn to Chapter 8.

Working with infinitives

The *infinitive* is another happy child of two different parts of speech. The infinitives' mother is the verb, and from her, infinitives inherit several important characteristics:

» Infinitives look like verbs, with the word *to* tacked on in front — *to dance, to dream, to be, to dally, to prosecute,* and so on.

» Words or phrases that usually describe verbs may also describe infinitives — to dance *divinely,* to dream *daily,* to be *in the kitchen,* to dally *for hours,* to prosecute *ferociously,* and so on.

» Similarly, the type of clause that usually describes verbs may also describe infinitives — to dance *until the cows come home,* to dream *when your heart is breaking,* to be *wherever you want to be,* to dally *even though homework awaits,* to prosecute *because justice demands action,* and so on.

» Infinitives may have objects or subject complements — to dance *a jig,* to dream *an impossible dream,* to be *silly,* to prosecute *Roger* for burglary, and so on.

The infinitive inherits its job in the sentence from the father. Who, you may ask, is the father of the infinitive? Well, the infinitive's mom has a very active social life, and the father may actually be any one of three parts of speech (shocking, isn't it?):

» Most infinitives act as subjects, objects, or subject complements. (Dad is a noun.)

» A few infinitives describe nouns. (Dad is an adjective.)

» A few infinitives describe verbs. (Dad is an adverb.)

Read these examples of infinitives in their natural habitat, the sentence. I italicized the infinitive and the words associated with it (the *infinitive phrase*, in technical terms):

> *To dance on a reality television show* is Lola's lifelong dream. *(to dance on a reality television show = subject of the verb is)*

> During cabinet meetings, Larry likes *to dream with his eyes open*. *(to dream with his eyes open = object of the verb likes)*

> Lulu's lifelong goal is *to be silly* when everyone else is serious. *(to be silly = subject complement of the verb is)*

> The case *to prosecute* is the one about the misplaced fire hose. *(to prosecute describes the noun case)*

> Ella went to that nightclub just *to dally*. *(to dally describes the verb went)*

TIP

Somewhere, sometime, someone came up with the idea that you shouldn't split an infinitive. That is, you shouldn't place any other word between *to* and the verb. This "rule," which many people still follow, may have arisen from the fact that in Latin (a language that has contributed much to English) the infinitive is a single word, which of course can't be split. In English, though, it's fine to insert a word between *to* and the verb:

> Greg tried to gently remove the bandage.

> To frequently wash the windshield is important in this dusty area.

One warning about splits: If you're writing for an authority figure who believes that split infinitives are wrong, you may be scolded for "breaking the rule," despite the fact that the rule doesn't exist. In such a situation, arguing may not help you. Reword the sentence if you can:

> Greg tried to remove the bandage gently.

> Frequent windshield-washing is important in this dusty area.

Participating with a participle

Last but not least of the verbals is the participle. *Participles* are actually parts of verbs (hence the amazingly original name). In some sentences participles act as part of the verb, but in those situations, they're not called verbals. I ignore the acting-as-verb participles here, but if you want more information about them, see Chapter 2. When participles are verbals, they, like gerunds and infinitives, inherit some important traits from their mom the verb:

>> Participles look like verb parts, though they may have several different forms. Some end with *-ing,* some with *-ed,* and some with other letters. Also, they may have helping verbs. *Driven, coping, elevated, having crossed,* and *gone* are a few examples of participles.

>> Words or phrases that usually describe verbs may also describe participles — driven *home,* coping *bravely,* elevated *to the position of Empress,* having crossed *illegally,* gone *with the wind,* and so on.

>> Similarly, the type of clause that usually describes verbs may also describe participles — driven *although he has two perfectly good feet,* coping *bravely when tragedy strikes,* elevated *because he bribed three officials,* having crossed *where no man has crossed before,* gone *after the sun sets,* and so on.

>> Participles may have objects or subject complements — elevated *Ella to the position of Empress,* having crossed *the road,* and so on.

From their father, the adjective, participles take one characteristic: They describe nouns and pronouns.

Participles may appear in several different spots in the sentence:

>> They may precede the noun or pronoun that they describe: *tired* feet (the participle *tired* describes the noun *feet*), *sneezing* toddlers (the participle *sneezing* describes the noun *toddlers*), *burped* baby (the participle *burped* describes the noun *baby*).

>> They may follow a linking verb, in which case they describe the subject. (A linking verb is a form of the verb *to be* or a sensory verb. See Chapter 2 for more information.)

> Ella is *exhausted.* (The participle *exhausted* follows the linking verb *is* and describes *Ella.*)

> Betsy's concerto sounds *enchanting.* (The participle *enchanting* follows the linking verb *sounds* and describes *concerto.*)

>> They may follow the noun or pronoun that they describe. In this position, participles often include descriptive words or objects. The participles and the words associated with them — the *participial phrases* — are italicized here:

> Norman, *having angered the herd of cattle,* is running for the fence at the speed of light. (*Having angered the herd of cattle* describes *Norman.*)

> I want to repeal the new anti-hacking law *passed by the senate.* (*Passed by the senate* describes *law.*)

>> Participles may begin the sentence, in which case they must describe the subject of the sentence:

> *Poked in the tummy,* the doll immediately said, "Watch it, Buster!" *(Poked in the tummy* describes *doll.)*

> *Having been smashed against the picture window,* Lola's nose looked sore. *(Having been smashed against the picture window* describes *nose.)*

REMEMBER

Participles have to appear in the right spot, or the meaning you're trying to express doesn't come across. (For more information on where to place these descriptions, read Chapter 21.) Standardized-test writers often check whether you know where a participle should appear.

Choosing the Correct Tense

Because verbals are partly made up of verbs, they have *tenses,* just as verbs do. In other words, verbals express time. In Chapter 6, I explain everything you need to know about tense as it applies to the verb of a sentence. Here I put verbals on the timeline.

Simultaneous events

Verbals often show up when two events take place at the same time. In the following sentences, check out the italicized verbals. Also keep your eye on the main verb, which is underlined. Notice that the same verbal matches with present, past, and future verbs and places the two actions at the same time or close enough in time to make the difference irrelevant. Also notice that none of the verbals are formed with the words *have* or *had.* (*Have* and *had* help to express actions taking place at different times. I explain this point in detail later in this section.)

> *Selecting* a handkerchief, Maya daintily <u>blows</u> her nose. (The *selecting* and the *blowing* take place at nearly the same time — in the present.)

> *Selecting* a handkerchief, Maya daintily <u>blew</u> her nose. (The *selecting* and the *blowing* took place at nearly the same time — in the past.)

> *Selecting* a handkerchief, Maya <u>will</u> daintily <u>blow</u> her nose. (The *selecting* and the *blowing* will take place at nearly the same time — in the future.)

Another variation:

> *To blow her nose daintily,* Maya <u>selects</u> a handkerchief. (The *blowing* and the *selecting* take place at nearly the same time — in the present.)

> *To blow her nose daintily,* Maya <u>selected</u> a handkerchief. (The *blowing* and the *selecting* took place at nearly the same time — in the past.)

> *To blow her nose daintily,* Maya <u>will select</u> a handkerchief. (The *blowing* and the *selecting* will take place at nearly the same time — in the future.)

No one in the known universe needs this information, so continue reading only if you love grammatical terms. *Participles* are verb forms that may act as adjectives. In the preceding example sentences, *selecting* is a present participle, and *selecting a handkerchief* is a participial phrase describing *Maya.* The action expressed by the present participle takes place at the same time (or nearly the same time) as the action expressed by the main verb. *To blow* is an infinitive, the basic form of a verb. Infinitives never function as verbs in the sentence. In the previous example sentences, *to blow her noise daintily* is an infinitive phrase describing *Maya.*

Different times

When verbals express actions or states of being that occur at different times, a helping verb *(having* or *have)* is involved.

For reasons that I can't begin to imagine, this topic is a favorite of standardized test-makers.

Check out this sentence:

> *Having sealed* the letter containing his job application, Nobrain *remembered* his name.

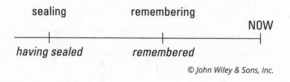

© *John Wiley & Sons, Inc.*

In other words, Nobrain's job application — unless he rips open the envelope — is anonymous because the *sealing* of the letter took place before the *remembering* of his name.

Here are additional examples:

> *Having finished* her homework, Elizabeth *turned* on the television to watch the algebra tournament. (Event 1: Elizabeth finishes her homework at 2 a.m. Event 2: The tournament begins at 3 a.m. The networks seem reluctant to broadcast the match during prime time. I'm not sure why.)

Having won all the votes, Lola named herself "Empress-in-Chief." (Event 1: Lola gets 100 percent of the votes. Event 2: Lola goes crown shopping.)

Having exhibited the painting in Mel's new gallery, Elizabeth considered herself an all-around artistic genius. (Event 1: Elizabeth convinces Mel to hang her *Homework Blues* portrait. Event 2: Elizabeth adds an art link to her Facebook page.)

If you have a life, skip this paragraph. If you like grammar, read on to learn the technical terms. The *present participle* (*finishing*, for example) combines with present, past, and future verbs to show two events happening at the same time or at nearly the same time. The *present perfect* form of the participle (*having finished*) combines with present, past, and future verbs to show two events happening at different times.

Another one of the verb-forms-that-aren't-verbs, the *infinitive*, may also show events happening at two different times. The *present perfect infinitive* (*to have finished*, for example) is the one that does this job. Don't worry about the name; just look for the *have*. Here's an example:

It was helpful *to have bought the cookbook* before the dinner party. (Event 1: Pre-party, panicked trip to the bookstore. Event 2: Guests arrive, unaware that they're about to eat Alfalfa-Stringbean Surprise.)

WARNING

The *have* form (the present perfect form) of the infinitive always places an event *before* another in the past. Don't use the *have* form unless you're putting events in order:

WRONG: I was wrong to have attended the party.

RIGHT: I was wrong to attend the party. The music was terrible and there was nothing to eat but overcooked vegetables.

ALSO RIGHT: I was wrong to have said I would attend the party before I got a chance to investigate the menu. Mark's cooking was terrible.

POP QUIZ

Which sentence shows two events happening at the same time, and which shows two events happening at different times?

A. Running up the clock, the mouse chatted with his friends.

B. Having run up the clock, the mouse chatted with his friends.

Answer: Sentence A shows two events happening at the same time. The mouse is running and chatting with his friends. Sentence B shows two events happening at different times. The mouse has arrived at the top of the clock and is now chatting with his friends. (Notice that the word *having* is involved, indicating that different events are occurring at different times.)

Sprucing Up Boring Sentences with Clauses and Verbals

A clause is any expression containing a subject and a verb. (For tons more detail about clauses, read Chapter 18.) In this section, I show you how to manipulate clauses and verbals to make your writing more interesting and sophisticated.

Here's what I mean. Read these two paragraphs. Which one sounds better?

Michael purchased a new spy camera. The camera was smaller than a grain of rice. Michael gave the camera to Lola. Lola is rather forgetful. She is especially forgetful now. Lola is planning a trip to Antarctica. Lola accidentally mixed the camera into her rice casserole along with bean sprouts and soy milk. The camera baked for 45 minutes. The camera became quite tender. Michael unknowingly ate the camera.

Michael purchased a new spy camera that was smaller than a grain of rice. Michael gave the camera to Lola, who is rather forgetful, especially now that she is planning a trip to Antarctica. Accidentally mixed into Lola's rice casserole along with bean sprouts and soy milk, the camera baked for 45 minutes. Michael unknowingly ate the camera, which was quite tender.

I'm going to take a guess; you said that the second paragraph was better, didn't you? It's a bit shorter (62 words instead of 69), but length isn't the issue. The first paragraph is composed of short, choppy sentences. The second one flows. Grammatically, the difference between the two is simple. The second paragraph has more subordinate clauses and verbals than the first.

You don't need to know how to find or label clauses or verbals. However, you should read your writing aloud from time to time to check how it sounds. The old saying, variety is the spice of life, applies to writing. Use this checklist to see whether your writing could use a little hot pepper:

» Do all your sentences follow the same basic pattern, subject-verb or subject-verb-complement?

» Have you strung a lot of short sentences together with *and* or a similar joining word?

» Are all your sentences more or less the same length?

If you answered yes to one or more of the preceding questions, your sentences need help. In this section, with a minimum of grammatical labels, I suggest some ways to add flavor to blah sentences.

TEST ALERT

If you're stuck with a writing section on a standardized exam — the AP tests, for example — pay extra attention to the information in this section. Graders of these exams like to see well placed clauses and verbals. These elements, used properly, make your writing sound more mature and raise your score.

The clause that refreshes

Are you a fan of home makeover shows? I confess that I am. I love to see a run-down, boring house magically turn into a palace with a new layout, fresh paint, and tasteful decorations. The rooms change from boring to interesting in 30 minutes, with time off for commercials. In this section, I suggest a couple of ways to renovate your sentences (not your house) with clauses.

Take a look at these before-and-after sentences. My insertions are subordinate clauses, which are italicized. (For more information on subordinate clauses, see Chapter 18.)

> BORING "BEFORE" VERSION: Max sat on a tuffet. Max did not know that he was sitting on a tuffet. Max had never seen a tuffet before. He was quite comfortable. Then Ms. Muffet came in and caused trouble.

> EXCITING "AFTER" VERSION: Max, *who was sitting on a tuffet,* did not know *what a tuffet was because he had never seen one before. Until Ms. Muffet came in and caused trouble,* Max was quite comfortable.

Doesn't the "after" paragraph sound better? It's two words shorter (33 instead of 35 words), but more important than length is the number of sentences. The before paragraph has five, and the after paragraph has two. Tucking more than one idea into a sentence saves words and makes your writing less choppy.

One more example:

> BORING "BEFORE" VERSION: The taxi sounded its horn. The taxi was traveling south. The intersection was clogged with trucks. The trucks were heading west. The taxi could not move. The traffic police finally arrived. They cleared the intersection.

> EXCITING "AFTER" VERSION: The taxi, *which was traveling south,* sounded its horn. *Because the intersection was clogged with trucks heading west,* the taxi could not move. The traffic police cleared the intersection *when they arrived.*

The "after" paragraph saves you only two words (34 for "before," 32 for "after"), but that's not the point. By combining sentences, you create a smoother flow of ideas. The writing sounds more mature, and therefore so do you.

Combine these sentences by creating subordinate clauses.

> The tea was very hot. The tea was not ready to drink. Catherine waited a few minutes.

Answer: You may combine these ideas in several different ways. Here's one, with the subordinate clauses italicized:

> The tea, *which was very hot*, was not ready to drink, so Catherine waited a few minutes.

Here's another possibility:

> *Because the tea, which was very hot, was not ready to drink,* Catherine waited a few minutes.

In the preceding answer, one subordinate clause (*which was very hot)* is tucked into another (*Because the tea was not ready to drink).*

Verbally speaking

Verbals pull a lot of information into a little package. After all, they represent a blend of two parts of speech, so they provide two different perspectives in just one word. Look at this sentence, taken from the gerund section, earlier in this chapter:

> Betsy gave *bribing the umpire* serious consideration when her team lost its 450th game in a row.

Without the gerund, you use more words to say the same thing:

> Betsy's team lost its 450th game in a row. Betsy thought about whether she should bribe the umpire. Betsy thought seriously about that possibility.

Okay, the gerund saved you seven words. Big deal! Well, it is a big deal over the course of a paragraph or a whole paper. But more important than word count is sentence structure. Verbals are just one more color in your crayon box when you're creating a picture. Who wants the same old eight colors? Isn't it fun to try something different? Gerunds, infinitives, and participles help you vary the pattern of your sentences. Here's a before-and-after example:

> BORING BEFORE VERSION: Lulu smacked Larry. Larry had stolen the antique toe hoop from Lulu's parrot. The toe hoop was discovered 100 years ago. Lulu's parrot likes to sharpen his beak on it.

EXCITING AFTER VERSION: *Smacking Larry* is Lulu's way of telling Larry that he should not have stolen the antique toe hoop from her parrot. *Discovered 100 years ago,* the toe hoop serves *to sharpen the parrot's beak.*

LABELS FOR THOSE WHO CARE: *Smacking Lulu* = gerund, *discovered 100 years ago* = participle, *to sharpen the parrot's beak* = infinitive.

Are you awake enough for another example? Take a look at this makeover. The verbal phrases are italicized:

BORING BEFORE VERSION: The sled slid down the hill. Luis was on the sled. He was excited. He forgot the brake.

EXCITING AFTER VERSION: *Sliding down the hill on the sled,* Luis was *excited* and forgot *to brake.*

LABELS FOR THOSE WHO CARE: *Sliding down the hill on the sled* = participle, *excited* = participle, *to brake* = infinitive.

POP QUIZ

Combine these ideas into one or more sentences.

Larry bakes infrequently. He bakes with enthusiasm. His best recipe is for king cake. King-cake batter must be stirred for three hours. Larry orders his cook to stir the batter. The cook stirs, and Larry adds the raisins. Sometimes Larry throws in a spoonful of vanilla.

Answer: Many combinations are possible, including the following:

Larry's *baking* is infrequent but enthusiastic. His best recipe, king cake, requires three hours of *stirring,* which Larry orders his cook to do. *Adding* raisins and the occasional spoonful of vanilla is Larry's job. (The italicized words are gerunds.)

Larry, who bakes infrequently but enthusiastically, excels at cooking king cake, which requires three hours of stirring. Ordering his cook to stir, Larry adds raisins and the occasional spoonful of vanilla. (*who bakes infrequently but enthusiastically* = subordinate clause, *cooking king cake* = gerund, *which requires three hours of stirring* = subordinate clause, *ordering his cook* = participle, *to stir* = infinitive)

Mixing It Up: Changing Sentence Patterns

To create interesting sentences, you can play around with clauses and verbals, as I explain in the preceding section. I can't leave this topic without giving two other tools for "redecorating" your sentences: pattern (what's where in the sentence) and length.

Scrambling word order

When you were little, you may have played a game called "Duck Duck Goose." It's a simple contest. Kids sit in a circle and the one who's "it" walks around the outside, tapping each child and saying "duck" — until suddenly the "it" kid changes the pattern and says "goose." I mention this game because it relies on surprise — the establishment of a pattern and then a break from it.

When you write, you probably follow the usual sentence pattern automatically: subject, verb, complement (a direct object, indirect object, or subject complement). Scan these examples, in which the major sentence elements are identified:

> Ali wants the stars. (*Ali* = subject, *wants* = verb, *stars* = direct object)
>
> He built a rocket in less than a year. (*He* = subject, *built* = verb, *rocket* = direct object)
>
> Ali traveled out of the Earth's atmosphere, across thousands of light years, to the planet Jupiter. (*Ali* = subject, *traveled* = verb, no complement)
>
> Ali is a national hero. (*Ali* = subject, *is* = verb, *hero* = complement)

That structure dominates because it's sturdy; it supports a ton of ideas. It's comforting. Readers are used to it, and they know what to expect. A change in routine, though, goes a long way toward improving your writing. Take a look at what happens when you shake up the word order:

> The stars, Ali wants. (*Ali* = subject, *wants* = verb, *stars* = direct object)
>
> A rocket in less than a year built he! (*He* = subject, *built* = verb, *rocket* = direct object)
>
> Out of the Earth's atmosphere, across thousands of light years, to the planet Jupiter traveled Ali. (*Ali* = subject, *traveled* = verb, no complement)
>
> A national hero, Ali is. (*Ali* = subject, *is* = verb, *hero* = complement)

WARNING

I wrote these example sentences to show you some possibilities, but don't change the usual sentence order too often. You can't play "Duck Duck Goose" unless you have some ducks — a lot of ducks! Placing too many unusual sentences in the same story would annoy your readers. Use scrambled word order for an occasional change of pace, not as a steady diet.

Going long or cutting it short

Pick up something you wrote recently and zero in on a random paragraph. Count the number of words in each sentence. What do you find? If your writing resembles most people's, you tend to place the same number of words in every sentence. Yet sentences can be as short as two words: "I quit!" or go on for pages and pages.

(Check out Virginia Woolf's or Charles Dickens's work to see some marathon statements.)

How do you mix it up, when it comes to sentence length? Try these techniques:

>> Combine some sentences by making the less important idea into a subordinate clause. Chapter 18 gives you the definition of a subordinate clause and provides examples. In this chapter, read "The clause that refreshes" to see some possible combination patterns.

>> Use a conjunction such as *and, but, or, nor,* or *for* to join two complete sentences that state ideas of equal importance. A bonus of this technique is that the conjunction may reveal the logic that leads from one sentence to the next.

>> Throw in a verbal to replace some less important ideas. "Verbally speaking" in this chapter provides some examples.

>> If you have a very long sentence — perhaps the result of combining several shorter sentences — consider following it with a short, emphatic statement. Look at this example:

> After the crowds left, when the remains of the meal had been cleared away, just before the band finished packing up its instruments, and while Katie was still opening her presents to see what she'd gotten for her birthday, the door opened. He'd arrived.

See what I mean? Doesn't that last sentence hit you right in the face? This long-short pattern doesn't work if you overuse it, but it's certainly a great choice for an occasional dramatic effect.

POP QUIZ

Take a crack at this paragraph. Change the sentence length and patterns using some or all of the suggestions in this section.

> Bill lit the candles. He bought flowers. He put the bank reports on the table. Tonight he would propose to Belle. Bill's company was very profitable. Belle's company was super-profitable. Bill was aware of her sales figures. Bill sought a merger. Bill hoped Belle would accept. Then their companies would combine. Bill and Belle would be very rich.

Answer: You can revise this paragraph in any one of about a million ways. Here's one, with an explanation in parentheses after each change:

> *Having lit the candles and bought flowers* (participles), Bill put the bank report on the table. Tonight he would propose to Belle, *whose company was super-profitable,* (subordinate clause) *as was Bill's* (subordinate clause). *Knowing her sales figures* (gerund) led Bill *to seek a merger* (infinitive). Bill hoped Belle would accept *combining their companies and making Bill and Belle very rich.* (gerunds)

>> **Being consistent in form, tense, and voice**

>> **Using pairs of conjunctions correctly**

>> **Keeping comparisons parallel**

Chapter **20**

Staying on Track: Parallelism

Taken any train trips recently? The tracks you see stretching before you are parallel — or they'd better be. If they aren't, your train goes off track and chaos quickly follows. In grammar, you have to stay on track also by creating parallel constructions — sentences and expressions that are balanced and consistent. In this chapter, I show you how to avoid several everyday errors of *parallelism*, also known as *faulty construction*.

Constructing Balanced Sentences

Dieticians tell you to eat a well-balanced diet. Grammarians are fans of balance, too. In grammar, though, the goal is a well-balanced sentence or expression. In other words, a sentence (or parts of a sentence) should be *parallel*. Before I give you the complete definition, see whether you can figure it out yourself. Can you spot the problem in this sentence?

> Larry wanted with all his heart to find a bride who was smart, beautiful, and had millions of dollars.

Not counting Larry's matrimonial ideas, the sentence has another problem: It's not parallel. Concentrate on the part of the sentence following the word *was*. Larry's dream bride needed these characteristics:

>> Smart

>> Beautiful

>> Had millions of dollars

Do you see that these three descriptions don't match? The first two are adjectives. The third consists of a verb *(had)* and an object *(millions of dollars)*. (For more information on adjectives, see Chapter 10. For more information on verbs, turn to Chapter 2. Complements show up in Chapter 6.) But all three descriptions are doing the same job in the sentence — describing Larry's dream bride. Because they're doing the same job, they should match, at least in the grammatical sense. If they match, they're *parallel.* Here's one revised, parallel list:

>> Smart

>> Beautiful

>> Rich

>> Nearsighted (I added this one because I've actually seen Larry and he looks better if he's a little blurry.)

And here's another:

>> Intelligence

>> Beauty

>> Millions of dollars

>> Bad eyesight

Both lists are fine. In the first set, all the characteristics of Larry's bride are adjectives. In the second set, all the characteristics are nouns. You can use either list. Just don't take some elements from one and some from another. Here are the revised sentences:

Larry wanted with all his heart to find a bride who was smart, beautiful, nearsighted, and rich.

Larry wanted with all his heart to find a bride with intelligence, beauty, bad eyesight, and millions of dollars.

The exam writers who come up with college admissions tests often test whether you can spot, correct, or create a parallel sentence. Be careful to keep your words on parallel tracks.

Parallelism is especially important when you're making a presentation or a bulleted list. If one item is a complete sentence, all the items should be. If you're listing nouns, make sure every item is a noun. (For more on bulleted lists, see Chapter 16.) Can you spot the error in the presentation slide?

This year's goals for employees of Upgrade Computer Systems, Inc. include the following:

>> To require as many upgrades as possible

>> Writing confusing directions for every download

>> Ensuring that help-desk employees have no knowledge of upgrades

Uh oh. One item doesn't match: *To require as many upgrades as possible.* In case you care, here's how the list appears to a grammarian: *to require* is an infinitive, but the next two items in the list, *writing* and *ensuring,* are gerunds. Though gerunds and infinitives are both *verbals* — forms of a verb that don't function as verbs in the sentence — you can't mix and match them freely. Here are three possible corrections for the list:

>> Requiring as many upgrades as possible

>> Writing confusing directions for every download

>> Ensuring that help-desk employees have no knowledge of upgrades

or

>> To require as many upgrades as possible

>> To write confusing directions for every download

>> To ensure that help-desk employees have no knowledge of upgrades

or

>> Full-time workers must create as many upgrades as possible.

>> Executives must write confusing directions for every download.

>> The employee with the least knowledge of upgrades will answer the most calls to the help desk.

TIP

Whenever you're writing a presentation slide or a sentence with more than one subject, object, or verb, make a list and check it twice, whether or not you believe in Santa Claus. Everything doing the same job must match grammatically.

Check out these additional examples:

NOT PARALLEL: Anna said that whenever anything went wrong, whenever someone let us down, or in case of disaster, she would "feel our pain."

WHAT'S WRONG: The three things that Anna said are not parallel. Two have subject–verb combinations *(anything went, someone let),* and one *(in case of disaster)* does not.

PARALLEL: Anna said that whenever anything went wrong, whenever someone let us down, or whenever disaster struck, she would "feel our pain."

WHY IT'S PARALLEL: Now the three things that Anna said are all subject–verb combinations.

ALSO PARALLEL: Anna said that in the event of mistakes, disloyalty, or disaster, she would "feel our pain."

WHY IT'S PARALLEL: Now the things that Anna said are all expressed as nouns: *mistakes, disloyalty, disaster.*

Another set for you to read:

NOT PARALLEL: Egbert, a gourmet cook and renowned for his no-cholesterol omelets, thinks that French cooking is "overrated."

WHAT'S WRONG: The *and* joins two descriptions of Egbert. One is a noun *(cook)* and one is a descriptive verb form *(renowned for his no-cholesterol omelets).*

PARALLEL: Egbert, a gourmet cook renowned for his no-cholesterol omelets, thinks that French cooking is "overrated."

WHY IT'S PARALLEL: When you remove the *and,* the problem is solved. Now the descriptive verb form *(renowned)* describes the noun *(cook).*

POP QUIZ

Identify the correct sentence(s).

A. Larry found a honeymoon suite that was restful, exotic, tasteful, and in the less-populated section of his kingdom.

B. Larry found a honeymoon suite that was restful, exotic, and tasteful. It was located in the less-populated section of his kingdom.

C. Larry found a honeymoon suite that was restful, exotic, tasteful, and remote.

Answer: Sentences B and C are correct. If you list the qualities of Larry's honeymoon suite as expressed in sentence A, you have

>> Restful

>> Exotic

>> Tasteful

>> In the less-populated section of his kingdom

The first three are adjectives, but the last is a prepositional phrase. (For more information about prepositional phrases, see Chapter 9.) Because they don't match, the sentence is not parallel. In sentence B, the three adjectives are alone in one sentence. The prepositional phrase is in its very own sentence. Sentence C expresses all the characteristics of Larry's honeymoon suite as adjectives.

TIP

To avoid parallelism errors, you don't have to know the correct grammatical terms. Just use your common sense and listen. A parallel sentence has balance. A non-parallel sentence doesn't.

Shifting Grammar into Gear: Avoiding Stalled Sentences

If you've ever ridden in a car with a stick shift, you know that smooth transitions are rare (at least when I'm driving). If something is just a little off, the car bucks like a mule. The same thing is true in sentences. You can, at times, shift tense, voice, or person, but even the slightest mistake stalls your sentence. In this section, I explain how to avoid unnecessary shifts and how to check your sentence for consistency.

Steering clear of a tense situation

Check out this sentence with multiple verbs:

> Larry begs Ella to marry him, offers her a crown and a private room, and finally won her hand.

Now make a list of the verbs in the sentence:

>> Begs

>> Offers

>> Won

The first two verbs are in present tense, but the third shifts into past for no valid reason. Stall! If the verbs in this sentence were gears in a stick shift, your car would conk out. All three verbs should be in present tense or all three should be in past tense. Here are the corrected versions of the sentence:

> Larry begs Ella to marry him, offers her a crown and a private room, and finally wins her hand. (All three verbs are in present tense.)

or

> Larry begged Ella to marry him, offered her a crown and a private room, and finally won her hand. (All three verbs are in past tense.)

TIP

Sometimes in telling a story, you must shift tense because the action of the story requires a change in time. For example:

> Betsy always *practices* for at least 10 hours a day, unless she *is giving* a concert. Last week she *flew* to Antarctica for a recital. When she *arrived,* the piano *froze.* Nevertheless, the show *went* on. Next week Betsy *will practice* 12 hours a day to make up for the time she *lost* last week.

Betsy's story has present *(practices)*, present progressive *(is giving)*, past *(flew, arrived, froze, went, lost)*, and future tenses *(will practice)*. Each change of tense is justified by the information in the story. (For more information on verb tense, see Chapter 6.) Here are some additional examples of justified and unjustified shifts in verb tense:

> WRONG: Max *slips* on the ice, and after obsessively checking every inch of his skull in the mirror, *decided* that he *had hurt* his head.

> WHY IT'S WRONG: The sentence shifts to past tense *(decided, had hurt)* but uses present *(slips)* for the first action on the timeline. That's not logical.

> RIGHT: Max *slipped* on the ice, and after obsessively checking every inch of his skull in the mirror, *decided* that he *had hurt* his head.

> WHY IT'S RIGHT: Two verbs *(slipped, decided)* are past tense. The other *(had hurt)* is past perfect. The past perfect tense talks about (you guessed it!) the past, placing

one event earlier than another. In this example sentence, *had hurt* occurs earlier than *decided*. Did I catch you with *checking?* That word looks like a verb, but in this sentence it's acting as a noun — a *gerund* — a grammatical element that has some characteristics of a noun and some of a verb. For more details about gerunds, turn to Chapter 19.

SENTENCE THAT LOOKS WRONG BUT ISN'T: Ralph *needs* a loan because he *bet* his entire paycheck on a horse that *came* in first in the eighth race. (Unfortunately, the horse *was running* in the seventh race.)

WHY IT LOOKS WRONG: The first verb *(needs)* is in present tense, and the next three are in past tense *(bet, came)* and past progressive *(was running)*.

WHY IT'S RIGHT: The shift in tenses is justified. The first part talks about Ralph now, explaining his present condition with a reference to the past. The other verbs refer to actions Max performed in the past. The meaning of the sentence makes the change from present to past or past progressive necessary.

POP QUIZ

Which sentence is correct?

A. Egbert scrambled to the finish line a half-second before the next fastest racer and then raised his arms in victory.

B. Egbert scrambles to the finish line a half-second before the next fastest racer and then raises his arms in victory.

Answer: Both sentences are correct. (Don't you hate trick questions?) In sentence A, both *scrambled* and *raised* are in past tense. No tense shift, no problem. In sentence B, both *scrambles* and *raises* are in present tense. Again no tense shift, again no problem.

Don't change tenses in a bulleted list (assuming you've got verbs there). If the bullet points mark off your summer achievements, don't mix *learned grammar* and *have more confidence*. Go for *learned grammar* and *gained confidence* or *know grammar* and *have more confidence*.

TIP

Keeping your voice steady

The voice of a verb — not baritone or soprano — is either *active* or *passive*. (For more information on voice, see Chapter 17.) Like tense, the voice of the verbs in a sentence ought to be consistent unless there's a good reason for a shift. I should point out that a shift in voice is not a grammar felony; think misdemeanor or maybe even parking ticket. Nevertheless, avoid unnecessary shifts if you can do so without writing yourself into a corner. Here's a sentence with an unjustified shift in voice:

> Larry *polished* the diamond engagement ring, *rechecked* the certificate of authenticity, and *was* completely *demolished* when his intended bride *said* no.

Do you see the problem? A checklist makes it obvious:

>> Polished

>> Rechecked

>> Was demolished

>> Said

The first two verbs and the last one are in active voice, but the third is in passive voice.

A number of changes can take care of the problem:

> Larry *polished* the diamond engagement ring, *rechecked* the certificate of authenticity, and *cried* like a baby when his intended bride *said* no.

or

> Larry *polished* the diamond engagement ring and *rechecked* the certificate of authenticity. His intended bride completely demolished him with her refusal.

WARNING

Notice that the list of verbs in the corrected sentences are all in active voice: *polished, rechecked, cried* and *polished, rechecked, demolished.* In general, active voice is better than passive. Listen to this clunker:

> The diamond engagement ring was polished and the certificate of authenticity was rechecked by Larry, and Larry was completely demolished when "no" was said to him by his intended bride.

Nope. I don't think so. The passive verbs create an awkward, wordy mess.

I should point out, though, that a parallel list of passive verbs may sometimes be the best option. Check out this example:

> The construction was done with care. The walls were stripped of wallpaper, patched, plastered, and repainted.

Do you really need to know who did the work? Unless you wish to emphasize someone's do-it-yourself skills or to promote a particular construction firm, the passive voice works fine here.

TIP

Bulleted lists containing verbs also need consistent voice. Don't switch from active to passive unnecessarily.

Which sentence is correct?

POP QUIZ

A. The cork had been popped from the champagne by Lulu, the chilled glasses had been reached for, and Lulu was shocked to learn that the caviar had been confiscated by customs officials.

B. Lulu popped the cork from the champagne, reached for the chilled glasses, and was shocked to learn that customs officials had confiscated the caviar.

C. Lulu popped the cork from the champagne, reached for the chilled glasses, and staggered in shock when she heard that customs officials had confiscated the caviar.

Answer: Sentence C is best because all of the verbs (*popped, reached, staggered, heard,* and *had confiscated*) are in active voice. Even without any grammar terminology (or knowledge), don't you think that Sentence C sounds better?

Knowing the right person

Ah, loyalty. It's one of the most celebrated virtues, in life as well as in grammar! Loyalty in grammar relates to what grammarians call *person*. In *first person*, the subject narrates the story: In other words, *I* or *we* acts as the subject of the sentence. In *second person*, the subject is being spoken to, and *you* (either singular or plural) is the subject. In *third person*, the subject is being spoken about, using *he, she, it, they,* or any other word that talks *about* someone or something.

To be grammatically loyal, don't start out talking from the point of view of one person and then switch to another point of view in a sentence, unless you have a valid reason for doing so. Here's an example of an unnecessary shift in person:

> To celebrate his marriage, Larry promised amnesty to all the criminals currently in his jails because you need to do something spectacular on such important occasions.

The first part of the sentence talks about *Larry*, so it's in third person. The second part of the sentence, which begins with the word *because*, shifts to *you* (second person). Making the correction is simple:

> To celebrate his marriage, *Larry* promised amnesty to all the criminals currently in his jails because *he* needs to do something spectacular on such an important occasion.

or

> To celebrate his marriage, *Larry* promised amnesty to all the criminals currently in his jails because *everyone* needs to do something spectacular on such important occasions.

or

> To celebrate his marriage, *Larry* promised amnesty to all the criminals currently in his jails because a *ruler* needs to do something spectacular on such important occasions.

All three of the preceding sentences are correct. Why? In the first, *Larry* is the subject of the first part of the sentence, and *he* is the subject of the second part. No problem. In the second correction, Larry (third person) is matched with *everyone* (a third-person pronoun). In the third correction example, third-person Larry is followed by *ruler*, another third-person noun.

Time for another round:

> WRONG: *I* am planning to pick up those coins; *you* can't pass up a chance for free money!

> WHY IT'S WRONG: The first part of the sentence is in first person *(I)*, and the second part of the sentence shifts to *you,* the second person form. Why shift?

> RIGHT: I am planning to pick up those coins; I can't pass up a chance for free money!

> ALSO RIGHT: I am planning to pick up those coins because no one can pass up a chance for free money.

> WHY IT'S ALSO RIGHT: The shift here is from first person *(I)* to third *(no one)*. This shift works because the speaker *(I)* is placing him- or herself in the context of a group.

Make sure your sentences are consistent in person. Unless there's a logical reason to shift, follow these guidelines:

>> If you begin with first person (*I* or *me*), stay in first person.

>> If you begin with second person (*you*), stay in second person.

>> If you begin with third person, talking about someone or something, make sure that you continue to talk about someone or something.

POP QUIZ

Which sentence is correct?

A. Whenever a person breaks a grammar rule, you get into trouble.

B. Whenever a person breaks a grammar rule, he or she gets into trouble.

C. Whenever a person breaks a grammar rule, they get into trouble.

Answer: Sentence B is correct. *A person* matches *he or she* because both talk about someone. In sentence A, *a person* does not match *you*. Sentence A shifts from third to second person for no logical reason. Sentence C is complicated. It stays in third person, talking about someone, but *a person* is singular and *they* is plural — sort of. For many centuries, grammarians and writers matched *they* with pronouns such as *someone, everybody,* and so forth, as well as with singular nouns with no obvious gender (*clerk, doctor, teacher,* for example). Then a well-meaning but misguided push to make *they, their, them* exclusively plural took place. Teachers and grammarians proclaimed that these pronouns couldn't pair up with singular nouns or other singular pronouns — not in formal English, anyway. The problem, of course, is that English needs a singular, nongendered pronoun to refer to a human being. So *they* is making a comeback as a singular pronoun. (For more information on singular and plural pronouns in general and this issue in particular, see Chapter 7.)

Try one more. Which is correct?

A. Everybody loves somebody sometime because all you need is love.

B. Everybody loves somebody sometime because all anybody needs is love.

Answer: Sentence B is correct. Sentence A shifts from third person (*everybody*) to second (*you*) for no reason. Sentence B stays in third person (*everybody, anybody*).

Seeing Double: Conjunction Pairs

Most joining words fly solo. Single words — *and, but, nor, or, because, although, since,* and so on — join sentences or parts of sentences. Some joining words, however, come in pairs. (In grammarspeak, joining words are called *conjunctions.*

Double conjunctions are called *correlatives.* Forget these facts immediately! Just remember how to use joining words properly.) Here are some of the most frequently used pairs:

>> Not only/but also

>> Either/or

>> Neither/nor

>> Whether/or

>> Both/and

WARNING

Some of these words show up in sentences without their partners. No problem! Just make sure that when they do act as conjunction pairs, they behave properly. Here's the rule: Whatever fills in the blanks after each half of a pair of conjunctions must have the same grammatical identity. The logic here is that conjunctions have partners, and so do the things they join. You may join two nouns, two sentences, two prepositional phrases — two whatevers! Just make sure the things that you join match. Check out this example:

Not only Larry but also his bride yearned for a day at the beach. (The conjunction pair joins two nouns, *Larry* and *his bride.*)

Either you or I must break the news about the fake diamond to Larry. (The conjunction pair joins two pronouns, *you* and *I.*)

TIP

Nouns and pronouns are equals when it comes to parallelism. Because pronouns take the place of nouns, you may mix them without ill effect:

Neither Ralph nor he has brought a proper present to Larry's wedding. (The conjunction pair joins a noun, *Ralph,* and a pronoun, *he.*)

Here's another example:

Both *because he stole the garter* and *because he lost the ring,* Roger is no longer welcome as best man. (This conjunction pair joins two subject–verb combinations.)

To help you spot parallelism errors in sentences with conjunction pairs, here are a few mismatches, along with their corrections:

NOT PARALLEL: Either *Lulu will go with Larry to the bachelor party* or *to the shower,* but she will not attend both.

WHY IT'S NOT PARALLEL: The first italicized section is a subject–verb combination. The second italicized section is a prepositional phrase.

PARALLEL: Lulu will go with Larry either *to the bachelor party* or *to the shower,* but she will not attend both. (Now you've got two prepositional phrases.)

NOT PARALLEL: Both *her lateness* and *that she was dressed in white leather* insulted the royal couple.

WHY IT'S NOT PARALLEL: First italicized section is a noun, but the second is a subject–verb combination.

PARALLEL BUT A LITTLE REPETITIVE: Both *the fact that she was late* and *the fact that she was dressed in white leather* insulted the royal couple. (Now the italicized sections are both subject–verb combinations.)

PARALLEL AND MORE CONCISE: Both *her lateness* and *her white leather clothing* insulted the royal couple. (Now the italicized sections are both nouns with a couple of descriptions attached — a more concise solution.)

POP QUIZ

Which sentence is correct?

A. Lulu neither mocked Larry nor his bride about the fact that the bride's mother has a slight but noticeable moustache.

B. Lulu mocked neither Larry nor his bride about the fact that the bride's mother has a slight but noticeable moustache.

Answer: Sentence B is correct. In sentence A, *neither* precedes a verb *(mocked)* but *nor* precedes a noun *(his bride)*. In sentence B, *neither* precedes a noun *(Larry)* and so does *nor (his bride)*.

Try another. Which sentence is best?

A. Both the way she danced and the way she sang convinced Michael to award Lola a starring role in Michael's new musical, *The Homework Blues.*

B. Both the way she danced and her superb singing convinced Michael to award Lola a starring role in Michael's new musical, *The Homework Blues.*

C. Both her graceful dancing and superb singing convinced Michael to award Lola a starring role in Michael's new musical, *The Homework Blues.*

Answer: Sentence C is best. Two nouns, *dancing* and *singing,* are linked by the conjunctions. True, sentence A is grammatically correct because a noun–subject–verb combination *(the way she danced, the way she sang)* follows both parts of the conjunction pair. However, sentence A is a little wordy; *the way* appears twice. In sentence B, the first half of the conjunction pair *(both)* is followed by a noun *(way)* and then a subject–verb combination (*she danced*). The second part of the conjunction pair (*and*) is followed only by a noun (*singing*).

REMEMBER

When you see a conjunction pair, underline (mentally) whatever follows each half of the pair. If they match, move on. If not, revise.

Avoiding Lopsided Comparisons

The grammar police will arrive, warrant in hand, if your comparisons aren't parallel. Comparisons to watch out for include the following:

>> More/than

>> But not

>> As well as

Comparisons with these words are tricky but not impossible. Just be sure that the elements you are comparing match grammatically. Check out these examples:

> Lulu was more *conservative* than *daring* in her choice of clothes for Larry's wedding.

> Even so, Larry liked *the way Lulu moved* but not *the way she looked*.

> Lulu enjoyed the ceremonial *garter-toss* as well as the ritual *bouquet-bonfire*.

The italicized words in each sentence pair off nicely. In the first sample sentence, *conservative* and *daring* are both descriptions. In the second sample sentence, *the way Lulu moved* and *the way she looked* are similar constructions — nouns described by adjective clauses, if you absolutely must know. In the third sample sentence, *garter-toss* and *bouquet-bonfire* are both nouns.

TIP

Treat nouns and pronouns as equals when you're checking for parallel comparisons. In other words, you can correctly say

> *He,* as well as Lola, failed to catch the garter.

because *He* (a pronoun) matches up with *Lola* (a noun) and makes a parallel comparison.

To illustrate parallel comparisons further, here are some incorrect and corrected pairs:

WRONG: Lola sang more forcefully than with the correct notes.

WHY IT'S WRONG: *forcefully* and *with the correct notes* don't match.

RIGHT: *Lola sang* more *forcefully* than *correctly*.

WHY IT'S RIGHT: The sentence compares two adverbs.

Here's another example:

WRONG: Ella assumed *that she would live in the same castle* but not *spending every hour with Larry.*

WHY IT'S WRONG: The words *but not* join a subject–verb combination and verb form.

RIGHT: Ella assumed *that she would live in the same castle* but not *that she would spend every hour with Larry.*

WHY IT'S RIGHT: The sentence compares two subject–verb combinations.

TIP

A question may have occurred to you: How do you know how many words of the sentence are being joined? In other words, in the preceding sample sentences, how did I figure out how much to italicize? The decision comes from the meaning of the sentence. Forget grammar for a moment and put yourself into reading-comprehension mode. Decide what you're comparing based on the ideas in the sentence. Now check the two ideas being compared and go back into grammar mode. Do the ideas match grammatically? If so, you're fine. If not, reword your sentence.

POP QUIZ

Which sentence is correct?

A. Michael told Max that the ceremony was canceled but not that the couple planned to elope.

B. Michael told Max that the ceremony was canceled but not about the planned elopement.

Answer: Sentence A is correct. *That the ceremony was canceled* matches *that the couple planned to elope.* In sentence B, *that the ceremony was canceled* has a subject–pair, but *about the elopement* is a prepositional phrase with no subject–verb pair.

Summon up your energy and try again. Which sentence is correct?

A. Lulu's assumption that the snake was more showy than dangerous proved fatally wrong.

B. Lulu's assumption that the snake was more putting on a show than it was dangerous proved fatally wrong.

Answer: Sentence A is correct. *Showy* matches *dangerous;* both are descriptions. In sentence B, *putting on a show* has a verb form but not a subject. Its partner, *it was dangerous,* has both a subject and a verb.

Chapter **21**

Meaning What You Say: Clarity

Pity the poor insurance agents reading accident reports. Far too often they run into statements like this one: "Driving along Calla Avenue, the stop sign and the red car came out of nowhere and we crashed." Huh? Who hit what, and how? No doubt the driver thinks this description of the accident makes sense. The rest of us would like a bit more clarity — the topic of this chapter. Specifically, here you see how to place descriptions in the proper place, make logical and clear comparisons, and ensure that the specific person, thing, or group the pronoun refers to is obvious. These tasks accomplished, your message will express your intended meaning.

On Location: Placing Descriptions Correctly

In some languages, word order isn't particularly important. You can write the equivalent of "cat dog bit" and the form of the word indicates which animal is the biter and which is the victim. English words have fewer forms (nice, right?), but location matters. To find out where to place every descriptive word or statement, read on.

Misplaced descriptions

One word to the left or two to the right can't matter much, right? Wrong. To see why, that a look at this sentence:

> Lulu put a ring in her pierced nose that she had bought last week.

The describing words *that she had bought last week* follow the word *nose.* The way the sentence is now, *that she had bought last week* describes *nose.* The Internet sells plenty of unusual items, but not noses (yet), though I imagine a website for plastic surgeons offering discount nose jobs is out there somewhere.

Here's the correction:

> In her pierced nose Lulu put a ring that she had bought last week.

Now *that she had bought last week* follows *ring,* which Lulu really did buy last week.

WARNING

If you encounter a misplaced description in your writing (or on a test), be sure that your revision doesn't create another error. Here's an example of a faulty revision, still working from the sentence about Lulu's nose:

> Lulu put a ring that she had bought last week in her pierced nose.

In this version Lulu's shopping took place inside her nose, which *is* rather large, but not spacious enough for a jewelry store. Why? Because *in her pierced nose* tells you where something happened. The sentence has two verbs, *put* and *had bought.* The description describes the nearest action, which, in the faulty revision, is *had bought.* In the true correction, *in her pierced nose* is at the beginning of the sentence, closer to *put* than to *had bought.*

I'm not a big fan of grammar terms, but if you're curious, here's the deal: The description *that she bought last week* is an adjective clause. It describes the noun *ring.* For more information on adjective clauses, see Chapter 18.

Here's another description that has wandered too far from home:

> Lulu also bought a genuine, 1950-model, pink Hoola Hoop with a credit card.

According to news reports, toddlers and dogs have received credit card applications, but not plastic toys — at least as far as I know. Yet the sentence says that the Hoola Hoop comes with a credit card. How to fix it? Move the description:

> With a credit card Lulu also bought a genuine, 1950-model, pink Hoola Hoop.

Granted, most people can figure out the meaning of the faulty sentence, even when the description is in the wrong place. Logic is a powerful force. But chances are your reader or listener will pause a moment to unravel what you've said. The next couple of sentences may be a washout because your audience is distracted.

The rule concerning description placement is simple: Place the description as close as possible to the word that it describes.

Maybe because professors are tired of moving descriptions around in student papers, college entrance tests (including the SAT and ACT) question you thoroughly on this topic.

Which sentence is correct?

A. Roger put the paper into his pocket with nuclear secrets written on it.

B. Roger put the paper with nuclear secrets written on it into his pocket.

Answer: Sentence B is correct because the paper has nuclear secrets written on it, not the pocket.

Try another. Which sentence is correct?

A. Anna pedaled to the mathematics contest on her ten-speed bicycle with a complete set of differential equations.

B. Anna pedaled on her ten-speed bicycle to the mathematics olympics with a complete set of differential equations.

C. With a complete set of differential equations, Anna pedaled on her ten-speed bicycle to the mathematics contest.

Answer: Sentence C is correct. In sentence A, the bicycle has ten speeds, two tires, and a set of equations — not very useful in climbing hills and swerving to avoid taxis! In sentence B, the mathematics contest has a complete set of differential equations. Perhaps so, but the sentence revolves around Anna, so the more likely meaning is that Anna has the equations. Only in sentence C does Anna have the equations. (By the way, she won a silver medal in the little known sport known as Pedal Solving. Contestants do math while riding exercise bikes.)

Just hanging out: Danglers

How can you describe something that isn't there? Descriptions must have something to describe. This idea seems simple, and it *is* simple when the description is one word attached to another. You're not likely to say,

> I want to buy a red.

when you're putting together a Santa Claus outfit for a holiday party. Instead you automatically declare,

> I want to buy a red suit.

In the preceding sentence, *red* describes *suit.* However, two types of descriptions tend to cause as many problems as a double-date with your ex: participles and infinitives. These descriptions look like verbs, but they don't function as verbs. In grammarspeak, they're known as *verbals.* (You can find out more about verbals in Chapter 19.)

In this section, I show you common mistakes with participles and infinitives. Don't worry about the names; you don't need them. Just place these descriptions properly.

First up is participles. Read this sentence:

> Munching a buttered sausage, the cholesterol really builds up.

As you see, the sentence begins with a verb form, *munching,* but *munching* isn't the verb in the sentence. It's a participle — a verb form that describes. (The real verb in the sentence is *builds.*) But participles have to describe something or someone. *Munching* must be tacked onto a muncher. So who is munching? You? Egbert? Everyone in the local diet club? In the sentence, no one is munching. Descriptive verb forms that have nothing appropriate to describe are called *danglers* or *dangling modifiers.* To correct the sentence, add a muncher:

> Munching a buttered sausage, Egbert smiled and waved to his cardiologist.

TIP

In sentences beginning with a descriptive verb form, such as a participle, the subject must perform the action mentioned in the descriptive verb form. In the sample sentence, *Egbert* is the subject of the sentence. The sentence begins with a descriptive verb form, *munching a buttered sausage.* Thus, *Egbert* is the one who is munching. (For more information on identifying the subject of a sentence, see Chapter 3.) If you want the cardiologist to munch, say

> Munching a buttered sausage, the cardiologist returned Egbert's wave.

Here's another example:

> Sitting on the park bench, the soaring space shuttle delighted the little boy.

Oh really? The space shuttle is sitting on a bench and soaring at the same time? Defies the laws of physics, don't you think? (Also, park rules clearly state that no intergalactic vehicles are allowed on benches.) Try again:

> Sitting on the park bench, the little boy was delighted by the soaring space shuttle.

Now *little boy* is the subject of the sentence, so the introductory description applies to him, not to the *space shuttle.* Another correction may be

> The soaring space shuttle delighted the little boy who was sitting on the park bench.

Now the descriptive words *sitting on the park bench* are placed next to little boy, who in fact is the one sitting, being delighted by the soaring space shuttle.

REMEMBER

This topic is so popular on standardized tests that it deserves another example. Here's a faulty sentence:

> Skidding over the icy pavement, the old oak tree couldn't escape the speeding sports car.

You spotted the problem, right? The *tree* is the subject of the sentence, but a tree can't be the thing *skidding over the icy pavement.* That sort of thing happens only in Harry Potter movies. Now for the better version:

> Skidding over the icy pavement, the speeding sports car slammed into the old oak tree.

Now the *speeding sports car* is skidding. No problem. Well, no grammar problem anyway. The traffic cop sees the situation a little differently.

POP QUIZ

Which one is correct?

A. Sailing swiftly across the sea, Samantha's boat was a beautiful sight.

B. Sailing swiftly across the sea, the sight of the beautiful boat made Samantha sob.

Answer: Sentence A is correct. *Sailing swiftly across the sea* describes Samantha's boat. Samantha's boat is performing that action. Sentence B is wrong because in sentence B *sight,* the subject, is sailing. (And of course, a *sight* can't sail.)

Another common dangler is an infinitive (to + verb) that begins a sentence.

> To sew well, a strong light is necessary.

This sentence may sound correct to you. After all, sewing in the dark is hard. But think about the meaning for a moment. Who is sewing? No one, at least the way the sentence is now written. Moving the infinitive may make the sentence sound better to your ears, but the move doesn't solve the problem:

> A strong light is necessary to sew well.

There's still no one sewing, so the sentence is still incorrect. To fix the problem, you must add a person:

> To sew well, you need a strong light. (*You* are sewing.)

> To sew well, sit near a strong light. (*You* is understood in this command sentence.)

> To sew well, everyone needs a strong light. (*Everyone* is sewing.)

> To sew well, Betsy insists on at least a 75-watt bulb. (*Betsy* is sewing.)

TIP

An infinitive at the beginning of a sentence *may* be legal. Check out this sentence:

> To sew well is Betsy's goal.

In the preceding sentence, *to sew well* isn't a description. It's an activity that is Betsy's goal. In other words, *to sew well* is the subject in this sentence. How do you tell the difference between a subject and a description? A subject pairs with a verb (*is* in the example sentence) and answers the questions *who? or what?* (For help finding the subject of a sentence, turn to Chapter 3.) A description is an add-on, contributing more information about something else in the sentence.

POP QUIZ

Which sentence is correct?

A. To enjoy a good cup of coffee, a clean coffeepot is essential.

B. A clean coffeepot is essential to enjoy a good cup of coffee.

Answer. Neither A nor B is correct. (I threw in one of those annoying teacher tricks just to keep you alert.) Neither sentence has a coffee drinker in it. So who's enjoying the coffee? No one. A true correction must add a person:

> To enjoy a good cup of coffee, *you* start with a clean coffeepot.

> To enjoy a good cup of coffee, caffeine *addicts* start with a clean coffeepot.

To enjoy a good cup of coffee, *Anna* starts with a clean coffeepot.

To enjoy a good cup of coffee, start with a clean coffeepot. (Now *you* [understood in this command sentence] are the coffee drinker.)

Avoiding confusing descriptions

Location, location, location! That's what real estate agents say matters, and it's also what grammarians declare. In this section, I examine the hot spot located between two actions. A descriptive word there may confuse your reader. Take a look at the following example:

The teacher that Roger annoyed often assigned detention to him.

What does the sentence mean? Did Roger *often annoy* the teacher? (I'm a teacher, and Roger would certainly annoy me. His burps alone . . . but back to grammar.) Perhaps the teacher *often assigned* detention to Roger. (Yup. Sounds like something Roger's teacher would do.)

Do you see the problem with the sample sentence? It has two distinct, possible meanings. Because *often* is between *annoying* and *assigning*, it may be linked to either of those two actions. The sentence violates a basic rule of description: All descriptions must be clear. You should never place a description where it may have two possible meanings.

How do you fix the sentence? You move *often* so that it is closer to one of the verbs, thus showing the reader which of two words *only* describes. Here are two correct versions, each with a different meaning:

The teacher that Roger often annoyed assigned detention to him.

In this sentence *often* is closer to *annoyed*. Thus, *often* describes *annoyed*. The sentence communicates to the reader that after 514 burps, the teacher lost her temper and assigned detention to Roger.

Here's a second possibility:

The teacher that Roger annoyed assigned detention to him often.

Now *often* is closer to *assigned*. The reader understands that *often* describes *assigned*. The sentence tells the reader that the teacher vowed "not to take anything from that little brat" and assigned detention to Roger every day of the school year, including winter break and Presidents' Day.

Correct or incorrect? You decide.

The pig chewing on pig chow happily burped and made us all run for gas masks.

Answer: Incorrect. You don't know if the pig is *chewing happily* or *burping happily*. Here's how to correct the sentence:

The pig chewing happily on pig chow burped and made us all run for gas masks.

or

The pig chewing on pig chow burped happily and made us all run for gas masks.

One other correction is possible here: the addition of a set of commas. If you set off the description with commas, the reader connects the description to the right verb. Therefore, these two sentences are also okay:

The pig, chewing on pig chow happily, burped and made us all run for gas masks.

The pig, chewing on pig chow, happily burped and made us all run for gas masks.

I have to warn you about the comma-correction. You can't always throw in a comma and fix a problem. In fact, sometimes you create an addition mistake by adding a comma! Check out Chapter 13 for comma advice, or fix the sentence by moving the description.

The most commonly misplaced descriptions are single words: *only, just, almost,* and *even.* See Chapter 22 for a complete explanation of how to place these descriptive words correctly.

Finding the Subject When Words Are Missing from the Sentence

In the never-ending human quest to save time, words are often chopped out of sentences, especially sentences texted while you're sipping a decaf, nonfat latte and running for a bus. (Bad idea on so many levels, by the way, as I explained to the lady who splashed me with her beverage recently.) The assumption is that the sentence is still understandable because the listener or reader supplies the missing piece. Not a bad assumption, as long as you understand what you can chop and what you need to leave alone. Check out these examples:

While sleeping, Johann dreamed that he was a giant frog.

Although screaming in rage, Lola managed to keep an eye on the clock.

If caught, Roger will probably deny everything.

Lulu snored when dreaming of little sheep.

Do you understand what these sentences mean? Here they are again, with the missing words inserted and italicized:

While *he was* sleeping, Johann dreamed that he was a giant frog.

Although *she was* screaming in rage, Lola managed to keep an eye on the clock.

If *he is* caught, Roger will probably deny everything.

Lulu snored when *she was* dreaming of little sheep.

As you see, the subject and part of the verb are missing in each of the sample sentences. The reader fills in both.

You need to remember only one rule for these sentences: The missing subject must be the same as the subject that is present. In other words, if your sentence lacks more information, the reader or listener will assume that you're talking about the same person or thing in both parts of the sentence. Here are some examples:

WRONG: While missing a shovel, the hole in Lulu's backyard was dug by a backhoe.

UNINTENDED MEANING: While the hole was missing a shovel, the hole in Lulu's backyard was dug by a backhoe.

CORRECTION: While missing a shovel, Lulu rented a backhoe to dig a hole in her backyard.

MEANING OF CORRECTED SENTENCE: While she was missing a shovel, Lulu rented a backhoe to dig a hole in her backyard.

WRONG: When showering, Roger's beauty routine requires industrial-strength cleaning products.

UNINTENDED MEANING: When Roger's beauty routine is showering, the beauty routine requires industrial-strength cleaning products.

CORRECTION: When showering, Roger requires industrial-strength cleaning products.

MEANING OF CORRECTED SENTENCE: For each of his twice-yearly showers, Roger has to apply the kind of glop that removes rust from old battleships.

Which sentence is correct?

A. Since conducting the leak test, Dripless's pipe has been watertight.

B. Since conducting the leak test, Dripless reported that the pipe was watertight.

C. Since he conducted the leak test, Dripless's pipe has been watertight.

Answer: Sentences B and C are both correct. The missing subject in sentences A and B is *Dripless*. In sentence A, *Dripless's pipe* is the subject of the second part of the sentence, so there is a mismatch between the two parts of the sentence. In sentence B, *Dripless* is the subject of the second part of the sentence. The two halves of the sentence match. In sentence C, a subject *(he)* is supplied, so the two halves of the sentences don't need to have the same subject.

Comparatively Speaking: Incomplete and Illogical Comparisons

Anyone with a sibling (or a friend, for that matter) understands the human need to compare. Whom does Mom love most? Who has more "likes" on that social media site? Who's the best cook? Comparisons are a part of life, and they're a part of grammar also — a part that writers often get wrong. In this section, you find out how to create proper comparisons.

Missing and presumed wrong

One of my many pet peeves is incomplete comparisons. Here's what I mean:

> Octavia screamed more chillingly.

Do you understand the meaning of this comparison? I doubt it. Take a look at these possible scenarios:

> Octavia screamed more chillingly. "Uh oh," thought Max, "yesterday I thought she would burst my eardrum. If she screams more chillingly today, I'd better get my earplugs out before it's time for tomorrow's lungfest."

or

Octavia screamed more chillingly. Max, rushing to aid Carmen, whose scream of terror had turned his blood to ice, stopped dead. "Octavia sounds even worse," he thought. "I'd better go to her first."

or

Octavia screamed more chillingly. "Please," said the director, "I know that you have just completed take 99 of this extremely taxing verbal exercise, but if you are going to star in my horror movie, you'll have to put a little more into it. Try again!"

I'm sure you see the problem. The comparison in the examples is incomplete. Octavia screamed more chillingly than . . . than what? Until you finish the sentence, your readers are left with as many possibilities as they can imagine. Bottom line: Don't stop explaining your comparison until you get your point across. Look at the following example:

WRONG: Octavia screamed more chillingly.

RIGHT: Octavia screamed more chillingly than I did the day Lulu drove a truck over my toe.

ALSO RIGHT: Octavia screamed more chillingly than she ever had before, and Max resolved to come to her aid after finishing his lunch.

RIGHT AGAIN: Octavia screamed more chillingly than she had in the previous takes, but the director still decided to hire a different actress.

Here's another comparison with a fatal error. Can you spot the problem?

Lulu loved sky-diving more than Lola.

Need another hint? Read on:

Lulu loved sky-diving more than Lola. Lola sobbed uncontrollably as she realized that Lulu, whom she had always considered her best friend, was on the way to the airport instead of on the way to Lola's birthday party. What a disappointment!

or

Lulu loved sky-diving more than Lola. Lola was fine for the first 409 jumps, but then her enthusiasm began to flag. Lulu, on the other hand, was climbing into the airplane eagerly, as if it were her first jump of the day.

See the problem? *Lulu loved sky-diving more than Lola* is incomplete. Your reader can understand the comparison in two different ways, as the two stories illustrate.

The rule here is simple: Don't omit words that are necessary to the meaning of the comparison.

> WRONG: Lulu loved sky-diving more than Lola.

> RIGHT: Lulu loved sky-diving more than she loved Lola.

> ALSO RIGHT: Lulu loved sky-diving more than Lola did.

One more time. What's the problem now?

> "My life is the best," explained Ralph.

This one is so easy that you don't need stories. *Best* how? In money, fame, love, health, lack of body odor, winning lottery tickets, number of Twitter followers? Ralph's friends may understand his statement, but no one else will.

REMEMBER In making a comparison, be clear and complete.

Which sentence is correct?

POP QUIZ

A. My cat Agatha slapped her tail more quickly.

B. My cat Agatha slapped her tail more quickly than Dorothy.

Answer: Both are wrong. (Sorry! Trick question.) The meaning is unclear in both A and B. In sentence A, the reader is left asking *more quickly than what?* In sentence B, the sentence may mean *my cat Agatha slapped her tail more quickly than she slapped Dorothy* or *my cat Agatha slapped her tail more quickly than Dorothy slapped the cat's tail.* Neither comparison is complete.

Illogical comparisons

Did you know that Babe Ruth played better than any baseball player? Before I continue, here's an explanation of that question for those of you who (gasp of pity here) don't like baseball. Babe Ruth was a baseball player. Actually, a great baseball player — one of the best, and a New York Yankee. So what's wrong with the first sentence of this section? It takes Babe Ruth out of the group of baseball players. It makes him a *non*-baseball player. To keep Babe Ruth in the sport, add *other*:

> WRONG: Babe Ruth played better than any baseball player.

> RIGHT: Babe Ruth played better than any other baseball player.

The rule for comparisons here is very simple: Use the word *other* or *else* when comparing someone or something to other members of the same group. Check out the following examples:

> WRONG: The star soprano of the Santa Lola Opera, Sarah Screema, sings louder than anyone in the cast.
>
> WHY IT'S WRONG: The sentence makes it clear that Sarah is in the cast, but the comparison implies that she's not in the cast. Illogical!
>
> RIGHT: The star soprano of the Santa Lola Opera, Sarah Screema, sings louder than anyone *else* in the cast.

> WRONG: That robot short-circuits more frequently than any mechanical device.
>
> WHY IT'S WRONG: A robot is, by definition, a mechanical device, but the comparison takes the robot out of the group of mechanical devices.
>
> RIGHT: That robot short-circuits more frequently than any *other* mechanical device.

Here's another problem. Can you find it?

> Max's nose is longer than Michael.

Okay, before you say anything, I should mention that Michael is tall — not skyscraper tall, but at least six-two. Now do you see what's wrong with the sentence? Max's nose, a real tourist attraction for its length *and* width (not including the pimple at the end) is about four inches long. It is *not* longer than Michael. It is longer than Michael's *nose*.

> WRONG: Max's nose is longer than Michael.
>
> RIGHT: Max's nose is longer than Michael's nose.
>
> ALSO RIGHT: Max's nose is longer than Michael's.

Here's the bottom line:

>> Make sure your comparisons are logical.

>> Check to see that you have compared what you want to compare — two things that are at least remotely related.

>> If the first part of the comparison involves a possessive noun or pronoun (showing ownership), the second part of the comparison probably needs a possessive also. For more information on possessive nouns, see Chapter 11. For more information on possessive pronouns, see Chapter 8.

Which is more difficult, the SAT Writing section or the ACT English section? I don't know. I do know that both test you on comparisons, highlighting the issues covered in this section.

Which sentence is correct?

A. The pug is cuter than any breed of dog.

B. The pug is cuter than any other breed of dog.

Answer: Sentence B is correct, at least in terms of grammar. (Please feel free to cross out "pug" and substitute your favorite dog breed.) By definition, a pug is a dog, and sentence A implies that pugs aren't. The word *other* in sentence B returns pugs to dogdom.

Another common error involves creating comparisons out of absolutes — characteristics that *can't* be compared. If I ask you whether this chapter is more unique than the previous chapter, the answer is definitely not. Why? Because nothing is *more unique.* The word *unique* means "one of a kind." Either something is one of a kind, or it's not. No halfway point, no degrees of uniqueness, no . . . well, you get the idea. You can't compare something that's unique to anything but itself. Check out the following examples:

> WRONG: The vase that Pete cracked was more unique than the Grecian urn.
>
> ALSO WRONG: The vase that Pete cracked was fairly unique.
>
> ALSO WRONG: The vase that Pete cracked was most unique.
>
> WRONG AGAIN: The vase that Pete cracked was very unique.
>
> RIGHT: The vase that Pete cracked was unique.
>
> ALSO RIGHT: The vase that Pete cracked was unique, as was the Grecian urn.
>
> RIGHT AGAIN: The vase that Pete cracked was more unusual than the Grecian urn.
>
> WHY IT'S RIGHT: *Unusual* is not an absolute term, so you can use it in comparisons.

The word *unique* is not unique. Several other words share its absolute quality. One is *perfect.* Something is perfect or not perfect; nothing is *very perfect* or *unbelievably perfect* or *somewhat perfect.* (I am bound, as a patriotic American, to point out one exception: The United States Constitution contains a statement of purpose citing the need to create "a more perfect union.") Another absolute word is *round.* Your shape is *round* or *not round.* Your shape isn't *a bit round, rounder,* or *roundest.* Here are some examples:

WRONG: "Lola is *extremely perfect* when it comes to grammar, as I am," said Lulu.

WHY IT'S WRONG: *Perfect* is absolute. There are no degrees of perfection.

RIGHT: "Lola is *nearly perfect* when it comes to grammar, as I am," said Lulu.

WHY IT'S RIGHT: You can approach an absolute quality, comparing how close someone or something comes to the quality. Lola and Lulu approach perfection, but neither achieves it.

ALSO RIGHT: "Lola is *perfect* when it comes to grammar, as I am," said Lulu.

WHY THEY'RE RIGHT: You may approach *perfect,* as in *nearly perfect.* You may also be *perfect,* without any qualifiers.

WRONG: Of the two circles drawn on the chalkboard, mine is rounder.

WHY IT'S WRONG: The shape is round or it's not round. It can't be *rounder.* Also, by definition circles are *round.*

RIGHT: Of the two *shapes* drawn on the chalkboard, mine is *more nearly round.*

RIGHT AGAIN: Neither of the two shapes drawn on the chalkboard is *round,* but mine approaches *roundness.*

As some of the "RIGHT" sentences in the preceding examples illustrate, you can't compare absolute qualities, but you can compare how close people or things come to having those qualities.

TIP

One more word causes all sorts of trouble in comparisons: *equally.* You hear the expression *equally as* quite frequently. You don't need the *as* because the word *equally* contains the idea of comparison. For example:

WRONG: Roger got a lighter sentence than Lulu, but he is *equally as* guilty because he stole as many doughnuts as she did.

RIGHT: Roger got a lighter sentence than Lulu, but he is *equally* guilty because he stole as many doughnuts as she did.

ALSO RIGHT: Roger got a lighter sentence than Lulu, but he is as guilty as she is because he stole the same number of doughnuts.

POP QUIZ

Find the correct sentence(s).

A. Michael's recent drama is even more unique than his last play.

B. Michael's recent drama is even more unusual than his last play.

C. Michael's recent drama is unique, as was his last play.

Answer: Sentences B and C are correct. Sentence A incorrectly compares an absolute (*unique*). In sentence B *more unusual* expresses a correct comparison. Sentence C tells you that Michael's recent drama is unique and that his last play was also unique. The absolute is not being compared but simply applied to two different things.

Steering Clear of Vague Pronouns

Pronouns, which stand in for nouns or other pronouns, attract problems as strongly as a newly scrubbed floor invites muddy footprints. In Chapter 8, I deal with pronoun case (whether to write *me* or *I*, for example). Here I show you how to ensure that every pronoun reference is clear and proper according to the standards of formal English.

Matching pronouns to antecedents

The *antecedent* of a pronoun is the word that the pronoun replaces. When you're speaking or writing, you know what meaning you're trying to convey. But your readers or listeners aren't mind readers. If you plop a pronoun into a sentence and don't make sure that the pronoun has a clear antecedent, you risk being misunderstood. For example, what do you think is going on in this sentence?

> Bob told Bill he had to leave.

Two possible interpretations come to mind:

> Bob shouted, "You've been here for three weeks. I can't stand it anymore. It's time to leave, Bill."

> Bob murmured, "I have had a great time playing baseball with you. I wish I could stay until the game is over. Unfortunately, I have leave. I can't miss my plane."

Both of these statements are possible expansions of the original, short sentence because the pronoun *he* could refer to either *Bill* or *Bob*. True, you may be talking to someone who knows that Bill has a tendency to overstay his welcome, in which case you don't need to clarify the pronoun antecedent. But why take a chance?

TIP

To clarify a pronoun, you can quote (as you see in the preceding examples). Another solution is to rewrite the sentence so that the vague pronoun is unnecessary:

> Bob told Bill to leave.

> Bob explained his reasons for leaving when he spoke with Bill.

Instead of two (or more) possible antecedents, some faulty sentences throw in a pronoun that has no antecedent at all. Penalty box! Also, you can't pair a pronoun with an antecedent that is almost, but not quite right. Scan this sentence:

Lola's a lawyer, and I want to study it.

What does *it* replace? *Law*, I suppose. But the word *law* is not in the sentence; *lawyer* is. *Law* and *lawyer* are close, but not close enough.

RIGHT: Lola's a lawyer, and I want to be one also.

WHY IT'S RIGHT: *One* refers to *lawyer.*

ALSO RIGHT: I'd like to study law, as Lola did.

WHY IT'S ALSO RIGHT: There's no pronoun in the sentence.

POP QUIZ

Which sentence is correct?

A. Lola and her sister are in Egypt because Lola is an archaeologist.

B. Lola and her sister went to Egypt because she's an archaeologist.

Answer: Sentence A is correct. In sentence B, the reader can't determine who *she* is — *Lola* or *her sister*. Sentence A, without the pronoun *she*, is clear.

One more. Which sentence is correct?

A. Lola has always been interested in archaeology because she thinks they spend a lot of time in the dirt.

B. Lola has always been interested in archaeology because she thinks archaeologists spend a lot of time in the dirt.

Answer: Sentence B is correct. In sentence A, no proper antecedent exists for *they*. Sentence B replaces *they* with the noun *archaeologists*.

One pronoun, one idea

One pronoun may refer to one noun. A plural pronoun may refer to more than one noun. But no pronoun may refer to a whole sentence or a whole paragraph. Consider the following scenario:

Lulu likes to arrive at school around 11 each day because she thinks that getting up at any hour earlier than 10 is ridiculous. The principal, not surprisingly, thinks that arriving two hours late each day is not a good idea. *This* is a problem.

IN THE PAPER IT SAYS . . .

Are you writing about literature or even trashy tabloid journalism? If so, beware of *it* and *they*. Some common errors follow those pronouns. Check out these examples:

> In *Hamlet,* it says that Claudius is a murderer.

Oh really? What does *it* mean? The play can't speak, and the author of the play (Shakespeare) is a *who*. Actually, in *Hamlet,* the ghost says that Claudius is a murderer, but even the ghost is a *he*. In other words, *it* has no antecedent. Reword the sentence:

> In *Hamlet* Claudius is a murderer.

> In *Hamlet* the ghost declares that Claudius is a murderer.

> My teacher says that in *Hamlet* Claudius is a murderer, but I'm not sure because I never understand Shakespeare's plays.

A variation of this error occurs in this sentence:

> In today's paper they say that more and more schools are dropping Shakespeare's plays from the curriculum.

Who is *they?* Perhaps the authors of an article, but the sentence doesn't make that fact clear. More likely the author of the sentence thinks that *they* is a good, all-purpose pronoun for talking about anonymous or nameless authors. In other words, the antecedent of *they* is "I don't know and I really don't care." Wrong! The antecedent of *they* must be a real, identifiable group of people. Here is one possible correction:

> Today's paper reports that more and more schools are dropping Shakespeare's plays from the curriculum.

Notice that the revised sentence eliminates the pronoun. No pronoun = no problem!

This certainly is a problem, and not because of Lulu's sleeping habits or the principal's beliefs. *This* is a problem because the antecedent of the word *this* is unclear. What does *this* mean? The fact that Lulu arrives around 11? That Lulu thinks getting up before 10 is out of the question? Or that the principal and Lulu are not, to put it mildly, in sync? Or all of the above?

The writer probably intends *this* to refer to *all of the above,* a perfectly good answer on those horrible multiple choice tests you have to take far too often.

Unfortunately, *all of the above* is not a good answer to the question, "What does the pronoun mean?"

Thus

> WRONG: The new orange dye Lola's hairdresser selected looks horrible, and the cut looks as though a kindergartener stole some scissors. *This* persuaded Lola to attend the dance wearing a wig.

> WHY IT'S WRONG: *This* is referring to the 20 words of the preceding sentence, not to one noun.

> RIGHT: Because the new orange dye Lola's hairdresser selected looks horrible and the cut looks as though a kindergartener stole some scissors, Lola decided to attend the dance wearing a wig.

> ALSO RIGHT: The fact that the new orange dye her hairdresser selected looks horrible and the cut looks as though a kindergartener stole some scissors persuaded Lola to attend the dance wearing a wig.

> WHY THEY'RE RIGHT: Eliminating *this* eliminates the problem.

TIP

As you see in the preceding example, sometimes the only way to avoid this sort of pronoun error is to write a sentence that needs no pronoun at all.

In ordinary speech (conversational English) you may use *this, which,* or *that* to refer to more than one word, as long as your meaning is clear. For example:

> Roger refused to defuse the explosive postage stamp, which angered all the postal workers.

The pronoun *which* in the preceding example refers to the fact that Roger refused to defuse the explosive stamp. Your audience grasps the meaning easily. However, grammatically, the sentence is incorrect because *which* should replace only one noun. Bottom line: In formal writing, you should follow the rule and reject the sentence. In informal situations, go ahead and use it.

POP QUIZ

Which sentence is correct?

A. The roof leaked and the floor creaked, which kept Ned up all night.

B. The leaky roof and the creaky floor kept Ned up all night.

Answer: Sentence B, lacking a pronoun, has no pronoun error. Sentence A is incorrect because *which* refers to two ideas, not to one noun.

EXTRA! EXTRA! DELETING ALL THAT'S EXTRA FROM YOUR SENTENCES

In your quest for clarity, don't go overboard and explain what's already evident. Here's an example of this practice:

> I live in Manhattan, an island surrounded by water. My 17-story apartment building is tall. It was built many years ago in 1929. I work as a teacher in a school. I write *For Dummies* books about grammar, which explain grammar to readers. I will also consider jumping from the roof of my tall apartment building if I have to write any more boring, repetitive, say-the-same-thing-at-least-twice sentences like these.

Overstuffed sentences sound silly and condescending. I mean, really. *An island surrounded by water* — that's clever. What surrounds other islands? Bagels? My *For Dummies books about grammar explain grammar to readers*. There's a shock. I'm sure you thought my grammar books explained Tai Chi or llama-raising. And once I wrote *repetitive*, I didn't have to tack on *say-the-same-thing-at-least-twice*. One word said it all. The moral of the story: Be clear, but don't repeat yourself.

Chapter **22**

Grammar Devils

D o you have a devil of a time with grammar? Probably not, if you've spent a few hours reading through the preceding chapters of *English Grammar For Dummies,* 3rd Edition (she said modestly). But even grammar experts trip up sometimes. This chapter introduces you to the little devils that can easily tug your writing away from the proper path. From double negatives to sound–alikes to words that appear correct but aren't, this chapter explains it all.

Deleting Double Negatives

In some lucky languages, the more negatives the better. In English, however, two negatives are a no-no. (By the way, no-no is *not* a double negative! It's just slang for something that's prohibited.) Two negative words logically create a positive statement. Take a look at these examples:

WHAT LENNY SAID: I didn't kill nobody.

WHAT LENNY THINKS THAT MEANS: I am not a murderer. I have killed no one.

WHAT IT REALLY MEANS: I am a murderer. I "didn't kill *nobody,* but I did kill *somebody."*

CORRECTED SENTENCE: I didn't kill anybody.

You can argue, and in part you'd be right, that most listeners or readers will understand that Lenny is trying to say he's innocent. In formal English, though, steer clear of double negatives.

One of the most common double negatives is *cannot help but.* How many times have you heard someone say something like

> Egbert *cannot help but* act in that dramatic style; he was trained by a real ham.

Unfortunately, this sentence is wrong. The *not* (inside the word *cannot*) and the *but* both express negative ideas. Use one or the other. Don't use both. Here is the correct version:

> Egbert *cannot help acting* in that dramatic style; he was trained by a real ham.

If you think this is one in a long list of useless grammar rules, think again. A double-negative mistake can completely wreck your sentence because in English, two negatives make a positive. So when you say *cannot help but,* you actually express the opposite of what you imagine you're saying (or writing). For example:

> WHAT MAX SAID TO THE BOSS: I cannot help but ask for a raise.
>
> WHAT HE THINKS HE SAID: I have to ask for a raise.
>
> WHAT HE REALLY SAID: I can't ask for a raise.

> WHAT THE BOSS SAID TO MAX: I cannot help but say no.
>
> WHAT THE BOSS THINKS SHE SAID: No.
>
> WHAT THE BOSS ACTUALLY SAID: Yes.

POP QUIZ

Which sentence has no double negative?

A. I cannot help but think that this double-negative rule is ridiculous.

B. I ain't got nobody.

C. I cannot help thinking that this double-negative rule is ridiculous.

Answer: Sentence C is double-negative free. Sentence A contains *cannot help but,* and sentence B has *ain't* (a slang form of *don't*) and *nobody.*

Another common double negative is *can't hardly.* That's a phrase in wide use in many areas, and it's fine in informal, friendly situations. When you're using formal English, though, stay away from this expression. *Can't* is short for *cannot,* which contains the negative *not. Hardly* is another negative word. If you combine them, by the logic of grammar, you've said the opposite of what you intended — the positive instead of the negative. Here are a few examples:

WHAT ROGER SAID: Lulu can't hardly count her tattoos.

WHAT ROGER THINKS HE SAID: Lulu can't count her tattoos.

WHAT ROGER ACTUALLY SAID: Lulu can count her tattoos.

WHAT EUGENE WROTE: According to Lola, Ella can't hardly wait until her divorce becomes final.

WHAT EUGENE THINKS THE SENTENCE MEANS: Ella is eager for her divorce to become final.

WHAT THE SENTENCE ACTUALLY MEANS: Ella can wait.

TIP

A variation of this double negative is *can't scarcely, aren't scarcely,* or *isn't scarcely.* Once again, *can't* is short for *cannot,* clearly a negative. *Aren't* and *isn't* are the negative forms of *are* and *is. Scarcely* is also negative. Use them together and you end up with a positive, not a super-negative.

Here's one more double negative, in a couple of forms: *hadn't only, haven't only, hasn't only, hadn't but, haven't but,* and *hasn't but.* All express positive ideas because the *not (n't)* part of the verb and the *only* or *but* are both negatives:

WRONG: Al *hadn't but* ten seconds to defuse the bomb before civilization as we know it ended.

WHY IT'S WRONG: As it reads now, the sentence says that Al had more than ten seconds to defuse the bomb, but the little red numbers on the trigger were at seven and decreasing rapidly.

RIGHT: Al *had but* ten seconds to defuse the bomb before civilization as we know it ended.

ALSO RIGHT: Al *had* only ten seconds to defuse the bomb before civilization as we know it ended.

WRONG: Roger *hasn't only* ten nuclear secrets.

WHY IT'S WRONG: The sentence now says that Roger has more than ten secrets, but he just counted them and there are ten.

RIGHT: Roger *has only* ten nuclear secrets.

POP QUIZ

Which sentence is correct?

A. Ella can't hardly understand those pesky grammar rules.

B. Ella can't help but be confused by those pesky grammar rules.

Answer: Both are wrong. (Did I fool you?) In sentence A, *can't hardly* is a double negative. In sentence B, *cannot help but* is a double negative.

Scoring D Minus

Many people are sloppy talkers. They say words quickly, often dropping letters. When you hear what a sloppy talker says, you probably guess the intended meaning. But if you reproduce those sounds when you're writing, you may end up with a misspelled word. The letter *D* is a prime example of this practice. Judging from the signs I often see on my walks around New York City, *D* stands for "dropped." Stores sell *grill cheese* (not *grilled*, as it should be) and *ice tea* (which is actually *iced)*. You may find these sentences familiar, too:

> Lola *was suppose* to take out the garbage, but she refused to do so.

> Ralph *use* to take out the trash, but after that unfortunate encounter with a raccoon, he is reluctant to go anywhere near the cans.

> George *is suppose* to do all kinds of things, but of course he never does anything he *is suppose* to do.

Each one is wrong. Check out the italicized verbs: *was suppose, use,* and *is suppose.* All represent what people hear but not what the speaker is actually trying to say. The correct words to use in these instances are *supposed* and *used* — past-tense forms.

I can't leave this topic without mentioning the opposite error, which is far less common but can lead to some silly errors. A small restaurant in my neighborhood posted a "Help Wanted" sign, asking *grilled men* to apply. No doubt they didn't want someone who'd sat on a barbecue, but rather someone who could cook on a grill. The added *D* makes quite a difference in meaning!

Distinguishing Between Word Twins and Triplets

I'm not sure who decided that it was a fine idea to have two words (and sometimes three) with completely different definitions, spelled in completely different ways, sounding exactly the same. (These word groups are known as *homonyms.*) But someone did, and you're stuck with the result. In this section, you see how to identify the twins or triplets and use them appropriately.

Three terrible twos

In English you find three "to's." And no, they don't add up to six. *To* may be part of an infinitive (*to speak, to dream*) or it may show movement towards someone or something (*to the store, to me*). *Two* is the number (*two eyes, two ears*). *Too* means "also" (*Are you going too?*) or "more than enough" (*too expensive, too wide*). In other words:

> If you *two* want *to* skip school and go *to* the ball game, today's a good day because the teacher will be *too* busy *to* check.

> The *two* basketballs that hit Larry in the head yesterday were *too* soft *to* do much damage, but Larry is suing anyway.

> *Two* things you should always remember before you decide *to* break a grammar rule: It is never *too* late *to* learn proper English, and you are never *too* old *to* get in trouble with your teacher.

Goldilocks and the three there's

There is a place. *Their* shows ownership. *They're* is short for *they are.* Some examples:

> "*They're* too short," muttered Egbert as he eyed the strips of bacon. (*They're* means *they are.*)

> "Why don't you take some longer strips from *their* plates," suggested Lola. (The plates belong to *them* — expressed by the possessive pronoun *their.*)

> "My arm is not long enough to reach over *there*," sighed Egbert. (*There* is a place.)

Your and you're: A problem

You're in trouble if *your* apostrophes are in the wrong place, especially when you're writing in the second person. (The second person is the form that uses *you*, *your*, *yours*, both singular and plural.) *You're* means *you are*. *Your* shows possession. These two words are not interchangeable. Some examples:

> "*You're* not going to eat that rotten pumpkin," declared Rachel. *(You are not going to eat.)*

> "*Your* refusal to eat the pumpkin means that you will be given mystery meat instead," commented Dean. (The refusal comes from *you,* so you need the possessive word *your*.)

> "*You're* going to wear that pumpkin if you threaten me," said Lola. *(You are going to wear.)*

> "I'm not afraid of *your* threats!" stated Art. (The threats come from *you*, so you need the possessive word *your*.)

The owl rule: Who's, whose

Whose shows ownership. It seldom causes any problems, except when it's confused with another word: *who's*. *Who's* is a contraction that is short for *who is*. In other words

> The boy *whose* hat was burning was last seen running down the street screaming, "*Who's* in charge of fire-fighting in this town?" (*Whose* shows that the boy possesses the hat, and *who's* means *who is in charge.*)

> *Whose* box of firecrackers is on the radiator? (*Who's* going to tell Egbert that his living room looks like the Fourth of July? *Whose* asks about possession, and *who's* means *who is going.*)

It's an its problem

I'm not talking about how a poison-ivy rash feels. I'm talking about a possessive pronoun *(its)* and a contraction *(it's)*. People who suffer from an *its* problem confuse the two words. Take heart: The remedy is simple. Just remember what each word means.

Its shows possession:

> The computer has exploded, and *its* screen is now decorating the ceiling.

It's means it is:

> *It's* raining cats and dogs, but I don't see any alligators.

So *it's* nice to know that grammar has *its* own rules. By the way, one of those rules is that *no possessive pronoun ever has an apostrophe*. Ever. Never. Never ever. Remember: If *it* owns something, dump the apostrophe.

POP QUIZ

Which sentences are correct?

A. Its going to rain.

B. Whose umbrella is this?

C. Did you lose you're umbrella?

D. The rain was to heavy, so we went inside.

Answer: Sentence B is correct. *Whose* is a possessive form. In Sentence A, you need *It's*, short for *is it*. Sentence C should read *your umbrella*, a possessive, not *you're* (*you are*). In Sentence D, the rain should be *too heavy*, not *to*.

Close, But Not Close Enough: Words That Resemble Each Other

Some words resemble each other so much that one is often mistaken for the other. In this section, you see these close relatives that are definitely *not* in the same family.

Continually (continuously?) making mistakes

Two description pairs trespass on each other's territory — *continuously/continuous* and *continually/continual*. Which pair should you turn to express your meaning? Read on.

Continual and *continually* refer to events that happen over and over again, but with breaks in between each instance. (*Continual* describes nouns, and *continually* describes verbs.) *Continuous* and *continuously* are for situations without gaps. (As you've probably guessed, *continuous* attaches to nouns, and *continuously* to verbs.) *Continuous* noise is steady, uninterrupted, like the drone of the electric generator in your local power plant. *Continual* noise is what you hear when I go bowling. You hear silence (when I stare at the pins), a little noise (when the ball rolls down the alley), and silence again (when the ball slides into the gutter without hitting anything). After an hour you hear noise (when I finally hit something and begin to cheer). In case you're wondering, I'm a very bad bowler.

Here are a couple of examples of these two descriptions in action:

> WRONG: Jim screams *continually* until Lola stuffs rags in his mouth.
>
> WHY IT'S WRONG: Jim's screams don't come and go. When he's upset, he's really upset, and nothing shuts him up except a gag.
>
> RIGHT: Jim screams *continuously* until Lola stuffs rags in his mouth.
>
> WHY IT'S RIGHT: In this version, Jim takes no breaks.

> WRONG: Ella's *continuous* attempts to impress Larry were unsuccessful. (Despite the fact that she sent him a fruit basket on Monday and flowers on Tuesday, Larry ignored her.)
>
> WHY IT'S WRONG: Ella's attempts stop and start. She does one thing on Monday, rests up, and then does another on Tuesday.
>
> RIGHT: Ella's *continual* attempts to impress Larry were unsuccessful.
>
> WHY IT'S RIGHT: Now the sentence talks about a recurring action.

By the way, this pair had a cameo appearance on a recent standardized test. Test-takers, refer to these examples *continually* so they'll remain in your memory *continuously*.

Are you affected? Or effected? Do you sit or set?

Has the study of grammar *affected* or *effected* your brain? Should you *set* or *sit* on the porch to think about this sentence? These two pairs of words are a complete annoyance, but once you learn them, you're all set. (And I do mean *set*.) Here are the definitions:

Affect versus *effect*: *Affect* is a verb. It means to influence. *Effect* is a noun meaning result. Hence

> Sunlight affects Pete's appetite; he never eats during the day.
>
> Lola thinks that pizza will positively affect her diet, but I think the effect will be disastrous.

Special note: *Affect* may also be a noun meaning "the way one relates to and shows emotions." *Effect* may act as a verb meaning "to cause a complete change." However, you rarely need these secondary meanings.

Sit versus *set*: *Sit* is a verb meaning "to plop yourself down on a chair, to take a load off your feet." *Set* means "to put something else down, to place something in a particular spot." Thus

> Ron seldom sits for more than two minutes.

> I'd like to sit down while I speak, but only if you promise not to set that plate of pickled fish in front of me.

Woulda, coulda, shoulda

Woulda, coulda, shoulda. These three "verbs" are potholes on the road to better grammar. Why? Because they don't exist. Here's the recipe for a grammatical felony.

1. Start with three real verb phrases: *would have*, *could have*, and *should have*.

2. Turn them into contractions: *would've*, *could've*, and *should've*.

3. Now turn them back into words. But don't turn them back into the words they actually represent. Instead, let your ears be your guide. (It helps if you have a lot of wax in your ears because the sounds don't quite match.)

4. Now say the following: *would of, could of, and should of.*

5. Cross out everything you've written, because these three phrases are never correct. Don't use them!

Take a look at these examples:

> WRONG: If George had asked me to join the spy ring, I would of said, "No way."

> RIGHT: If George had asked me to join the spy ring, I would have said, "No way."

> ALSO RIGHT: If George had asked me to join the spy ring, I would've said, "No way."

Here's another set:

> WRONG: When I heard about the spy ring, I should of told the Central Intelligence Agency.

RIGHT: When I heard about the spy ring, I should have told the Central Intelligence Agency.

ALSO RIGHT: When I heard about the spy ring, I should've told the Central Intelligence Agency.

You gotta problem with grammar?

If you speak proper English all the time, and few people do, you probably don't say *gotta, gonna, gotcha,* or *hisself.* You never use *done* all by itself as the verb in the sentence. These expressions come from various regional accents and customs (similar to the one that makes New Yorkers shop at a store on *Toidy-toid and Toid* — Thirty-third and Third, for those of you from other parts of the world). Although saying *gotta* when you're chatting with a friend is perfectly okay, it isn't okay when you're speaking to a teacher, a boss, a television interviewer, the supreme ruler of the universe, and anyone else in authority. Thus,

WRONG: You *gonna* wait for Cedric? He bought *hisself* a new car, and he might give us a ride.

RIGHT: *Are* you *going* to wait for Cedric? He bought a new car for himself, and he might give us a ride.

WRONG: No, I *gotta* go.

RIGHT: No, I *have to* go.

WRONG: We *done* nothing today!

RIGHT: We *have done* nothing today! (or, We *haven't done* anything today!)

WRONG: *Gotcha.* Next week we'll go bowling.

RIGHT: *I understand.* Next week we'll go bowling.

I'd add another sample conversation, but it's almost time for lunch. I gotta go.

Accepting the difference

Only two letters separate *accept* from *except,* but those two letters make a big difference. *Accept* is "to say yes to, to agree, to receive." *Except* means "everything but." *Except* excludes, and *accepts* welcomes. Therefore,

Please *accept* my apology. I cleaned everything in the kitchen *except* for the oven. I ran out of time.

Marge *accepted* all her in-laws *except* for Larry. She hated him!

Hanged or hung up on grammar

To hang is a verb meaning *to suspend*. In the present tense the same verb does double duty. You *hang* a picture and you also *hang* a murderer, at least in countries with that form of capital punishment. Past tense is different; in general, people are *hanged* and objects are *hung*. Therefore

> In Michael's new movie, Lulu stars as the righteous rebel leader *hanged* by the opposition.

> After the stirring execution scene, the rebels rally, inspired by a picture of Lulu that someone *hung* on the wall of their headquarters.

The farther or further of our country

Farther refers to distance. If you need to travel *farther*, you have more miles to cover. *Further* also has a sense of "more" in it, but not more distance. Instead, *further* means "additional." *Further* is for time, ideas, activities, and lots more. Some examples:

> Abe needs *further* work on his online profile, but he's too lazy to update it.

> Mimi flew *farther* than anyone else in the club, even though she's afraid of heights.

> They believe *further* discussion is silly, because everyone's mind is already made up.

> The *farther* Jim walks, the more his shoes hurt.

POP QUIZ

Which sentences are correct?

A. He hanged the painting on the wall.

B. I except the nomination for president.

C. That donation to my campaign has no effect on my political views.

D. The continuous sound from that machine is driving me crazy! It never stops!

E. Jose would of attended the meeting, but his plane was delayed.

Answer: Sentences C and D are correct because *effect* is "a consequence or result," and a *continuous sound* never stops. In sentence A, *hung* is the verb you want. In sentence B, *accept* is correct. Sentence E should read *would have* or *would've*.

Roaming Descriptions

A couple of small words pack a huge punch when it comes to meaning. Specifically, when you see *even, almost, nearly, only,* or *just,* watch out! Errors pop up if you plop them into the wrong spot.

Placing "even"

Even is one of the sneaky modifiers that can land any place in a sentence — and change the meaning of what you're saying. Take a look at this example:

It's two hours before the grand opening of the school show. Lulu and George have been rehearsing for weeks. They know all the dances, and Lulu has only one faint bruise left from George's tricky elbow maneuver. Suddenly, George's evil twin Lester, mad with jealousy, "accidentally" places his foot in George's path. George is down! His ankle is sprained! What will happen to the show?

>> Possibility 1: Lulu shouts, "We can still go on! *Even Lester* knows the dances."

>> Possibility 2: Lulu shouts, "We can still go on! Lester *even knows* the dances."

>> Possibility 3: Lulu shouts, "We can still go on! Lester knows *even the dances.*"

What's going on here? These three statements look almost the same, but they aren't. Here's what each one means:

>> Possibility 1: Lulu surveys the 15 boys gathered around George. She knows that any one of them could step in at a moment's notice. After all, the dances are very easy. *Even Lester,* the clumsiest boy in the class, knows the dances. If *even Lester* can perform the role, it will be a piece of cake for everyone else.

>> Possibility 2: Lulu surveys the 15 boys gathered around George. It doesn't look good. Most of them would be willing, but they've been busy learning other parts. There's no time to teach them George's role. Then she spies Lester. With a gasp, she realizes that Lester has been watching George every minute of rehearsal. Although the curtain will go up very soon, the show can still be saved. Lester doesn't have to practice; he doesn't have to learn something new. Lester *even knows* the dances.

>> Possibility 3: The whole group looks at Lester almost as soon as George hits the floor. Yes, Lester knows the words. He's been reciting George's lines for weeks now, helping George learn the part. Yes, Lester can sing; everyone's heard him. But what about the dances? There's no time to teach him. Just then, Lester begins to twirl around the stage. Lulu sighs with relief. Lester knows *even the dances.* The show will go on!

Got it? *Even* is a description; *even* describes the words that follow it. To put it another way, *even* begins a comparison:

>> Possibility 1: *even* Lester (as well as everyone else)

>> Possibility 2: *even* knows (doesn't have to learn)

>> Possibility 3: *even* the dances (as well as the songs and words)

So here's the rule. Put *even* at the beginning of the comparison implied in the sentence.

Placing "almost" and "nearly"

Almost and *nearly* are tricky descriptions. Here's an example:

> Last night Lulu wrote for *almost* (or *nearly*) an hour and then went rollerblading.

and

> Last night Lulu *almost* (or *nearly*) wrote for an hour and then went rollerblading.

In the first sentence, Lulu wrote for 55 minutes and then stopped. In the second sentence, Lulu intended to write, but every time she sat down at the computer, she remembered that she hadn't watered the plants, called her best friend Lola, made a sandwich, and so forth. After an hour of wasted time and without one word on the screen, she grabbed her rollerblades and left.

Almost and *nearly* begin the comparison. Lulu *almost wrote* (or *nearly wrote*), but she didn't. Or Lulu wrote for *almost an hour* (or *nearly an hour*), but not for a *whole hour*. In deciding where to put these words, add the missing ideas and see whether the position of the word makes sense. (I discuss comparisons further in Chapter 20.)

Placing "only" and "just"

If only the word *only* were simpler to understand! If everyone thought about the word *just* for *just* a minute. Like the other tricky words in this section, *only* and *just* change the meaning of the sentence every time their positions are altered. Here are examples of *only* and *just* in action:

> *Only* (or *just*) Lex went to Iceland. (No one else went.)

> Lex *only* went to Iceland. (He didn't do anything else.)

Lex *just* went to Iceland. (The ink on his passport is still wet. *Just* may mean *recently*.)

Lex went *only* (or *just*) to Iceland. (He skipped Antarctica.)

TIP

Many people place *only* in front of a verb and assume that it applies to another idea in the sentence. I see t-shirts all the time with slogans like "My dad went to NYC and only bought me a lousy t-shirt." The *only* should be in front of *a lousy t-shirt* because the sentence implies that Dad should have bought more — the Empire State Building, perhaps. The original wording describes a terrible trip: Zoom in from the airport, buy a t-shirt, and zoom back home.

POP QUIZ

Which sentence is correct?

A. I only want one reindeer for my trip to the North Pole, not all of them.

B. Greg nearly bought that hat, but at the last minute we persuaded him that it was too expensive.

C. Just Allen attended the opera; he didn't have time for the party afterward.

Answer: Sentence B is correct. In sentence A, the number of reindeer is an issue, so *only* belongs in front of *one*, not before *want*. In Sentence C, *the opera* and the *party* are the focus, so *just* should precede *the opera*, not *attended*.

Pairs of Trouble: Complicated Verbs

Whenever I'm trying to set up a new piece of technology, I think about the person who wrote the manual. In my imagination, the writer is sitting in a windowless room, laughing at the trouble the complicated instructions cause buyers. The same sort of person, I think, also created a few pairs of verbs that are guaranteed to give you a headache — unless you read this section.

Rise and raise

Rise means "to stand," "to get out of bed," or "to move to a higher rank" under one's own power. *Raise* means "to lift something or someone else up" or "to bring up children or animals." Check out these verbs in action:

Egbert *rises* when a poultry expert enters the room.

Egbert is currently an apprentice, but he hopes to *rise* to the rank of master poultry-breeder some day.

He *raises* roosters on his farm, delighting the neighbors every morning at sunrise.

When a nest is too low, Egbert *raises* it to a higher shelf.

Here's another way to think about this pair: *Rise* is a self-contained action. The subject acts upon him- or herself. *Raise* is an action that begins with one person (or thing) and move to another person or thing. You *rise* by yourself; you *raise* something else.

Lie and lay

Whoever invented the verbs *lie* and *lay* had an evil sense of humor. Besides meaning "not to tell the truth," *lie* also means "to rest or to plop yourself down, ready for a snooze" or "to remain." *Lay* means "to put something down, to place something." Here are some examples:

Sheila likes to *lie* down for an hour after lunch. Before she hits the couch, she *lays* a soft sheet over the upholstery.

Roger *lies* in wait behind those bushes. When unsuspecting tourists *lay* down their picnic blankets, he swoops in and steals their lunches.

So far, this topic isn't too complicated. The problem — and the truly devilish part — comes in the past tense. The past tense of *lie* (to rest, to recline, to remain) is *lay*. The past tense of *lay* (to put or place) is *laid.* Check out these examples:

Sheila *lay* down yesterday, but a car alarm disturbed her rest. She immediately went to the street and *laid* a carpet of nails in front of the offending vehicle.

Yesterday, while Roger *lay* in wait, a police officer *laid* a hand on Roger's shoulder. "You are under arrest," intoned the cop.

One more complication: When you add *has, had,* or *have* to the verb *lie* (to rest, to recline, to remain), you say *has lain, had lain, have lain.* When you add *has, had,* or *have* to the verb *lay* (to put or place), you say *has laid, had laid, have laid.* In other words:

Sheila *has lain* in the hammock all morning, and her brothers *have laid* a basket of red ants on the ground beneath her. When Sheila gets up, she'll be surprised!

Roger *has lain* in the lumpy bunk all night, but no one *has laid* a blanket over him.

Lose and loose

To lose is "not to win, to come up short." *Lose* also means that you can't find something or have had to give something up. *Loose* is nearly always used as a description meaning "roomy, not tight." As a verb, *to loose* is "to set free," but you seldom see the word used this way. Read these example sentences:

> If you *lose* the game, your team will ask for a rematch.

> That uniform is too *loose;* tighten your belt!

> *Loose* the giant hound, Sherlock. He's been tied up too long.

> Jim often *loses* when he plays that video game.

POP QUIZ

Which sentence is correct?

A. The loose belt shows that Roger does not need to lose more weight.

B. Sam can't find the stuffing recipe; he always looses something.

C. After dinner, Sam laid down for a nap.

Answer: Sentence A is correct. The belt is not tight, and he doesn't have to get rid of excess weight. In sentence B, *looses* should be *loses.* In sentence C, *laid* should be *lay.*

Two Not for the Price of One

Here's a spelling tip: The following words are often written as one — incorrectly! Always write them as two separate words: *a lot, all right, each other.*

> Ella has *a lot* of trouble distinguishing between the sounds of "l" and "r," so she tries to avoid the expression *"all right"* whenever possible.

> Ella and Larry (who also has pronunciation trouble) help *each other* prepare state-of-the-union speeches every January.

Here's another tip: You can write the following words as one or two words, but with two different meanings: *altogether* means "extremely, entirely." *All together* means "as one."

> Daniel was *altogether* disgusted with the way the entire flock of dodo birds sang *all together.*

Another pair of tricky words: *Sometime* means "at a certain point in time," and *some time* means "a period of time."

> Lex said that he would visit Lulu *sometime,* but not now because he has to spend *some time* in jail for murdering the English language.

Still more: *Someplace* means "an unspecified place" and describes an action, but *some place* means "a place" and refers to a physical space.

> Lex screamed, "I have to go *someplace* now!"

> Lulu thinks he headed for *some place* near the railroad station where the pizza is hot and no one asks any questions.

And another pair: *Everyday* means "ordinary, common." *Every day* means "occurring daily."

> Larry loves *everyday* activities such as cooking, cleaning, and sewing.

> He has the palace staff perform all of those duties *every day.*

Last set, I promise: *Anyway* means "in any event." *Any way* means "a way, some sort of way."

> *"Anyway,"* added Roy, "I don't think there is *any way* to avoid jail for tax evasion."

POP QUIZ

Which sentence is correct?

A. This fork belongs to Lola's every day set of silverware.

B. Do you have some time to help Roger with his algebra homework?

C. Please sing the chorus altogether.

Answer: Sentence B is correct because the question is about a period of time. In sentence A, *everyday* (ordinary) is the word you want. In sentence C, the chorus should sing as one, or *all together.*

Four for the Road: Other Common Errors

If you made it this far into the chapter, you've cleared up (I hope!) a few confusing grammar points. Time to hit you with four last mistakes that appear often — and that are super easy to correct.

Me, myself, and I

You can use *I* as a subject, but not *me* or *myself*.

> WRONG: Bill and me are going to rob that bank. Bill and myself will soon be in jail.

> RIGHT: Bill and I are going to rob that bank. Bill and I will soon be in jail.

Me doesn't perform actions; it receives actions. To put this rule another way: *Me* is an object of some action or form of attention: He gave the check to *me*.

Myself is appropriate only for actions that double back on the person performing the action:

> I told *myself* not to be such a nerd!

> I ask *myself* that question often, but I never answer.

Myself may also be used for emphasis (though some grammarians object to the repetition), along with the word *I*:

> I *myself* will disclose the secret to the tabloid offering the most bucks.

In the group: Between/among

Between and *among* are two tricky prepositions that are often used incorrectly. To choose the appropriate preposition, decide how many people or things you're talking about. If the answer is two, you want *between*, as in this sentence:

> Lola was completely unable to choose *between* the biker magazine and *Poetry for Weightlifters*. (two magazines only)

If you're talking about more than two, *among* is the appropriate word:

> Lola strolled *among* the parked motorcycles, reading poetry aloud. (more than two motorcycles)

One exception: Treaties are made *between* nations, even if more than two countries sign:

> The treaty to outlaw bubble gum was negotiated *between* Libya, the United States, Russia, and Ecuador.

Being that I like grammar

Many people say *being that* to introduce a reason. Unfortunately, *being that* is a grammatical felony in the first degree (if there are degrees of grammatical felonies — I'm a grammarian, not a lawyer). Here's the issue: People use *being that* as a subordinate conjunction, but *being that* is not acceptable, at least in formal English usage. Try *because* or *given that*. For example:

WRONG: *Being that* it was Thanksgiving, Mel bought a turkey.

RIGHT: *Because* it was Thanksgiving, Mel bought a turkey.

ALSO RIGHT: *Given that* it was Thanksgiving, Mel bought a turkey.

WRONG: The turkey shed a tear or two, *being that* it was Thanksgiving.

RIGHT: The turkey shed a tear or two, *because* it was Thanksgiving.

ALSO RIGHT: The turkey shed a tear or two, *given that* it was Thanksgiving.

WARNING

Irregardless is in the same category as *being that* — something a lot of people say but totally unacceptable in formal English. Recently, some publications have begun to see *irregardless* as part of the language and therefore not a grammatical felony. If you want to be sure that everyone views your language as proper, try *regardless* or *nevertheless*. Steer clear of *irregardless* unless you know your reader or listener doesn't object.

Try and figure these out: Verbs and infinitives

Now that you've read this heading, do you see what's wrong with it? *Try and* means that you're going to do two different things: *try* (first task) and *figure out* (second task). But you don't have two tasks in mind, do you? *Try and* is a common expression but not a correct one. Here's what you really mean: *try to figure this one out*. *Try to* follows the normal English pattern of a verb and an infinitive. *Try to remember* the verb-infinitive rule and *try to forget* about *try and*. Some examples:

Try to remember where you parked the car.

Jack tried to tie the car to a tree, but someone stole the Mercedes anyway.

Which sentence is correct?

A. Being that I'm the most determined person on the planet, I have only one message for you: Try and stop me! I bet you can't!

B. Among the 15 club members there was little agreement.

C. Jack and myself went up the hill, but he fell.

Answer: Sentence B is correct because *among* is the word you want for a group larger than two. In sentence A, *being that* should be replaced by *because. Try and* should be *try to.* In sentence C, *myself* should change to *I.*

5

The Part of Tens

IN THIS PART . . .

Discover ten ways to boost your proofreading power, so your final writing product reflects the best grammar and style.

Examine ten "rules" of proper English that you *don't* have to follow.

Chapter **23**

Ten Ways ~~Two~~ to Improve Your Proofreading

You clicked the "Send" button. Then you sat there, heart pounding. Was the message good enough? Had you explained yourself well? How would the recipient react? Unable to calm your fears, you sat down to read the text. And that's when you finally saw it — an error. Not a little error, but a big one. An embarrassing one. The grammatical equivalent of a pimple on the tip of your nose.

Sound familiar? A situation like the one above has happened to all of us. In this chapter, I give you ten tricks to improve that all-important final check.

Reread

Okay, I know this one sounds obvious, but it's far too easy to send something off, especially a text or a tweet, without checking it for both content and grammar. You don't have to spend an hour revising, but you should go back to see which words actually made it to the screen (or paper, for those of you who still use it), and fix anything that displeases you. Also, computer programs and apps tend to substitute what the coding says is correct, without having a clue about what you're actually trying to say. "Autocorrect" is often "auto-mistake." Speech-to-text apps, which "hear" your voice and put it into written form, are even less reliable. Bottom line: Reread what you write before anyone else does!

Wait a While

Your work is done, you've read it, and you've made the corrections. Now what do you do? Save the draft and then put it away and do something else. Go water-skiing, run for president, or clean the closet. Then come back to the writing — refreshed and equipped with a new point of view. You'll see your work with new eyes — and find mistakes.

Of course, this method works only if you've left some time before the deadline. If you finish your report three nanoseconds before your boss or teacher wants to see it, you'll have to forgo this method of proofreading.

Read It Aloud

I know, I know. You don't want to sound like an idiot. But reading aloud helps you *hear* your writing in a different way. So blast some music and lock yourself in the bathroom. Read your writing in a normal speaking voice. Did you stumble any-where? If so, you may have come across an error. Stop, circle or make a note of that spot. Later, check all places you hesitated. Chances are you'll find something that should be different.

Check the Commas

When you're typing on your phone, it can be a pain to insert a comma. You may have to change to a punctuation screen and then switch back to letters. Bad use of time? Not really. The meaning of a statement can change drastically according to the insertion or omission of a comma. Perhaps your writing includes commas where none are needed. So go back and check each sentence. Is there a reason to insert a comma? If you can't identify a reason, omit this punctuation mark. If you need one, put a comma in, even if you have to tap a few extra times.

Swap with a Friend

The best proofreading comes from a fresh pair of eyes. After you've written your essay, report, parole petition, or whatever, swap with a friend. You'll see possible errors in your friend's writing, and he or she will see some in yours. Each of you should underline the potential errors before returning the paper. Make sure you check those sections with special care.

Let the Computer Program Help

Not foolproof, by any means, computer grammar- and spell-checks are nevertheless helpful. After you've finished writing, go back and check the red and green lines (or whatever signal your computer supplies). Don't trust the computer to make the corrections for you; the machine makes too many mistakes. The computer identifies only *possible* mistakes and misses many errors (homonyms, for example). Let your own knowledge of grammar and a good dictionary, as well as *English Grammar For Dummies,* 3rd Edition, help you decide whether you need to change something.

Check the Verbs

Traps sprinkled in every sentence — that's the way you should look at verbs. Give your work an extra verb-check before you declare it finished. Consider *number:* Should the verb be singular or plural? Consider *tense:* Have you chosen the correct one? In formal writing, check whether you have any sentences without verbs. If you're texting or tweeting, determine whether you need a verb to make your meaning absolutely clear. Then fix any problems you've found.

Check the Pronouns

Pronouns present potential pitfalls and are also worthy of their own special moment. Give your work an extra once over, this time checking all the pronouns. Singular or plural — did you select the appropriate number? Does each pronoun refer to a specific noun? Did you avoid sexist pronoun usage? Did you give a subject pronoun a job suited to an object pronoun, or vice versa?

Know Your Typing Style

I have a tendency to hit a comma when I want a period and to type *ever* when I intended to write *even.* The word-processing program mostly takes care of these mistakes, but not always. But I do, because I look carefully for these typos. Do you have a mistake that results from your typing style? Notice when you have to backspace as you type and then check for similar errors when you finish writing.

The Usual Suspects

Look at your earlier writing, preferably something that was corrected by a teacher or someone else in a position to point out your mistakes. Where is the red ink concentrated? Those red-ink areas are the usual suspects that you should identify in future writing. For instance, if you have a number of run-on sentences in an old paper, chances are you'll put a few in a new paper. Put "run-on" on your personal list of common errors. Don't let any piece of writing leave your desk until you've searched specifically for those errors.

Chapter **24**

Relax Already! Grammar Rules You Can Stop Worrying About

D o alligators live in city sewers? Is the Washington Monument for sale? Has the Tooth Fairy left some cash under your pillow? If you answered yes to any of these questions, you may be vulnerable to all sorts of myths, including some that concern grammar — ten, to be exact. In this chapter, I show you "rules" that never existed, as well as a couple that have passed their expiration date. In other words, when you face any of the situations described in this chapter, relax!

To Not Split an Infinitive

In Latin and many other languages, an *infinitive* is a single word, the "family name" of a group of verb forms. In English, an infinitive is written this way: *to walk, to eat, to study,* and so forth. You can't split an infinitive when it's a single word. But when you have *to* and a verb, can you "split" it by inserting a description — *to slowly walk, to never eat, to sometimes study*? Despite the fact that some influential 19th century grammarians banned split infinitives, few writers care about this bogus "rule."

After all, the captains of all the *Star Trek* ships were on a mission "to boldly go" into unexplored territory. You can follow!

A Good Part of Speech to End a Sentence With

Another "rule" that is (or should be) dead on arrival is the idea that no sentence may end with a preposition, a part of speech that includes *up, down, at, about, by, in,* and similar words. If you follow this standard, you can't ask a question like this one: "What did he text about?" *About* is a preposition, and as you see, in that perfectly normal sentence it sits at the end. Instead, followers of the no-prep-at-the-end want you to ask, "About what did he text?" See the problem? The "correct" version sounds stilted and stuffy. The "incorrect" version sounds natural. Go for natural, with the assurance that you're not breaking any real rule of grammar.

What Can or May I Do?

How many times have you had a conversation resembling this one:

> YOU: Can I go to the party this weekend, Mom?
>
> MOM: You *can* go, but your verb is wrong. Ask again.
>
> YOU: *May* I go to the party this weekend?
>
> MOM: No, you *may* not. You don't have my permission.

Mom has the final say over party attendance, but not grammar. The traditional distinction between *can* (ability) and *may* (permission) has largely faded. Unless you're talking with someone who is stricter about grammar than your great-aunt's English teacher, use *can* and *may* (and their relatives, *could* and *might*) interchangeably.

Formal Greetings in Emails and Texts

If you're writing a business letter on paper, you probably begin with a formal greeting such as *Dear Mr. Spock* or something similar. But if you're typing on electronic media (emails, texts, instant messages), you can skip these formalities.

Readers know that the content is directed to them because it lands in their inbox or on their phone screens. No need to identify the recipient.

Addresses and Dates in Electronic Communication

In texts, tweets, emails and instant messages, you don't have to worry about the *To* and *From* lines (except to write the correct address of the recipient) because the device you're writing on formats those elements automatically. Nor do you have to worry about the date: The computer inserts it. Isn't it wonderful to have less to worry about?

Periods and Commas in Some Electronic Messages

You can often bend, ignore, or break traditional punctuation and capitalization rules when you're writing a text, tweet, or instant message to a friend. Emails are a bit more formal, but they too may diverge from the usual English-teacher format. Specifically, you may often ignore periods and commas when you're pressed for time or space. *Note:* Everything you just wrote is subject to one important rule. If your reader may misunderstand what you're trying to communicate, you're in trouble. There's a big difference between "Meet soon?" and "Meet soon." (Chapter 16 goes into detail about these issues.)

The Jury Are Out on This Rule

A collective noun is a word that names a group (*jury, team, parliament, committee,* and so forth). Once upon a time — and even now in the strictest grammatical circles — a collective noun was deemed singular if the group was acting as a unit: "The team plays its last game tomorrow." The collective noun, traditionally, was plural if the members of the group were acting individually or in disagreement: "The jury are arguing about the verdict."

In the United Kingdom, this rule is often observed, but in the United States, it's fallen into the category of "the good old days." My advice? In a situation in which the group acts as individuals or disagrees, dump the collective noun and refer to the members instead: "The jury members are arguing about the verdict."

That? Who?

Lots of writers obsess about *who* and *that* — specifically, whether the pronoun *that* may refer to human beings. If you're one of those writers, stop worrying. *That* works for both people and things, though *who* is more common for people. Therefore, these sentences are both correct: "The traffic cops that write tickets earn more than their salary in fines." (*that = traffic cops*) "The cop who warned that bicyclist to follow traffic laws is my hero." (*who = cop*)

To refer to a specific person by name, go for *who*, not *that*: "Mary, who raises lambs, wears nothing but fleece."

Don't use *who* or *whom* for things: "The fleece that Mary wears is as white as snow."

Who/Whom Is Correct?

Okay, I admit that I find it difficult to let go of *whom* and its variation, *whomever*. Traditionally, these pronouns are objects, as in these sentences:

> To whom are you speaking?

> Choose whomever you like for that job.

In conversational English, though, many people these days drop *whom* and *whomever* and substitute the subject pronouns *who* and *whoever* for every job in a sentence. My advice is to relax about *whom/whomever* in speech. In formal writing, though, I recommend that you follow the traditional rules.

Hopefully This Rule Has Faded

Did you know that *nice* once meant "neat"? Now, of course, *nice* means "friendly and helpful." *Nice*, like many words, evolved. Once a critical mass of people accept the definition that used to be wrong, the definition becomes the *right* definition. So if you hear that *hopefully* means "with hope in voice or manner" and not "to be hoped that," smile. You know better! You can say, "Hopefully, it won't rain tomorrow" without violating any grammar rules.

Index

Symbols

! (exclamation point), 62, 145, 191–192

. . . (ellipses), 52, 63, 195

. (periods)
  after interjections, 145
  in electronic communication, 359
  overview, 62, 63
  in quotations, 186, 187

". . ." (quotation marks)
  capitalization rules, 226
  with exclamation points, 191–192
  overview, 184, 185
  with question marks, 190–191
  quotations inside of quotations, 192–193
  sanitizing, using, 195–196
  with semicolons, 192
  single, 192–193
  with speaker tags, 185–188
  for titles, 196–198
  without speaker tags, 189

: (colons)
  bulleted list introductions, 252
  business letters or email, addressing, 220–221
  lists, introducing, 221–222
  long quotations, introducing, 222–224
  overview, 220

; (semicolons), 54, 55, 192, 278

? (question marks), 62, 190–191

[ ] (brackets), 195

' (apostrophes)
  compound plural possessives, 173–174
  contractions, 179–181
  hyphenated words, 175
  irregular plural possessives, 172
  overview, 169
  plural possessives, 171–174
  possession, showing, 170–174
  possessive nouns ending in s, 176–177

  in possessive pronouns, 136–137, 337
  pronouns, common errors with, 177–178
  proper nouns, possession with, 174–175
  single possessives, 170–171
  would have/could have/should have, 180–181

— (em dashes), 215, 216

– (en dashes), 215, 216–217

'. . .' (single quotation marks), 192–193

, (commas)
  in addresses, 209–210
  adjectives, separating with, 202–204
  appositives, 207–208
  checking, when proofreading, 354
  clauses, placing after, 212–213
  conjunctions, placing before, 213–214, 278
  conjunctive adverbs, placing after, 54
  in dates, 211
  in descriptions, 318
  direct address, 208–209
  in electronic communication, 359
  essential and nonessential, 204–207
  interjections, placing after, 145
  introductory, 212–213
  in lists, 200–202
  overview, 199
  phrases, placing after, 212–213
  in quotations, 186, 187
  untangling clauses when deciding where to put, 277

A

a lot, 346

a/an, 150–151

abbreviations
  capitalization of, 236–237
  in electronic communication, 241–242

absolutes, creating comparisons out of, 324–325

accept, 340

acronyms, 237

overview, 331

person, shifting, 303–305

pronouns, 326–329

separate words often written as one, 346–347

tense, shifting, 299–301

verb-infinitive rule, 349–350

voice, shifting, 301–303

words resembling each other, 337–341

essays, punctuating titles of, 197–198

essential commas, 204–207

-est endings, forming comparisons with, 160–163

eternal truths, correct use of tenses in, 95

ethnicity, capitalization of, 230

even, 342–343

every, 116

everyday/every day, 347

except, 340

exclamation point (!), 62, 145, 191–192

F

Facebook, 249–250

fake subjects, 41–42

fake verbs, 39, 40–41

family relationships, capitalization of, 228–229

farther, 341

faulty construction

balanced sentences, constructing, 295–299

in bulleted lists, 253

comparisons, 308–310

conjunction pairs, 305–308

overview, 295

person, shifting, 303–305

subject complements, mixing, 70–71

tense, shifting, 299–301

voice, shifting, 301–303

feel, 21–22

first person, 303

formal English

in electronic communication, 240–243, 358–359

general discussion, 12–13

fractions, hyphenating, 219

fragments

appropriate, 60–61

inappropriate, 61–62

overview, 47, 59

subordinate clauses, 272

friendly letters, 221

friendspeak, 10–11, 13, 240, 241

From line, in email, 359

further, 341

future perfect progressive tense, 86–87

future perfect tense

correct use of, 92–93

general discussion, 86–87

subject-verb agreement, 105

"to be" in, 98

future progressive tense, 80–82, 83–84, 105

future tense

correct use of, 83–84

general discussion, 80–82

subject-verb agreement, 105

"to be" in, 98

G

gender, pronoun, 104, 119, 121–123

geographic features, capitalization of, 230–232

gerund phrase, 282

gerunds

general discussion, 282–283

parallelism, 297

possessive pronouns in front of, 137–138

God, capitalization of, 226

gonna, 340

good, 157–158, 164–165

gotcha, 340

gotta, 340

grammar. *See also* errors/mistakes

common usage problems, 15–16

conversational English, 11–12, 13

defined, 7

formal English, 12–13

friendspeak, 10–11, 13, 240, 241

history of, 7

rules, mythical or antiquated, 357–360

software, checking with, 14–15

versus style, 8–9

style, 8–9

three Englishes, 9–13

grammar school, 7

grammar checks, 355

greetings in emails and texts, 247, 358–359

grow, 19–20

H

"had", forming subjunctives with, 264

hang, 341

he or she, 122–123

heading, in email, 246

headlines, 196–198, 233–234

helping verbs

done, 29

for future tense, 80, 81

in negative statements, 25–27

overview, 25

in questions, 25–27

shades of meaning, adding with, 27–28

subjects in questions with, 40

time frame, creating with, 25

verbal tense, 287–288

here, 41–42, 110

hieroglyphs, 242

him and her, 122–123

his, 119–120, 121

his or her, 122–123

hisself, 340

historic events and eras, capitalization of, 235–236

historical present, 95–96

homonyms, 335–337

hopefully, evolution of, 360

hung, 341

hyphenated words

ethnicity and race, terms related to, 230

plural nouns, 44–45

possession, showing with apostrophes, 175

titles, capitalization of, 228

hyphens

for compound words, 218–219

dividing words with, 217–218

in numbers, 219

overview, 217

two-word descriptions, 220

I

I

agreement, 113

capitalization of, 226

erroneous use of, 348

as subject, 38

icons, used in book, 2

if statements, 264

illogical comparisons, 322–326

imperative mood, 261–262

implied comparisons, 129–130

incomplete comparisons, 320–322

independent clauses

general discussion, 55–56

joining subordinate clauses and, 279–280

versus subordinate clauses, 271–273

untangling subordinate clauses and, 276–277

indicative mood, 261

indirect objects

general discussion, 68–69

locating, 72–74

pronouns, 131

infinitive phrase, 284

infinitives

as descriptions, 314, 316–317

overview, 31, 50

parallelism, 297

split, 284, 357–358

tense, 287, 288

verb-infinitive rule, 349–350

informal English, 10–11, 13, 240–243

"-ing" nouns, possessive pronouns and, 137–138

Instagram, 249–250

instant messages

abbreviations in, 236–237

addresses and dates in, 359

apostrophe errors in, 178, 181

character limits, creativity within, 243–245

commas in, 201, 209

conversational English, 11–12

emoticons and emoji, 242

endmarks in, 63

formal or informal language, choosing, 240–243

Notes

Notes

Notes

Notes

About the Author

Geraldine Woods has taught every level of English from 5th grade through AP. She's the author of more than 50 books, including *Basic English Grammar For Dummies, English Grammar Workbook For Dummies*, 2nd Edition, *1001 Grammar Practice Questions For Dummies, SAT For Dummies* (all published by Wiley), and *Webster's New World Punctuation: Simplified and Applied* (Webster's New World). She blogs on grammar and language at www.grammarianinthecity.com.

Author's Acknowledgments

I owe thanks to my elementary school teachers, nuns who taught me how to diagram every conceivable sentence and, despite that fact, also taught me to love language and literature. I appreciate the efforts of Tim Gallan, my project editor, Lindsay Lefevere, Wiley's acquisitions editor, Cindy Kaplan, the technical reviewer, and Sophia Seidner, my agent, who worked to make this third edition possible.

Dedication

To H, the bravest man I know. The best is yet to be.

Publisher's Acknowledgments

Executive Editor: Lindsay Lefevere

Project Editor: Tim Gallan

Technical Reviewer: Cindy Kaplan

Production Editor: Siddique Shaik

Cover Image: © nadtytok/Getty Images

Math & Science

Algebra I For Dummies,
2nd Edition
978-0-470-55964-2

Anatomy and Physiology
For Dummies, 2nd Edition
978-0-470-92326-9

Astronomy For Dummies,
3rd Edition
978-1-118-37697-3

Biology For Dummies,
2nd Edition
978-0-470-59875-7

Chemistry For Dummies,
2nd Edition
978-1-118-00730-3

1001 Algebra II Practice
Problems For Dummies
978-1-118-44662-1

Microsoft Office

Excel 2013 For Dummies
978-1-118-51012-4

Office 2013 All-in-One
For Dummies
978-1-118-51636-2

PowerPoint 2013
For Dummies
978-1-118-50253-2

Word 2013 For Dummies
978-1-118-49123-2

Music

Blues Harmonica
For Dummies
978-1-118-25269-7

Guitar For Dummies,
3rd Edition
978-1-118-11554-1

iPod & iTunes
For Dummies, 10th Edition
978-1-118-50864-0

Programming

Beginning Programming
with C For Dummies
978-1-118-73763-7

Excel VBA Programming
For Dummies, 3rd Edition
978-1-118-49037-2

Java For Dummies,
6th Edition
978-1-118-40780-6

Religion & Inspiration

The Bible For Dummies
978-0-7645-5296-0

Buddhism For Dummies,
2nd Edition
978-1-118-02379-2

Catholicism For Dummies,
2nd Edition
978-1-118-07778-8

Self-Help & Relationships

Beating Sugar Addiction
For Dummies
978-1-118-54645-1

Meditation For Dummies,
3rd Edition
978-1-118-29144-3

Seniors

Laptops For Seniors
For Dummies, 3rd Edition
978-1-118-71105-7

Computers For Seniors
For Dummies, 3rd Edition
978-1-118-11553-4

iPad For Seniors
For Dummies, 6th Edition
978-1-118-72826-0

Social Security
For Dummies
978-1-118-20573-0

Smartphones & Tablets

Android Phones
For Dummies, 2nd Edition
978-1-118-72030-1

Nexus Tablets
For Dummies
978-1-118-77243-0

Samsung Galaxy S 4
For Dummies
978-1-118-64222-1

Samsung Galaxy Tabs
For Dummies
978-1-118-77294-2

Test Prep

ACT For Dummies,
5th Edition
978-1-118-01259-8

ASVAB For Dummies,
3rd Edition
978-0-470-63760-9

GRE For Dummies,
7th Edition
978-0-470-88921-3

Officer Candidate Tests
For Dummies
978-0-470-59876-4

Physician's Assistant Exam
For Dummies
978-1-118-11556-5

Series 7 Exam For Dummie
978-0-470-09932-2

Windows 8

Windows 8.1 All-in-One
For Dummies
978-1-118-82087-2

Windows 8.1 For Dummies
978-1-118-82121-3

Windows 8.1 For Dummies
Book + DVD Bundle
978-1-118-82107-7

Available in print and e-book formats.

Available wherever books are sold. **For more information or to order direct visit www.dummies.com**

Take Dummies with you everywhere you go!

Whether you are excited about e-books, want more from the web, must have your mobile apps, or are swept up in social media, Dummies makes everything easier.

For Dummies is the global leader in the reference category and one of the most trusted and highly regarded brands in the world. No longer just focused on books, customers now have access to the For Dummies content they need in the format they want. Let us help you develop a solution that will fit your brand and help you connect with your customers.

Advertising & Sponsorships

Connect with an engaged audience on a powerful multimedia site, and position your message alongside expert how-to content.

Targeted ads · Video · Email marketing · Microsites · Sweepstakes sponsorship

Custom Publishing

Reach a global audience in any language by creating a solution that will differentiate you from competitors, amplify your message, and encourage customers to make a buying decision.

Apps • Books • eBooks • Video • Audio • Webinars

Brand Licensing & Content

Leverage the strength of the world's most popular reference brand to reach new audiences and channels of distribution.

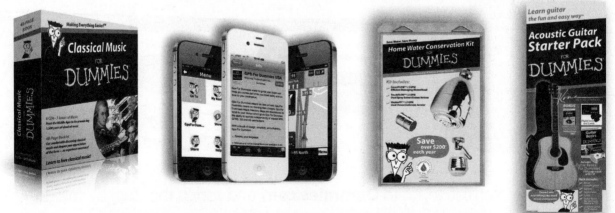

For more information, visit www.Dummies.com/biz

A Wiley Brand

Dummies products make life easier!

- DIY
- Consumer Electronics
- Crafts
- Software
- Cookware
- Hobbies
- Videos
- Music
- Games
- and More!

For more information, go to **Dummies.com** and search the store by category.

FOR
DUMMIES
A Wiley Brand